LESSONS FROM THE CROSSROADS

Finding My Authentic Path

Ed Poole

*To recover his heart's desire a man needs to get away
from the noise and distraction of his daily life for
time with his own soul. He needs to head into the
wilderness, to silence and solitude. Alone with
himself, he allows whatever is there to come to
the surface. Sometimes it is grief for so much
lost time. There, beneath the grief, are desires
long forsaken.*

John Eldredge - Wild At Heart

*What our spirits desperately need is time
away for comfort, restoration, and transformation.*

Bruce Wilkinson - The Dream Giver

*The act of storytelling helps create community;
the storyteller's job is to do community maintenance.*

Len Cabral

Foreword

I have had the privilege and pleasure of assisting Ed Poole with his transformation from professor at a major university to Professor of Life Skills at the University of Life. I met Ed at a large seminar I was hosting, where he asked me if I would mentor him to become a transformational speaker. I have witnessed Ed's quantum leaps as a writer, speaker, life coach, and leader, and I am proud to say he is unequivocally one of the finest students I have ever had the opportunity to collaborate with. His newest book, *Lessons from the Crossroads,* is a book all entrepreneurs, salespeople, and business owners deserve to own and pass on to their teammates, friends, and colleagues.

Ed has a story of "climbing the corporate ladder to success, then hitting the emotional bottom of despair" that gives you, the reader, a better awareness of how to overcome your own personal challenges. As a storyteller, Ed's unique style will allow you to better understand the story in all of us. His message will allow you to transform a set of conditions that limit your prosperity into a new set of beliefs that will allow you to live a more prosperous life. You deserve to receive these insights so that you can become the person you deserve to be. Ed is the leader you are looking for!

- Jeffery Combs
President, Golden Mastermind Seminars, Inc.

...My Greatest Hope...

This book is dedicated to those four individuals in my life who hold my greatest hope for wonderfully exciting journeys – my grandchildren: Allie, Aimee, Emma, and Kate. Several years ago your dad and Uncle Eric taught me a lesson he learned during his bike riding days – a lesson I've never forgotten. He said we have to ride the uphills in life to enjoy the downhills. I wish you enough uphills in life to help you understand who you are and why you were placed on this earth. You will struggle with the uphills. Your hearts will be pumping and your legs will grow weary. But the climbs will give you character and resolve to continue on your journeys. There will be times when getting to the tops of the hills seems too hard. Just keep strugglin' and pedalin' – you'll make it. The top of the hill is just around that next curve. The grace of the downhills that follows will bring understanding and will help you know why the uphill rides were so very hard. May the grace you feel going downhill find its way into your heart long enough to allow you to pick up the speed, courage, and faith you will need for your next uphill adventure. Savor them both as you chase your dreams.

There is one other lesson about faith, courage, hope, and perseverance I want you to remember. A unique wave with each of your names on it found you when you were born. These waves are yours and yours alone. No one will ever have your unique wave. While treating it with love and respect, make sure above all else you give it one heckuva ride!

With so much love and hope,
Gramps/Papaw

...With Gratitude...

So many individuals contributed to *Lessons from the Crossroads*. Even though Ruth and Harley Poole are no longer living, they continue to give me the faith and courage to write. This faith and courage, transferred to my life, are the greatest gifts I could have received from them.

My family encouraged me to tell my story. They have always supported my journey toward once again finding my authentic self. Without their faith in their husband, father, and father-in-law, the book would never have been written.

Without the diligent editing by Ellen and Dale LaGow the finished product could not be the quality we all three desired. I have always had such confidence and trust in their skills and hearts to greatly improve upon my words, helping both the reader and me improve our understanding of my journey.

As with my first book, John Cassano used his creativity to design the front and back jacket covers. His image of the tower at the crossroads sharpened my own awareness of the importance of my quest to find my way out of that crossroads. Thank you, John, for the talent, support, and love you shared with me during this writing as well as the last twenty-six years of our lives.

My publisher, More Heart than Talent, provided the technical expertise to produce the book and put it into your hands. I especially want to thank Erica Combs whose assistance was invaluable in translating the manuscript into the finished product.

I am grateful Jeffery Combs came into my life in January, 2006, as my professional coach, mentor, and friend. His guidance and questions have helped beyond measure in reinventing myself as an entrepreneur, an author, a public speaker, and a coach. He has been a wonderful model of selflessness, a personal attribute I have struggled with for years. I could not have finished this book without Jeff's constant encouragement and faith in me as a human being.

Finally, I am so grateful to God for the continued patience and love He gives me. I am learning to listen more carefully to the messages and questions He sends me, which, for so many years, I ignored. I'm reminded of the words of Elie Weisel, "God created man because he loves his stories."

Ed Poole
October, 2006

Thank You!

At the very beginning, I want to say that I have
made many new friends during my
retreats. What genuine, sincere, caring,
and fun-loving folks they are – to the person. I want
to acknowledge in particular two
new friends I met: Charlie Alber and
Art Janhke. Without their friendship, generous gifts of time, and
their wonderful stories, the product that comes from my
own journey would have been stripped of much of
its richness and meaning. These two most vividly reflect that genuineness,
honesty, and caring I'm searching for and
their stories are truly gifts to me.
I also want to thank my friends and family who sensed
my need for time away without understanding why.
Their encouragement made it all possible.

Ed Poole
3108 S. Route 59 - Suite 124-213
Naperville, IL 60564
epooleiu71@aol.com - (630) 674-4480

ISBN: 0-9720740-1-5

Published by
More Heart Than Talent Publishing, Inc.
6507 Pacific Ave #329
Stockton, CA 95207 USA
Toll Free: 800-208-2260
www.MoreHeartThanTalentPublishing.com

Copyright © 2007 Ed Poole
All Rights Reserved.

Printed in the United States of America

This book is full of stories, tales I heard from others, tales that are now a part of my own life. I had the patience to listen and the wisdom to learn. Doing so affirmed a thought I've carried with me a long time: The story of any one of us is, in part, the story of all of us. By telling the story of my experiences of reclaiming my authentic path, I hope you will discover humor, joy, laughter, personal meaning for you in your life, some sadness, but above all, a sense of hope, love, forgiveness, and personal excitement for those times you want and need opportunities to learn your lessons from your own crossroad experiences. Please know as I speak to you I am also speaking to myself, one who continues to struggle along my own journey. And I am happy to be able to tell you this. *Lessons from the Crossroads: Finding My Authentic Path* is a sequel to my earlier book, *Lessons from the Porch: A Gathering Place for Telling Our Stories.* I did not begin this book expecting to continue that earlier writing. It just happened that way. I've learned, however, that my writing – just as my life – is cyclical and interdependent. Writing, just as everything in our lives, is an evolving, nonlinear process. I could not write this book without remembering what I wrote in my earlier book, taking personal note of how I have changed in the last ten years.

When I began writing this book, I had no predetermined organization in mind. I had no outline. I knew the writing would evolve from the experiences I had. Since I did not know, at the outset, what these experiences might be, I wrote about them as they appeared in my life. Parts of the book were written chronologically as

I experienced and wrote about my journey. Other parts of the book are reflections on my past, present, and future journeys. As I reread the manuscript, these reflections took the form of lessons rather than a chronological perspective.

While reading *Lessons from the Crossroads*, you will become aware of the changes in my life. You will find that I feel differently about certain struggles, concepts, and feelings as I share my insights throughout the book. As I write, I grow through the process of writing, and I grow amidst the writing. Such is the joy of telling our stories.

CONTENTS

Introduction	Here's How It All Got Started	15
1	My Adventure Begins	29
2	Reclaiming My Authentic Self from the Depths of Depression	39
3	Beginning to Find Some Connections Toward My Authentic Self	45
4	Closed but (Still) Open as Charlie Begins His Story	57
5	Encouraging Others by Extending Care and Understanding	69
6	Saturday: My "Travels with Charlie" and Findin' Home	81
7	Oh, No! My Second Week Is Already Here	91
8	Finding the Hole in My Sidewalk	105
9	Back to a (true? or false?) Sense of Reality	123
10	And the Beat Goes On	131
11	A Tug of War to Relocate My Authentic Path	139
12	The Hero's Journey: Providential Moments	167
13	My Ongoing Pilgrimage Toward My Authentic Path	181
14	Is the Third Time the Charm?	189
15	Lessons from Art and Charlie	199
16	My Desert Oasis	207
17	Understanding My Authentic Path Didn't Remove the Fears	225
18	Lessons from the Crossroads	243
Epilogue	A Talk with God	265

INTRODUCTION
Here's How It All Got Started

It is hard to imagine making any important change in life without an inward journey... It is on the inward journey, taken over time, that we develop the capacity for intimacy with ourselves and with others.
Peter Block - *The Answer to How Is Yes: Acting on What Matters*

For many months that tiny voice deep within my soul was sending me a mixed message. The unclear message had to do with whether or not I needed a major change in my life. The one message said I didn't want a change, that I just wanted to go along each and every day as I knew it. I was comfortable, passing time, not worrying about my life and its meaning. The other message told me not to be afraid to dream my dreams and to believe I can be anything I want to be. I was beginning to feel I was at a point where my current life just didn't make sense anymore. For two years I struggled with these messages, and then I knew the only way to find which message to honor was to take an inward journey, a journey I had not taken for ten years.

In March 2004, I was released from my second hospitalization with clinical depression. In late 1996 and into early 1997 I spent four months in a psychiatric care unit with clinical depression. One of the gifts of those four months was my first book *Lessons from the Porch: A Gathering Place for Telling Our Stories*. I felt better as a result of my time in the hospital in 2004 because I had lost my soul and needed to find it. Although I didn't know it, I began my journey while in the hospital. As a result of my second time-out in the hospital I again became acquainted with Ed Poole, a person I had lost contact with for almost ten years. *Lessons from the Crossroads: Finding My Authentic Path* began forming in my mind during that second hospitalization. I had lost contact with Ed Poole because I mistakenly thought I had learned all my life's lessons while writing the first book. As in early 1997 I called a second time-out in my life in the spring of 2004, trying once again to find my lost soul. I find it interesting that my books came as the result of my two experiences with clinical depression.

In April of that year, in an effort to continue searching for my lost soul, I began reading a book by Jon Katz, *Running to the Mountain,* in which he chronicles a significant part of his journey – a journey seeking inward change.

As Katz approached his fiftieth birthday, he was overwhelmed with feeling he needed to alter his life. About ten years earlier, the little voice inside Katz was sending him the same two messages I received. After struggling with these messages, he finally left a lucrative and (at the time) self-fulfilling job as executive producer of the two-hour program, *The CBS Morning News*, working with celebrities such as Phyllis George and Diane Sawyer. Katz described walking into his office one day, locking the door, putting his head on his desk, and just sobbing, the tears streaming down his face. On that day he closed and locked his office and walked away from what he thought he should be doing with his life, to discover what he wanted to do with his life. Katz reflects, "I had reached a rung in life a lot of people would have coveted, and I would rather have thrown myself off a bridge than stay there for another month." He decided he wanted and needed to write, and during the intervening years between his decision and the publication of *Running to the Mountain,* he did just that. He listened to the voice of change, not the one encouraging him to stay in the rut he had been stuck in for several years.

Co-authors Janice Brewi and Ann Brennan, in their book *Mid-Life*, identified Katz's and my struggles using these words: "When, one day in mid-life, one comes to doubt oneself, and all one's relationships and commitments, and when the pain and anxiety of this dragging away of… energy from all that formerly was so life-giving begins to overwhelm, there surfaces the depth question: *Why bother?* Lucky the one who lets that question stand." Katz and I lived with that question. Katz's personal struggles helped him find the answer. By telling the story of my struggles, I hoped to find the answers I too was seeking.

Like the trigger for my own inner journey, the greater pain of not changing was what compelled Katz to run to the mountain in the summer of 1997. The pain in his current life became unbearable, forcing him to consider a new calling, what he called "change in the service of risk and discovery. Change in search of what…Thomas Merton called the interior life – change in the pursuit of hope, faith, spiritual meaning." Like Katz, I had to be willing to let go of the life I had accepted and felt comfortable with so that I could find the life waiting for me. Although I had some thoughts about what I wanted to do, I did not know if I could face the changes required to find that life.

Change invades all our lives, whether the change involves switching careers, dissolving a marriage, moving to a different town, having children, purchasing a new pet, sending our kids off to college, and/or struggling with who we are and what we should be doing with our lives. However, change in anyone's life can also include hopes and possibilities. Where I find hope, I will find my life. Where I find my life, I will find possibilities. And where I find these possibilities, I can make dreams into realities.

To discover my dreams for the future, chase them, and create my reality from the pursuit defined the goal I sought. Because life's changes and our reaction to these changes are different for each of us, it's impossible to compare the changes in one person's life to those in others'. My changes may be similar to yours, but they are mine, with their own peculiar personal characteristics and descriptions.

However, regardless of the *kinds* of changes we might experience, all occur within fairly common themes. There is always an ending, then a neutral zone, followed by a new beginning. Sometimes it's those "in-between times" – those neutral zones between an ending and a new beginning – that are particularly onerous. As changes evolve in our lives, endings and new beginnings sometimes get blurred, with overlapping boundaries and uncertain feelings. In her wonderful book *Refuge: An Unnatural History of Family and Place* Terry Tempest Williams said, "It's strange to feel change coming. It's easy to ignore. An underlying restlessness seems to accompany it like birds flocking before a storm. We go about our business with the usual alacrity, while in the pit of our stomach there is a sense of something tenuous." I felt that tenuous, uneasy feeling as I went about easing the pain from within.

Change, regardless of its relative size, always requires risk taking: It requires courage to admit the change may or may not have been what we thought it would be. Experiencing change means a willingness to "go out not knowing" (my own definition for faith), the strength to appear the fool for awhile in the new beginning because we are moving into the unknown. Moving into the unknown puts us in a new place in life and necessitates our knowledge that initially our lives will probably get worse before they get better. As Bruce Wilkinson asked in *The Dream Giver*, "Are you ready to seem ridiculous, take risks, feel weak and small so that God's power and goodness will be made clear to all?" Change tests us and requires faith in the process.

For Jon Katz, his definition of faith was daring to dream and then risking many parts of his life in pursuing those dreams. Katz said, "Change is the way we progress from having dreams to achieving them. The run to the mountain was, to my mind, a drama of faith and change, a compelling necessity, part of a lifelong struggle for peace, balance, and purpose. Change promised all those things but guaranteed none."

We begin changing our lives with questions, and I was struggling with many: Should I leave the field of education to write and speak full time? How would I feel if I seized the opportunity to live these two callings? Can I remember the excitement, joy, sense of fulfillment, and inner peace I experienced as I wrote my first book, *Lessons from the Porch*? Was that writing a one-time experience, from one who did not consider himself a writer? Had I forgotten the opportunities to speak to groups about my journey and my enjoyment of those opportunities? When do I feel my best? Do I feel good about the way I am living my life? Can I believe in myself as much as others believe in me? These questions identified my struggles. I could not answer any of them when I once again began my writing. I didn't remember the skills that I used while writing my first book.

As I write, the words of others often provide clarity for my own words. One of my many favorite writers is Rainer Maria Rilke. I have read his works for over twenty years. Rilke struggled mightily in his life. He never had much money, and he constantly wandered from place to place, searching for himself and hoping to find the gifts he had in his soul. Currently, his book that speaks to me about my writing is *Letters to a Young Poet*. This book contains ten letters written by Rilke to a young and aspiring writer, Franz Kappus, who was questioning his calling to become a writer.

The very first letter to Kappus includes thoughts that were so relevant to my struggles. I want to quote a long portion of that first letter, written in 1903, in order to capture the essence of my inner conflict.

> You are looking outward, and that above all you should not do now… There is only one single way. Go into yourself. Search for the reason that bids you write; find out whether it is spreading out its roots in the deepest places of your heart, acknowledge to yourself whether you would have to die if it were denied you to write. This above all – ask yourself in the stillest hour of your night: *must* I write? If you may meet this earnest question with a strong and simple "*I must*," then build your life according to this necessity…Then draw near to nature…describe your sorrows and desires, passing thoughts and the belief in some sort of beauty – describe all these with loving, quiet, humble sincerity, and use, to express yourself, the things in your environment.

As I struggled with my ability to write and speak, *if* I should write and speak and *where* these activities might occur, Rilke gave me much to ponder.

A few paragraphs back, I said change begins with questions, and I identified those that defined my struggles. The questions defined the quest to once again find my authentic self. They were the roadmap. The way to an authentic self is an inward journey along an authentic path. Rediscovering this path encourages my heart to be open to the messages and questions God sends me. This openness, then, gives my soul the sense of inner peace and inner control God desires for me.

No small task, huh? However, the task was somewhat less formidable because I felt an abiding sense of synchronicity among those questions. They were not stand-alone questions. Only by considering them as interconnecting parts of a much larger whole could I make sense of such immensely deep and abiding questions. The questions provided the context and foundation for my lived experiences throughout my writing. Separating the questions removed my obligation of returning to them at several points in the book. Highlighting their inextricable relationships provided me quite a different map for my journey. These questions seemed impossible to answer. However, I knew of no better way to grow intellectually and spiritually than to ask them daily.

To better understand my questions, I reversed a saying I knew growing up. I often heard someone say, "I'll believe it when I see it." Remember this thought? In my life I've learned to turn that saying around to "I'll *see it* when I *believe it*." For me, I need to believe something – feel it in my heart – before I can really see it. I have to internalize the thought, concept, or idea, and it has to become a part of me. Only then can I see it. Then I understand.

On a vacation trip to North Carolina, my friend Dan Hammond told me a story that increased my understanding of the relationship between *seeing* and *believing*. The Hammonds have a neighbor, a twelve-year-old boy named Georgie Pocheptsov, who has been painting since he was six. This very young lad is an impressionistic painter who earned $500,000 last year selling his paintings. Recently former Secretary of State Colin Powell commissioned a painting from this young

Introduction - Here's How It All Got Started

North Carolinian, and the U.N. displayed four of his latest works in 2005.

When Georgie and his parents moved to this country, they settled in New York City. Shortly after they arrived, Georgie's father was diagnosed with cancer. Georgie's mother gave her son crayons and paper to occupy his time while she tended to his dad. He drew then and has continued to draw today. After his father died, Georgie and his mother moved to Wilmington, North Carolina, where they live today, just down the street from the Hammonds. This young Picasso fishes with Dan in the pond, and Dan, in many ways, has become a father figure to a young boy who lost his own father when he was much too young. To thank the Hammonds for their kindness, Georgie created a beautiful, impressionistic painting of the Hammond family and gave it to them as a gift – again, no small gift from an artist who can get as much as $30,000 for a single painting. In the painting one of the two Hammond dogs is shown standing upright on his hind legs playing a violin. Dan asked Georgie, "Why is Murphy playing a violin?"

Georgie said, "To me, Murphy seems like a barnyard rooster, always struttin' around. He likes to be front and center, so I painted him up on his hind legs playing a violin."

"Oh, now I *see* it," exclaimed Dan. "I had to *feel* it first!" Dan's feelings allowed him to finally see what Georgie meant.

I needed to examine my beliefs so I could improve my sight, to find out if I *was* doing what I liked, if I *was* following my calling in life, and if my passion *was* where my heart was. I knew the task was not going to be easy. But I gave myself permission to just begin a process that I was certain would take a lifetime, and it was the journey I wanted to enjoy, not the destination.

Landing in the Crossroads

The weight of my questions came to me one day as I reflected on them. I felt as though I had been propelled smack in the middle of a crossroads, as if I had been shoved unwillingly out the open door of a helicopter, which hovered fifteen feet above the ground. I ached all over from the fall. After lying there awhile, I knew the pain not only was on the surface but also went deep into the recesses of my soul. As I shook my head to clear my mind, I realized an overwhelming sense of fear and uncertainty, feelings that unexpectedly stimulated my imagination.

As soon as I started this mental journey, I noticed a tall, stone, foursquare tower about twenty-five feet from where I was pushed into the crossroads. I knew I was supposed to walk over to that tower, but getting back on my feet was difficult. The ache I felt in my soul as I struggled to get to my feet brought my divided life into a sense of wholeness I had never felt before. Regaining my footing was difficult because I felt I was on the shifting sands of midlife.

As my eyes regained focus and I was able to pull myself into a standing position, I walked toward the tall tower. As I walked around the tower, I looked up and saw a window atop each of the four sides. A door took me inside the tower where I found a long flight of cold, winding, stone steps leading to the top. As I climbed to the top, I counted the steps. There were seventy-one. My legs were heavy, and I was out of breath as I reached the top of the tower; still I was anxious to look out the four tall windows. As I walked from window to window, I realized each looked out on a different landscape with its own unique path, full of its own stories. For a moment, my fear had subsided, and I was totally inside that tower.

To the north, the countryside was a blue haze. I saw witches, demons, and angels. I also saw princes and princesses. I could barely see the road sign for this path. After some time, I made out the word "Spiritual" on the road marker. I realized the five different images were there to remind me of the thoughts and feelings I've had throughout my life about the meaning of spirituality, some fearful and others peaceful and comforting.

To the east I saw adventures. There were highwaymen, warriors, knights in shining armor. I saw images of my family and friends along this path. Some were quiet, a few were arguing, and others had a look of fear on their faces I had never seen before. But I also saw a peacemaker and guide among the people. She had long, flowing blonde hair that glistened in the sun. Looking through the window, I watched those times when the peacemaker showed people how to find their common ground along the path, a place they could all walk together, hand in hand. I finally saw the road sign for this path: "Personal." In my personal life there have been times when my family and friends have thought, felt, and spoken with one mind. There have most assuredly been times when head-to-head, knock down drag-out fights have occurred. I knew why the peacemaker was on this path.

To the south the landscape was more familiar. The terrain was hilly, and the path was full of sharp twists and turns. I recognized some of the people as co-workers I have met over the years. Some were shouting advice and directions to each other, uncertain where they were going and wanting someone else to make their decisions, telling them what was best for them in their lives. Others seemed to have a level of self-assurance that allowed them to complete their tasks, uninterrupted by others. This path was marked with the road sign "Professional."

The view from the west window was very hazy. I had great difficulty seeing the events taking place there. I finally located an unreadable road sign. I was confused. The other three paths seemed so clear that I was noticeably shaken by the absolute lack of clarity out this fourth window. Suddenly I became obsessed with finding the name on that fourth sign. I knew the only way to find that name was to take a journey. I stayed atop the tower for what seemed like hours, watching, thinking, and wondering. I hoped by telling my story from the crossroads I could find the clarity and enlightenment that were now missing.

I descended the long flight of winding steps, arrived at the bottom, and walked back outside into the crossroads. The dust had not settled, and confusion replaced the clarity I found up top. I tried to re-enter for a second look through the windows, but the heavy door was locked. I knew immediately that remembering the crystal views I found at the top of the tower was going to be difficult. I could no longer see the four paths I saw while in the tower, but I was sure they represented the paths of my life. I felt I had traveled them as an adult but only as separate paths. I recognized the images I saw through the three windows because they defined the experiences I had as I walked them as an adult. Up to this very point at the crossroads, I did not see any connections among the paths because I did not believe they were there. By treating them separately, I didn't see the relationships among those individual paths. I lived my life in parts, not as a whole. I was a different person as I moved along each separate path. Therefore, I was confused about who Ed Poole was.

Right after being released from four months of treatment for clinical depression I called a time out in my life. I knew I had to answer the question that troubled me as I left the hospital: What have I learned during my hospitalization? I spent a year and a half trying to answer that question and the answer came in the form of the twenty-two lessons in my first book. Why twenty-two lessons and not some other number? I went to those parts of me where I felt the most pain when I realized I did not know myself. Those areas of pain in part concerned: a willingness to move from the known into the unknown; a need to become trustworthy so others could trust me; the ability to begin finding my inner self and not depend on others' expectations for how I should have been leading my life; the desire to stand still and face my problems rather than running from them; the importance of matching what I do with what I say; the absolute necessity of shedding the masks I had worn my entire life – masks that didn't allow me to know myself; the need to learn humility.

I forgot many of these lessons as my paths separated and became hidden in the clouds. The wholeness I felt when I finished my first book was lost along the way.

My plunge into the crossroads gave me the realization that not only did I need to revisit those original twenty-two lessons, but also identify new lessons I learned during those ten intervening years between beginning the first book and this one. However, because my drop into the middle of the intersection was so sudden and painful, I couldn't distinguish one path from the others, and I did not know why I was there. Even as my head became untangled, I could not find that one road I knew held my dreams and my future. I was at a total loss, not having a clue about finding that road marker. Somehow I knew if this road became clear to me, the other three might wind their way into it, and my journey would become simpler, more focused, and whole once again. If I didn't find my fourth path, I knew I would feel like Parker Palmer, who said in his book *A Hidden Wholeness: The Journey toward an Undivided Life*, "Slowly, and with some reluctance, I began to see that what I feared was the impending collision of my age, vocation, and survival." I felt that collision in the middle of the crossroads, but at that time I didn't know the pain I felt from the fall was really coming from deep within, and, like Palmer, I was afraid.

One of my fears centered in my professional life. When I plummeted into the crossroads, my professional path was leading me away from, not toward, the other three. I have been in education for forty years, and I am currently an associate professor at a university not far from Chicago. Standing in the middle of the crossroads, I realized how disconnected I felt from my lifetime profession. I was seeking to rediscover my authentic, individual path at the same time my profession was moving me in an opposite direction, a path I knew I could not follow.

I loved teaching and working with graduate students at my little university. However, I didn't enjoy other, sometimes time-consuming aspects of my job. My goal was to decide what I wanted to do about those parts of my work I found distasteful.

Another disconnect among the three paths was between my professional life and my spiritual life. For years, as an educator, I was told to leave "me" outside the classroom door as I entered. I was not supposed to let my students get to know me as a human being. Educators were to use only their teacher's voice when interacting with students. In higher education this personal/professional relationship is somewhat more connected. However, the many years I left myself outside the classroom door made it difficult to allow my human side to enter with me.

Finally, my personal and spiritual paths were two, not one. The religious beliefs handed to me early in life no longer matched my spiritual beliefs as an adult. That early, religious indoctrination was so deep within that I had difficulty letting it go to nurture more congruent beliefs that allowed me to live an integrated, adult life. I grew up knowing about a God who focused on what I did wrong rather than the good in my life. He was a watchdog to see what He could record in His big, black book to guarantee I was going to hell. I hated this God I first knew. My life now is full of a loving, caring, understanding, encouraging, and forgiving God. The beliefs I have internalized encouraged me to become my true self as I wrote *Lessons from the Porch*.

As some of my friends heard me speak about my first book, they told me how honest and genuine I sounded and how they could tell from my voice and the way my eyes danced that my love and passion were in the stories from that book. As I talk about the part of my journey ending with the publication of *Lessons from the Porch*, I realized I was at a more authentic place in my life than I was when I began this book. I wondered if I lost that unidentifiable path in the maze of all other paths I traveled in the last several years. I got off that path, thus feeling separated and not integrated with my personal, professional, and spiritual paths. I did not recognize I had been traveling down roads that prevented my integrated life.

As I began this book, I felt this disconnect and I struggled to accept a new calling, once again to find that path and to see it as preparation for a future God saw for me. I struggled with the angst, fighting to remember Peter Block's words in *The Answer to How is Yes: Acting on What Matters*: "Each of us has a calling, something that pulls us." For me, the "something" was asking God to make me aware of the messages and questions He sends me so I could risk finding my authentic self while moving so decisively down the path God wants me to travel.

Having become comfortable with what I had done professionally for many years, I was reluctant to follow a new path. I lived by the one message telling me to stay with the known and discouraging me from venturing into the unknown. Change is difficult, and the pain had not yet reached the point of being unbearable. Throughout all the struggling, I needed some way to help me understand my feelings, fears, and frustrations, so I wrote a poem to explain the reasons I listened to that one message from deep within.

Introduction - Here's How It All Got Started

How <u>Dare</u> You
An unwanted, unknown, uninvited, disruptive calling
seeps into the pores of my soul.
Who are you?
What do you want of me?
How did you find me?
How dare you interrupt and complicate my life!
When I ignore you long enough, you'll leave me alone.
Are you a sham, disguised in God-like remnants?
Or are you an angel with hidden wings,
waiting to teach me to fly?
Honestly, I don't really care.
I've grown comfortable in my world. I can predict.
I can cope. I'm settled in and content.
I can fool others by feigning happiness. Why can't I fool you?
My masks serve me well. How can you see behind them,
when no one else can? You may think you can lure
me into your mysteries. You can't!
I won't let you do this to me so late in my life.
In short, hit the road!
So, why are you still in my soul? Didn't you hear me?
I'm fine right here, right now, and I will
not listen to what you tell me are yearnings for
uncharted seas when I hear the unrelenting waves pounding the shore.
Why can't I ignore you, like all those other interlopers?

Ed Poole

This poem *is* my life as I've known it. I've avoided a lot of pain along the way, but I have also missed opportunities for excitement and meaning in my life by ignoring the "soul-tuggers" and staying wrapped in my cocoon of comfort, not seeing the hidden angel's wings. I've been afraid to discover what I wanted to do beyond my role as an educator and then do it. I had lost the authentic path I was on ten years ago. I also knew the sham in God-like clothing. I met him often in my adult years. But the sham I knew was put there by me, not by God. I viewed His part in my life through my own lenses. The masks were like old friends. I put them on and took them off at will as I jumped from one path to another, seldom removing my masks long enough to walk my authentic path. The masks had not only disguised me but also the authentic path I was on and then lost. I did not know what to do.

CHAPTER 1
My Adventure Begins

Throw a loaf of bread and a pound of tea in an old sack and jump over the back fence.
John Muir

My First Adventure: Finding a Place
I remembered once again that it was as much about the way I found my site as it was the site itself.
Ian Shamir - *Poet Tree: The Wilderness I Am*

Where could I go to find the solitude Jon Katz found at his mountain retreat to heal my confused and painful heart, and discover the unidentifiable path I saw atop the tower? I began asking myself this very overwhelming question in April 2004 after finishing Katz's book. Time, however, was running short. I had only a brief window of time for my two weeks alone. I was teaching a doctoral class in mid-July and had already made other plans for the remainder of the summer. Trying to think of a place I could go for my mini-retreat, my sabbatical, I remembered some dear friends, Deb and Tom, who live in North Carolina and had built a mountain home a few years ago as their get-away retreat.

I called Tom, only to find they had sold the mountain home and purchased a new retreat, a cottage clear across the state close to the ocean. Their cottage by the ocean was rented for the summer. Then I called a dear and long-time friend in Colorado Springs. While Dick was excited for my planned adventure, he didn't have a place to suggest. He did, however, convince me that I *absolutely must take* one specific book on my trip: *A Walk in the Woods: Rediscovering America on the Appalachian Trail* by Bill Bryson. Dick was so insistent I decided I had to purchase the book. He made me promise, though, that I would not read it until I located my retreat setting.

While debating what to do, I realized even more that I did need to spend this time with myself. Since neither Tom nor Dick had a place to recommend, I called the Lodge at Brown County State Park in Indiana, hoping beyond hope that all their cabins had not been rented for the busy summer. I wanted to find a cabin at the state park because it is located fifteen miles from where I grew up in Columbus, Indiana. Having made many visits to the park from a very young age and continuing all through high school, I knew the peaceful setting was perfect for the writing, reading, and thinking I needed to do.

As it turned out, there was a cabin available during the time I was able to take my trip. I booked it immediately, about three weeks prior to my departure. I felt very lucky, for Brown County State Park seemed to be the place I should be heading.

Once I booked the cabin, my excitement about the trip engulfed my every waking moment. As friends asked about my summer plans, I could not wait to tell them the news. I thought about the trip all the time, what to take to wear; what to take to read; what to expect from the weather; what to take for play; and how to prepare myself for this first-in-a-lifetime excursion. Each person with whom I shared my good news could see the dancing in my eyes and hear the elevation, resolve, and excitement in my voice as I talked about my trip.

What to Pack!

Right before leaving for Brown County I had to pack a bag. I do *not* like to pack for trips. Consequently, I always put that job off until the very last minute, often closing the bag as I'm running out the door to catch a plane. Because I don't like to pack, I am not a careful packer. I don't really think too much about what to take. Sometimes I take the wrong clothes, and invariably much more ends up in my bag than I need.

While packing for this trip, however, I wanted to make certain I included some very important items. Of course, I placed some clothes in my bag, but I also "packed" attitudes and beliefs that I hoped would help me.

First, I wanted to have a clear and open mind and an accepting heart while there. I prepared for this openness before I left home by trying to let go of the stressors connected with my job. I taught at the graduate level for several years. I absolutely loved working with graduate students who were interested in the field of education. But, as in many professions, education changed over the years. When I began my university teaching in 1971, I had total freedom in what and how I taught. As higher education moved to standardization of instructional content, I lost my personal freedom. My college was in the midst of program changes which ran counter to my own personal set of beliefs. I wondered if my retreat would cause me to say it was time to leave my profession.

Second, I packed self-confidence, determined to leave a constant nemesis, my self-doubt, at home. I needed to be open to the additional meanings the experience could have in my life. I wanted to believe that my best was yet to come, and I wanted to be confident I could find the best in me to pursue my dreams.

The third item I packed was an open heart. For one of the few times in my life, I wanted to listen to what my heart had to say. I hoped that doing so would give me the patience and resolve to act on what my heart told me and to find comfort in what I heard. I can manipulate my thoughts, but my heart speaks the truth. Not often in my life have my heart and my mind told me the same things at the very same time. Could I have that experience there? When I feel it in my heart, I can work it out in my mind.

Fourthly, I wanted to be "in community" while in the woods, so I carefully packed my relational self. When we are in relation with others, we are there to help and to serve them with their needs while, in the process, having our own needs addressed. When I stay within myself and don't interact with people around me,

I deny knowing important parts of who I am. Community means experiencing life together. During my life, I look forward to opportunities to be with people, friends, family, my graduate students, and people I haven't met yet. I was excited about this latter group as I packed my bag.

Finally, I wanted to bring my faith to the woods. I needed to take my faith in God. I needed an open mind and heart, and to remove the self doubt, I had to be willing to have faith that God would provide the direction that would lead me to some answers to the questions I took with me. God does not lead me down a wrong path. Because I have been given free will, I make the choice of whether or not to walk down the paths he puts before me. But if I have unconditional faith in my Higher Power, I have to make the decision to listen to Him, trust Him, and have faith in Him.

Because my faith is often in others and not myself, I have not acknowledged that dreams can become a way to find my authentic self. However, if those dreams were not there when I planned my first retreat, I would not have run to the woods searching for a clearer understanding of what God's purpose is for my life, and I would not have realized, as I discovered that purpose, I would once again journey down that path I could not identify from the tower. If I let myself go and commit to having faith in God, He will help me have the faith I need in myself. He will also help me see that my hopes for the future are greater than the dream itself, or me, as one part of that dream.

As I approached Brown County State Park, outside Nashville, Indiana, I passed through a beautiful, white, aging covered bridge built in 1838 by Aaron Wolf. Doing so seemed appropriate since, among other titles, Indiana is known as "the covered bridge state." By crossing it, I knew the bridge was taking my heart from the known into the unknown. I hesitated a moment before beginning my drive through the bridge, riding on its floor of thick, heavy wooden planks. I did not know what to expect from my upcoming adventure once I reached the other side. I knew the drive through the covered bridge would open me to beautiful scenery. Even more, I also realized it symbolized a letting go and arriving on the other side at my moment of readiness.

As I drove through the bridge, I remembered some lines from an old Brown County song I heard years ago: "And I don't regret a single move I'm makin'. Life's like a game of checkers don't you know. Don't fool yourself with strategy and fakin'. Make your move and then just let it go." I knew so much of my life had gone by, but I also felt in many ways – as I crossed the bridge – my life was just beginning. When I was almost through the bridge, I knew I had gone there with an aching in my heart for direction and guidance. I was longing for new adventure, adventure that had been waiting there, just for me to arrive. The time had come to make my move, let go and let God help me rediscover the authentic self deep inside me.

At the guard gate I paid my one-time $5 entrance fee. What a gorgeous drive to the Lodge up and down the "Hills of Brown," a local term used in reference to the beauty of this hilly countryside. Driving along the narrow road, I couldn't help but notice how the tall, old trees formed a canopy across the road as the upper branches from each side met at their tiptops. I saw only spots along the road where the sun found its way through those tall trees to highlight my drive. Each spot of sunlight was as unique as the special wave I wish for each of my four granddaughters. The joining of the trees' branches was exactly the convergence – toward a sense of connections and wholeness – I sought from all sides of my life. I checked in at the Abe Martin Lodge, secured the key to my cabin, and drove to the special parking spot identified for the "Tawny Apple #1" cabin.

Opened in 1929, Brown County is the largest Indiana State Park, covering 15,696 acres. On June 1, 1934, the Civilian Conservation Corps Company 1557 began its work, building cabins, including mine, and planting black locust, black walnut, various pines, and spruces, giving nature a helping hand in healing extreme erosion.

Brown County State Park is 15 miles west of my hometown Columbus, Indiana, and 20 miles east of Bloomington, Indiana, home to Indiana University. The park is in the rolling hills of southern Indiana, and its beauty is almost unmatched in the Midwest.

On that sunny Sunday afternoon in southern Indiana, I sat on the front porch of my cabin, looking in all directions and seeing nothing but beautiful, inviting woods. The birds were chirping, the ground squirrels were playing just below my porch, and the bugs were winning their battle with me. Where was that spray can of *OFF* I brought as an outer protection for the inner work I planned to do? The sun streamed through the stately trees, their shadows dancing in the late afternoon. The sun was making its daily journey from east to west. I breathed in the fresh air that surrounded me, and I felt at peace. While in Brown County, I hoped the trees and paths would lead me to a meaningful understanding of my place in the exciting web of life.

To say the least, my cabin was rustic. As I walked in the front door, some friendly (I later discovered) animals greeted me as they scurried around the floor. I left the door open a few minutes, and they were happy to find their way to freedom outside the cabin and off the porch.

Tawny Apple #1 had a welcoming, musty smell. There were two rooms. The larger room was about 10' x 10'. A full size bed took up much of the space. Also in this room were two pea-green chairs, covered with simulated leather. A small round table stood in one corner of the room, along with a dresser where I unloaded my clothes and carefully placed on top of the dresser those five specially packed items: a clear and open mind, my self-confidence, an open heart, a sense of community, and my faith. One dim light hung overhead, with two small lamps placed in nonstrategic locations. Three windows enhanced the light in the cabin. Two windows opened inward, and the third dropped down. Quaint old frames made of wood surrounded the windows and blended somewhat with the room.

The bathroom was all of 5' x 6'. It provided a shower stall, a toilet, and a sink. The shower was not even big enough to allow me to dry off while standing inside. We're talkin' about a small place here!

I had wanted "rustic," but as I surveyed my new surroundings, I found myself asking, "Why am I here, and what will I do without all those creature comforts I've grown so accustomed to? No TV, no phone, and therefore no Internet access. How was I going to stay in touch with my family, friends, and colleagues at work? What about all those important calls I get every day at the office? How could I check e-mails and keep in touch with all those individuals who depended on me to respond to their messages?"

Despite these haunting questions, in my heart the cabin soon became a castle. I forgot about the dark paneled walls, the dirty, old green carpet, the pea-green chairs, the tiny, cramped rooms, and the dim lights. It was all mine for two weeks!

My porch was about 5' x 7', built of old wooden planks, each about 8 inches wide. The cracks between the planks allowed me to see the ground below and the scampering animals that came to check out the stranger invading their territory.

While sitting on the porch and surveying my surroundings, I knew I had made the absolute right choice to run to the woods for two weeks. I got exactly what I wanted: me alone – with myself, my books, my laptop, my hikin' boots, my journal and a beautiful 15,000+ acre state park to provide the very kind of pastoral setting I needed.

Could I Do This?

The problem was, with all the descriptions I just wrote, I never had that kind of adventure before, and I was scared. I was scared to be by myself for two weeks with no agenda, no expectations, and no planned days. Could I stand to be with me for that long? I've said for years that I don't do "alone" very well. When I am alone with myself, I often think I have to be *doing* something, anything to avoid being with me. I normally do not take such opportunities to rest, refresh, and reflect. I didn't know if I could spend two weeks nourished with only my thoughts, my books, and my laptop. But I was sure as hell going to try. When nothing is sure, everything is possible.

In thinking about my decision to go to the woods in Brown County, I realized something: I believe God allowed me to choose Brown County, not only because a cabin was available during my limited window of time but also because it is very close to two places I know well – my hometown, Columbus, and my favorite university, Indiana. At least there I knew the lay of the land. I could find my way around, and in my aloneness I had comfort in being close to places I knew. I wanted my adventure and newness to have some familiarity to them.

Unlike Jon Katz, who spent months and months alone with his two white labs, Julius and Stanley, I spent a mere two weeks alone, a far less challenging time span. Still, for me it was a big deal! Although the time span was less challenging, the newness of the experience, the uncertainty that awaited me, and the fear that gripped me were overwhelming.

As Katz struggled with his decision about whether or not to buy the $67,000 house atop the mountain, so many events were happening around him, telling him he shouldn't buy his dream retreat. He developed so many doubts, almost convincing himself not to buy it. But something always convinced him to "go for it" and buy the house. Each obstacle he faced turned out to be an opportunity. Every time he thought of giving up, something happened to change his mind. I was so taken by his courage and his risk-taking. Amidst all my doubts and fears, events fell into place, giving me the courage finally to say, "I can do this."

My Expectations

The main purpose for my retreat to the woods was to search for the hazy path I saw at the top of the tower but lost again when I descended the stairs and got outside, lost in the dust of the crossroads. Beyond this primary quest, I decided early on that I was not going to Brown County with a long list of other expectations. As Thomas Merton said in his book *Contemplation in a World of Action*, "The imagination should be allowed a certain amount of time to browse around." I wanted to browse along the paths in Brown County, hoping to reclaim my authentic self, leaving behind any expectations for how and when this reclamation might reveal itself to me. In his book *A Short History of Nearly Everything* Bill Bryson suggested, "It is easy to overlook this thought that life just is. As humans we are inclined to feel that life must have a point. We have plans and aspirations and desires. We want to take constant advantage of all the intoxicating existence we've been endowed with… Life, in short, just wants to be."

I simply wanted to be in the moment for once in my life and see what each day had in store for me. I did not want a rigid schedule to follow each day. I knew I wanted to read, do some writing, take some hikes along the marked paths in the woods, swim in the park's pool, and, most of all, reflect on my life. I remembered some lines from a favorite Eagles song:

> Lighten up while you still can.
> Don't even try to understand.
> Just find a place to make your stand,
> And take it easy.

I made my two-week stand at Brown County State Park. I hoped to lighten up while I still could. I did not yet understand all the obsessive thoughts compelling me to make my stand there. But I wanted to take it easy as I tried to gain new insights about Ed Poole. In their own time, those insights would find me.

CHAPTER 2
Reclaiming My Authentic Self from the Depths of Depression

Ten years ago my life was on cruise control, and I was skimmin' along like a beautiful sailboat on a clear azure-blue lake where the water is as smooth as glass. I had always secured the jobs I wanted when I wanted them. I was a public school administrator, had climbed the "ladder of success" (or so I thought), and was making that coveted six-figure salary for a school administrator. I surrounded myself with many of those material possessions by which I measured my success. I lived in a beautiful up-scale community in one of Chicago's most affluent western suburbs. Life was good.

My son and daughter were grown, through college, married, and living happy lives of their own. Those major responsibilities of raising children and nurturing them into early adulthood were over.

All of these outward signs that I was leading the good life masked the fact that on the inside my life was falling apart around me. I was a lost soul. I couldn't eat; I couldn't sleep; I lost my ability to focus on *anything* – my work, my play, and the meaning of my life in general. I didn't want to engage in activities with family or friends. After reading a newspaper article, I could not remember many details I had just read. I was irritable.

I began spending the hour-long commute to and from my job looking at cement mixers and eighteen wheelers, thinking if I would just turn the steering wheel a little to the left, take off my seat belt, and pick up speed, there was no way I would survive the crash. Because of the size and weight of these two massive machines I knew the driver would probably not be hurt at all. As the months went by, these thoughts began to occupy more and more of my thinking. I didn't know why the thoughts were there, and, thank goodness, I got scared!

After a period of time spent entertaining these thoughts, seeing my fear grow to the point of panic, and visiting various doctors, I received the diagnosis of clinical depression. How could I be clinically depressed? I had pulled inward, as if in a cocoon, and I did not know how to become a butterfly.

When I first became aware of my depression in 1996, many on-going life issues came together for the first time in my life. Developmentally I was entering the mid-point in my life. This transition was natural, but at the time I didn't know it was occurring. My work and the moments of confusion in my life about who I was as a person became intrusive events, contributing to the crisis. I was tormented internally because of my inability to understand, and hence cope, with my life at that point in time. The one coping mechanism I considered was suicide. Fortunately for me, I found others while in the hospital.

I now realize I have been at a crossroads several times in my life. I landed in that first crossroads because my life before college was full of uncertainty and confusion. I grew up in a home where Mom was the dominant role model. She saw that same primary role model in her mother, so Mom assumed this same position in my home. I stayed attached to my mother and never identified with my dad as a male role model. I did not know my masculine role as I prepared to leave for college. In my home I seldom saw my parents show affection for one another: a few hugs perhaps, but no kisses, no public arguments, and no "I love you" expressed verbally in my presence. I also did not share my emotions with anyone. I kept them deep inside me because I didn't know how to express my feelings. I couldn't escape those early, confusing memories even if I tried. As author Eleanor Farjeon said, "The events of childhood do not pass but reveal themselves like seasons of the year."

My initial crossroads experience continued into my college years. I missed my home, my mother, and was totally unprepared with an inadequate self-esteem and a modicum of self-confidence. After only one semester I packed my belongings and headed home, fully expecting to stay there until I decided if I really wanted to go to college and if so where? Although academically successful in high school, I felt totally unprepared to meet the challenges of the academic program in college. I felt the same pain and confusion then that I internalized before I left for college. During that semester break I decided, for once in my life, to face my fears and uncertainties and return to school. As a young adult, I didn't even know I was at a crossroads and needed to decide where to travel.

I plummeted into a crossroads the second time when I graduated from college. There was no tower at this crossroads, just as there was none at the first crossroads landing. When I left college, I was still clueless about my four paths. I just knew I was a confused 22-year-old man, unable to understand my life. It took me two years to release the fears I felt when I left home. However during my last two years in college I broke through the comfort zone, leaving the uncertainty and fear of leaving home and attending college behind. Those last two years were more comfortable and enjoyable. My grades improved, and I met the girl I would eventually marry.

My third landing at a crossroads occurred several years later, in the early nineties, when I was a superintendent of schools in northern Indiana. I spent night after night sitting alone in my dark basement, without realizing I was trying to find my way out of that particular crossroads because the four paths were not even intersecting at a crossroads. The paths were as far apart as they had ever been up to that point in my life.

In 1996, when I contemplated suicide, my life became what author Sue Monk Kidd described as "a holy summons to cross a threshold… both a leaving behind and a stepping toward, a separation and an opportunity." Toward the end of 1996, I entered the psychiatric care unit with clinical depression, the fourth time I fell in the middle of a crossroads, not knowing what to do and once again feeling so afraid. The staff at the hospital and my friends who were also patients along with me helped me redefine my authentic self at that point in my life. I called a halt to everything around me and wrote *Lessons from the Porch.*

As time passed, after I left the hospital and began writing, my depression became a gift from God. I was forced to call a "time out" and try to understand what had just happened. I needed to slow down to understand; because I had been such a human "doing," I did not know how to act as a human "being." At previous crossroads I got the message that I needed to ask God for help. During the thirty years between my first and fourth times in the middle of the crossroads, I did not ask God for help because I didn't know how, and I was rebelling against the God I knew in my early life.

While my hospitalization helped me realize I did not know Ed Poole outside my job titles, I found little pieces of myself as I wrote *Lessons from the Porch.* But I lost Ed Poole as I pushed forward with my professional life and completely ignored the other personal, spiritual, and authentic paths. In his book *Living an Undivided Life,* Parker Palmer said it so well: "As we become more obsessed with succeeding, or at least surviving…we lose touch with our souls and disappear into our roles." I had climbed that ladder of success I mentioned earlier, only to find the ladder was leaning up against the wrong wall. The wall was wrong because almost every brick used to build it was made from others' expectations for me and for the way I should be living out my life through my work. I felt I only existed as a reflection in other people's eyes and the resulting need I felt to please everyone. Very few bricks in my "wall of success" contained my own expectations for who I was and what I should be doing with my life and, in the process, to be happy.

Sometimes my life has been a matter of performing the scripts written for me by others: society, family, church, job, friends, and traditions – I played them out in full costume and mask, those masks I saw looking out the windows of the tower. In *Turning toward the World* Thomas Merton wrote these words: "Struggle in my heart all week. My own moral conflict never ceases. Knowing I cannot and must not simply submit to the standards imposed on me, and merely conform as 'they' would like. This I am convinced is wrong – but the pressure never ceases."

For Merton, it became imperative to rid himself of others' expectations and not succumb to the pressure of the outside world. Like Merton, doing so for me has been very difficult. The difficulty increased because my compass and the light for my path were neither in my hand nor my heart and soul. Rather, that light was in the hands of others because they defined me and established their expectations for my life and what I should be doing with it. During my hospitalization and since, I've spent a lot of time getting acquainted with Ed Poole, trying to find that common light in my heart and soul as I try to understand where I've been, what happened to me, and why I was at that particular point along my journey.

The lessons in my previous book are "from the porch" because the porch became a metaphor for how I accept, or fail to accept, change in my life, the same quest for change both Jon Katz and I embarked on. When I was a little boy growing up in Columbus, Indiana, how I wish Mom had said, "Eddie, it's a beautiful day out there. Go find some friends to play with and just explore the world. When you get thirsty, come home and get something to drink. When you get hungry, we'll have some lunch, and if you get tired, come home, sit in the porch swing, and rest a spell."

Instead, Mom always cautioned me, "Eddie, don't get too close to the edge of the porch because if you do, you might fall off." This normal cautioning from a mother to her child stayed with me for many, too many years. Her concern for my safety was there deep inside me because I allowed it to remain there.

New Sight from my Granddaughter

Recently, Mom's cautioning was viewed through a different set of eyes – mine! My one-year-old granddaughter, Emma, and I were on the back patio of her parents' home, enjoying the beautiful day. She was sitting atop the black, heavy, circular wrought iron table, enjoying her new view of the world. The day was sunny, 73 degrees, with a slight breeze – a perfect day for exploring. At one point, Emma decided she wanted to crawl around on the tabletop. As she reached one critical point, without a moment's hesitation, I said, "Emma, don't get too close to the edge of the table; you might fall off."

Emma pulled herself back into a sitting position, away from the edge of that circular patio table. Soon after she moved away from the edge, I asked, "Emma, are you ready to get off now?" With that, I extended my hands to her, she raised her little arms over her head, and I knew she was ready to explore other places.

At that very moment I realized something that, for my entire life, I was unable to see: Mom never said to me, "Eddie, don't get *off* the porch." She just didn't want me to get too close to the edge, fall off, and crack my head on the sidewalk.

The part about *staying on* the porch was my view, not Mom's. I'm amazed that it took this interaction with Emma to cause my eyes to open to an unintended message from my mother, a message I've carried with me for over fifty years. I misinterpreted Mom's caution. She wanted to keep me safe while I was on the porch. I thought her concern meant she didn't even want me to leave the porch.

I remembered a saying I read some years ago by Marcel Proust: "The real voyage of discovery consists not in seeking new landscapes but in having new eyes." That day with Emma, I internalized Mom's cautioning from my own new eyes. I also came to understand that if I look through new eyes, perhaps even those paths I've been following will appear new. Maybe I'm on a path that is right for me at this moment, and I'm trying to find new eyes with which to see my way.

CHAPTER 3

Beginning to Find Some Connections Toward My Authentic Self

Do What You Like
Like What You Do

After I got settled into my cabin, I took the short drive into Nashville, the tiny village three miles from the park. I used to live in this little hamlet, so I was familiar with my surroundings. I parked my car and began exploring the familiar shops in town. As I walked into a T-shirt shop, I was immediately reminded why I came to the woods. The shop's logo is "Life is Good." I found a shirt with the shop's logo on the front and a very powerful thought on the back: "Do what you like. Like what you do." As the owner put my new purchase in a bag, I thought this shirt, front and back, defined why I was there: to remind myself that life *is* good and to be sure I do what I like and like what I do. Katz wanted to discover what he wanted to do with his life as he retreated to his mountain cabin, and so did I.

As Katz went for solitude to his mountain retreat in upstate New York, he quickly realized that solitude meant being alone, but it also meant interacting with others. In his book *A Hidden Wholeness*, Parker Palmer shared similar thoughts. He wrote, "Of course, solitude is essential to personal integration...but because we are communal creatures who need each other's support – and because, left to our own devices, we have an endless capacity for self-absorption and self-deception – community is equally essential to rejoining soul and role." Katz spent a lot of time in his new cabin retreat, but he had to go into his little town to be with others. Those same two aspects of solitude, being alone and being in community, very quickly became evident to me in the hills of Brown County. I needed my time alone, but I also needed to be in community. Doing so helped bring definition to those times I spent in silence and gave me clues to my authentic self.

I found my community at a hotel I entered after leaving the shop. I had such a great time. Entering the bar, I felt like I was at Cheers, a place where everybody knows your name. The friends gathered around the bar were sharing stories of the day and their plans for the upcoming week.

Shortly they brought me into the conversation, asking me who I was, where I lived, and why I had come to the park for two weeks – all appropriate questions when a stranger interrupts a small inner circle of friends. Art, a long-time Brown County resident, bought a round of drinks for those of us at the bar. I chuckled to myself that Norm (from Cheers) would have been overjoyed someone was buying a round for the bar. I could just hear him saying, "Sam, do *not* put *this* beer on my tab. By the way, Sam, isn't my tab all paid up?" After enjoying the connections I felt with my new friends, I headed back to Tawny Apple and went to bed in the peace and quiet of the woods of Brown County. My trip to Brown County could not have had a better beginning.

An Almost Perfect Day

My first full day in Brown County was an almost-perfect day. When I went to bed, I decided I would not set an alarm clock. I would just see what time I woke up. Fortunately, I awakened around 6:30, just in time to see the sun beginning to appear through the beautiful forest of tall, stately trees that surrounded the cabin. What a breath-taking sight! I sat on my front porch for a long time, just watching the sun blink through different clusters of the forest, climbing its way from the east, and I thanked God for leading me to this place.

After sitting a long time in awe of this beauty, I read my daily devotional and threw on some clothes for a trip to my favorite coffee house in Nashville, The Daily Grind, a place so special to me because when my son and daughter were undergraduates at Indiana University, we made many trips to Nashville and never, ever missed going to my favorite place for coffee. Arriving there around 8:00, I was the only one in the shop, except for the wait help. I ordered a large cup of coffee, and the waiter told me the owners have a variety of daily papers for customers to read, which I knew from my previous visits.

I took my coffee to a table, grabbed a couple of local papers, and spent the next hour and a half sipping, reading, observing, and enjoying! The coffee shop was warm and inviting, just like its coffee. As I drank my coffee and read the papers, customers began drifting in to get their morning cup of java. The setting reminded me of the many memories and the wonderful conversations I had with Eric and Tracie during their undergraduate years. What a way to start my day!

After finishing my coffee, I returned to the cabin, wanting to read and write. I realized that, even though I was staying in a castle, I was beginning to feel claustrophobic in such cramped quarters. The cabin was great for sleeping, thinking, and enjoying the beauty all around me but not good for the reading and writing I wanted to do. Even the can of *OFF* wasn't providing an impenetrable shield from the bugs, so I gathered my laptop and my books and headed to the lodge.

The Abe Martin Lodge is built of solid, rustic Indiana limestone mined from the quarries in Bedford, Indiana, just a short drive from the state park. Large, one-foot-square, solid log beams support a very spacious entry. As I walked through the huge heavy doors, my eyes immediately were drawn to a long wooden table on the left, lined with books by local authors and full of endearing, humorous stories about some of the characters who lived in the "hills and hollers" around here over the past 150 years.

I walked up a half flight of stairs, settling in the mezzanine level, with overstuffed sofas and chairs and a huge 20' x 50' stone fireplace that I enjoyed during past winter visits. The chairs and sofas were comfortably arranged in clusters, facilitating the many intimate conversations shared among friends. Unlike my pea-green imitation leather chairs at the cabin, these chairs and sofas were made of fine, comfortable fabric, with lots of reds, greens, and blues. Above the fireplace was a framed picture of Kin Hubbard, the creator of the Abe Martin cartoon character after whom the lodge is named. The room was spacious, with an open, beamed ceiling built of logs and supported by heavy, black, iron L-braces. The braces hold the beams in place with some of the biggest nuts and bolts I have ever seen. To give you an idea of the expanse of this spacious level, the room itself overpowered that huge fireplace. We're talkin' big here!

At the other end of the room, opposite Kin Hubbard's picture, was an old map of Indiana, so old the paper had turned brown. Both of these large frames at either end of the mezzanine were surrounded by paintings of southern Indiana's beautiful fall leaves, as well known and admired here as the fall colors in New England. Other paintings captured images of the beautiful wolves found in this part of the country.

Similar to my visit to the coffee shop, *I was the only person in the area!* I opened my laptop and began writing. I wrote for a long time, then closed down the laptop and opened a book to read. While I knew I eventually would once again find my own authentic self by answering the questions I brought with me, I also knew the thoughts and ideas of others would help me answer those questions. The words of other writers challenge my ideas and beliefs, and I like the internal struggle of comparing their thoughts to mine. Doing the comparing is both confusing and frustrating as I read what others say about their quests for the meaning of authenticity in their lives and what they did along the way to find that meaning. I knew that out of my confusion and frustration the dust and clouds would begin to lift.

I knew rediscovering my authentic self was a combination of work from the outside in and the inside out. As long as I'm struggling and confused, I'm still learning. I truly believe the struggle and confusion were part of what God expected of me. I wish sometimes it might be easier and simpler, but I know in my heart God doesn't work with me in easier and simpler ways.

These thoughts were whizzing through my mind. I needed a break to let them settle. Just outside the mezzanine was a lush courtyard, filled with a beautiful rainbow of flowers. The sun was beaming down on the flowers, and they were smiling. The courtyard was a quiet place to rest, refresh, reflect and let my soul be at peace, surrounded by wisteria, tulips, snapdragons, peonies, roses, the Queen Anne's lace and lilac's grace. I sat in the courtyard a long time. When my heart was filled with the floral beauty surrounding me, I returned to my writing.

Blending Work with Play:
A Relatively New Experience

Throughout life, I've relied on work alone, my professional path, to define my journey. Experiencing both work and play that first day caused me to realize I must have both to help me find my authentic self. After finishing my thoughts on the laptop and reading for a while, I reversed my steps to the cabin, donned my bathing suit, and went for a swim at the pool. I loved it! The sun was bright, causing sparkling diamonds to dance on the top of the pool. The water was a perfect temperature, and again I reflected on how lucky I was to be in that place at that very time in my life. I took time out from my reading and writing, just to relax and try to be in the moment. I was reminded of a statement made by author Sam Shemitz:

> It is too nice to write today.
> You may beg and plead, but still no way.
> I'm going outside to play while it is light.
> Maybe I'll write some more when it is night.

After a leisurely, invigorating hour poolside, I returned to the cabin, grabbed my laptop and books, and headed back to the quietness and vastness of the mezzanine. I couldn't stay away from the writing too long. As I allowed the day to unfold in its logical order, I captured in writing the events I found. The three paths I was able to identify at the crossroads – personal, professional, and spiritual – remained unconnected as I progressed through the day. I wrote as if they were separate, the way I have most often experienced them in my life. I continued to feel an urging to find the fourth path so I could lead the authentic life God wanted for me. But I took this strong desire to keep reading, writing, and reflecting as an indication that the way to my soul and to authenticity was still inside me, begging to find a way out. I was glad I played, but I wanted to continue writing. As the afternoon drifted away into the early evening, I felt it was time to play some more. I went into town, made some new friends, and got better acquainted with those I met the previous day.

During my trip to Nashville I thought again of Jon Katz and his double meaning for the word solitude, being alone and being in community with others. Last night while having dinner at the Hotel Nashville, I met the managers of a local winery in Nashville, the Chateau Thomas Winery. I promised I would stop by this afternoon. After tasting some wine (I bought a bottle of their locally-made Merlot) and meeting more very nice, congenial folks, I headed back to the Hotel Nashville for dinner.

Entering the bar, I saw Art and Charlie from last night and met more people, all from Nashville. I spent three hours talking to Art, an 84-year-old gentleman who lives in the hotel. What an interesting guy! He served in the Navy where he met his wife. After leaving the Navy, Art and his wife lived for many years in New Mexico. He had wonderful stories to tell.

Art is almost six feet tall, and our eyes meet when we're both standing. His frame is slight, and he weighed 150 pounds, the same as when he graduated from high school. He stood straight and proud with snow-white, curly hair that, like mine, receded from his forehead. Art's hair was combed straight back, and its length emphasized the curls.

The southwestern influence Art brought with him to Nashville was still evident in the clothes he wore. On this particular evening, he wore a beautiful turquoise, long-sleeved shirt and jet-black jeans. Around his neck was a rope-like lanyard, held together by a medallion with two Kokopellis in the middle, which immediately caught my attention. I became acquainted with this ancient character through my son, Eric, and daughter-in-law, Stacy. They have long-admired this mythical person and helped me understand its symbolic meaning.

In ancient Indian legend, Kokopelli, the flute player, was the symbol of happiness and joy. He talked to the wind and the sky, his flute audible in the spring breeze, bringing warmth after the winter cold. The legend of Kokopelli represents everything pure and spiritual. He was also thought of as a traveling prankster. He visited villages, playing his flute and carrying his songs on his back. Everyone sang and danced the night away. In the morning, when he left, the crops were plentiful, the sun came out, the snow melted, the green grass grew, and the birds came out and began to sing. Just as the T-shirt from the Life is Good store, the legend of the Kokopelli was symbolic of my trip to Brown County. I hoped my retreat would represent everything pure and spiritual in my heart and my soul. As I visited with others I didn't play a flute; my songs were heard in the stories I told and those I heard. I wanted to sing and dance the night away with my writing, my reading, and my visits with my new friends. I hoped when I left the lessons in my heart would be plentiful, the sun would be shining, the grass would be green, and the birds would be singing. Art's happy personality and clothing represented all the wonderful stories about the Kokopelli.

After a long while into our wonderful conversation, Art excused himself to go to his room and bring back some items for me to see. He returned with two over-stuffed three-ring binders and a brief article he wrote on "The Chronology of Aging."

The first binder he opened was devoted solely to his friendship with Bob Knight, who coached men's basketball at Indiana University for over 20 years and is now head coach at Texas Tech University. I have long-admired what Coach Knight stands for relative to interscholastic basketball and life in general, and I so enjoyed reading the personal correspondence between Art and "Coach." Glancing through the folder brought me closer to a man I have long admired and a man I was beginning to admire.

The second binder contained a history of Art's professional life with Western Electric in Indianapolis, the job that brought Art and his wife to the Midwest from New Mexico. Page after page acknowledged the work and many contributions Art accomplished while there. Art was responsible for beginning many new programs to assist other employees. One that struck my heart was the adult education program, designed to help employees attain their high school diplomas.

What I found myself taking away from that evening's conversation was how honored I felt that Art, so quickly, was comfortable sharing some of his very personal memoirs and stories with me. But I decided that's just the kind of guy he is. Our conversation connected an old friend, the Coach, with my new friend, Art. He talked with his heart. I hope he felt I had done the same.

I finished my day enjoying a couple more drinks with Art, Charlie, and the friendly folks from the winery. We laughed and shared more stories. I left around 10:00 and returned to my cabin. I sat on the front porch, looking through the trees at the bright moon overhead, and thought of the words of writer and storyteller Thomas Berry: "If you have a wonderful sense of the divine, it is because we live amid such awesome magnificence." I was amid the overpowering beauty of my surroundings, and there I sought a sense of the divine as I searched for my authentic self.

Finding Connections

For a long time I have felt there are no coincidences in life. Events happen for a reason, perhaps unknown at the time of the event. I knew my wonderful day was defined by the experiences I had and those experiences did not happen by accident. I enjoyed the beauty of nature, found solitude in a rustic building that stimulated my writing, reading, and thinking, relaxed my body and mind, enjoyed good wine, and shared wonderful conversations with genuinely good people.

Those experiences also connected me to the questions I brought with me and helped ease the pain of landing in the middle of the crossroads, seeing the crossroads clearly from the tower, then losing their distinctions as I came back to the crossroads. Bathed from the moonlight on the porch and wrapped in a soft blanket of peace, I realized my questions couldn't be understood in a vacuum, separated from each other and from my experiences in the woods. They were so intrinsically interrelated and must be considered in total. When my heart touched one question, it touched them all. For example, all the questions required me to be open to the messages and questions God was trying to send me, which demanded my serious thought about the others. As I tried to better understand my journey toward an authentic life, I could not do so without an open heart.

In my adult life, my heart was only open to other people, allowing them to define me. I was not open to my own voice or to God's voice. I've usually taken my cues from others, without listening closely for the unique messages and questions God sends only to me. I've come to realize that God keeps sending me these messages, which I keep ignoring. If I ignore them often enough, the messages He sends return in the form of problems: lack self-esteem and self-confidence, a reliance on others to influence my journeys, and an unwillingness to be open and honest with others – family, colleagues, and friends. As God keeps sending problems, and I keep ignoring those as well, He begins to send me not messages, not problems, but crises. An example of this sequence occurred when I was hospitalized with clinical depression. If I could have understood the messages and then the problems God sent me, the crises of my subsequent crossroads experiences might have been avoided. But, in all honesty, perhaps God intended me to remain unaware of any messages because the overriding, critically important message came when I realized it was no coincidence I spent four months at that time in my life hospitalized with clinical depression.

Could I become the person God sees, without having the sense of self-control and inner peace he wants for me? As I've said, most often my life has been full of others' expectations for me, not my own. I've allowed those expectations to govern much of my behavior and many of my decisions. I often took jobs because those whom I respected in education thought doing so would advance my career. Usually I accepted new positions before taking time to consider if the position was one I truly desired, thereby matching where I thought my career should go.

One job I did not want to pursue early in my career was that of high school principal. However, when that job became available at my home high school in Columbus, I jumped at the opportunity because I was returning to a high school I loved during my years there. That decision took me down a path I never thought I would travel. I enjoyed my time in a job I didn't expect to have. However, another job those same respected friends wanted me to consider was the superintendency. As I wrote earlier, I took this job and regretted it from the moment I signed the contract. I had a miserable experience and could not wait to leave for another position, one I wanted to find for myself.

The time as superintendent was the first opportunity I took to look deeply inward, search my soul, and ask God to direct me. That job, however, had bright spots: For a brief time I found my inner self while enmeshed in a job I did not want. While in that job, I spent hours in the basement talking to my imaginary inner guide Joshua. I asked my friend questions about why I was there and how I could have made such a poor decision about a career move. Joshua helped me see that in my life following paths I didn't choose is perhaps more important than finding paths which are right for me at the time. However, my propensity has been to forget the lessons when I move on and get busy again.

Once I realized I did not know Ed Poole when all my fancy job titles were stripped away, I knew that my control and peace were not "self" and "inner" but were formed by expectations, hopes, and desires from outside me. Those expectations that came at me from without appealed to my ego and made me feel important. If others whom I respected thought I was capable of handling a position with more responsibility, why shouldn't I just accept their praise and give it a try? Maybe those expectations, hopes, and desires matched mine, but I had no way of knowing. Parker Palmer (*To Know as We Are Known: A Spirituality of Education*) said, "It is the Christian tradition, whose central claim is not that God takes us out of ourselves and our world into ethereal realms, but that God broke in to reveal us and our world as we are." How could I quit living for others and live for myself? I couldn't follow my own dreams if I listened to the dreams others had for me. How should I listen for God's voice to help me find the calmness, patience, and openness I needed, to feel at peace with myself, to feel in control of my own life and the decisions that emanate from within? How could I find connections among those four paths I saw from the tower?

Living with life's connections is a topic Vaclav Havel, a playwright, dissident, prisoner, and former president of the Czech Republic, viewed in an interesting way. In an article titled "The Quiver of a Shrub in California," he used these words to describe the interconnectedness in life.

> Being, nature, the universe – they are all one infinitely complex and mysterious metaorganism of which we are but a part, though a unique one. Everyone of us is a crossroads of thousands of relations, links, influences, and communications – physical, chemical, biological, and others of which we know nothing... And while each of us is a very special and complex network of space, time, matter, and energy, we are nothing more than their network. None of us knows how the quiver of a shrub in California affects the mental state of a coal miner in North Bohemia or how his mental state affects the quivering of the shrub.

In *Memoirs of a Geisha*, Arthur Golden shared his view of connections in our universe: "We must use whatever methods we can to understand the movement of the universe around us and time our actions so that we are not fighting the currents, but moving with them."

Robert Raines, a former Methodist minister, offers yet another view on life's connections. In his book *Living the Questions* Raines encourages his reader to live with the questions in life and find connectedness within the questions. Doing so requires much patience and practice. I've had trouble living with the questions. Usually I want to jump too quickly to answers that will be inadequate, because the questions have not been within me long enough to provide comfortable, inclusive, and connected answers. The answers are also incomplete if I have not yet seen the interrelatedness of the questions, those same connections between the shrub and the coal miner, between the universe and myself, and between my experiences in the woods and my authentic self.

The fast pace with which we lead our lives often makes it difficult to be patient with the questions. Living with the questions long enough to find their deeper meaning causes us, once again, to consider *changing* our lives. Change itself can be synchronistic, depending on its meaning to each person's experience. And meaning is found within the questions.

CHAPTER 4

Closed but (Still) Open as Charlie Begins His "Story"

My second day in the woods began with another beautiful sunrise. Again I awakened around 6:30, taking advantage of my built-in alarm clock, sat on the porch and watched the sun beaming a simultaneous combination of light and shadows through "my" trees surrounding the cabin. The light dew on the leaves highlighted their intricate and beautiful structures. While sitting amidst the beauty, I read my daily devotional and put myself in a place to receive the events of the day.

Those events began with another trip to the Daily Grind for that first cup of steaming hot, delicious coffee. I got to the coffee shop, only to find it *closed*! The sign on the door read "Open daily from 8:00 to 6:00." Well, this day was a part of "daily," and my watch said it was 8:30, so why wasn't my favorite coffee shop open? I reminded myself that this is southern Indiana where life moves a bit slower than in suburban Chicago. I sat a few more minutes, finally realizing, as much as I wanted the shop to open, it was going to stay closed. Then I thought, even if my coffee shop was closed, I could still be open to the day's adventures.

After achieving this happier state of mind, I returned to the park and walked up the hill to the lodge where I found a free cup of coffee out of a machine,

<u>not</u> the same quality as The Daily Grind but coffee just the same.

After finishing my coffee, I took a three-mile hike along one of the many marked paths throughout the park, a beautiful, meandering trail through the woods. As I hiked, I was torn between looking up to find the sun through the treetops and looking down to make sure I didn't miss the beauty at my feet. What a gift! I also realized, while tromping through the woods, I was trying to find God by finding myself.

Near the end of my walk, I ran into two young boys, accompanied by two adults, just beginning their hike. One boy seemed to be about six and the other a bit younger. As I approached them, I said "Hi, guys." (I've been reminded here in southern Indiana everyone makes eye contact with the approaching person and says "Hi" or "How ya doin?" or "Hey.") The older boy said, "Hi, Grandpa." The younger greeted me with "Hi, Gramps." Now, I *am* a "Papaw" and a "Gramps" to four beautiful granddaughters – Allie, Aimie, Kate, and Emma. But for some reason I didn't want to appear to be a "grandpa" to two youngsters I had never seen before – a nice dose of reality and humility for me that morning. Then I thought those two boys probably love their grandfather, so I should feel honored they felt like giving me that title as we met briefly on the path.

I thought about the greeting from those boys and the reality of my age as I went to the mezzanine and began writing. My age was on my mind because I was in my mid-fifties when I began taking that backward look at my life, and ten years later I once again tried to find my authentic self as I began *Lessons from the Crossroads*. These thoughts consumed me all afternoon. By late afternoon I decided to have dinner. The restaurant at the Hotel Nashville is closed on Tuesday and Wednesday nights. Last night Art told me The Seasons, a local hotel close to the park, always has a fried chicken buffet on Tuesday nights. I thought of my dad, who always, *always* ordered fried chicken on those rare occasions when our family ate in a restaurant as I was growing up. Dad's favorite dinner soon became mine. I went and enjoyed my chicken dinner, thinking Dad would have enjoyed it too.

I returned to Tawny Apple #1, did some more reading, and finished writing about the events of my second full day in the woods. I again said a big "thank you" to God for inspiring me to make this sojourn, to return to my childhood home, and to enjoy its southern hospitality. Most importantly, I was open to the day and all its possibilities. While The Daily Grind was closed, I remained open, and I had another wonderful day. My openness allowed the day to unfold as it was supposed to. I had no agenda. That day I felt in tune with one of my primary reasons for going to Brown County: I continued my inward journey toward understanding the angst and confusion about my life that took me there.

Another Day Toward My Authentic Self

It was pouring down rain at 6:45 when I opened the drapes in my cabin. I was *very* tempted just to crawl back into bed and sleep some more, but then I remembered I was not there to sleep but to spend time finding me.

I walked out onto the porch in the rain, still in my "sleepin' togs." Those same stately tree columns surrounded me, and the rain gave a fresh smell to all the lush, green growth. Returning inside, I read my daily devotional, got dressed and headed into town for my coffee. YEA, the Daily Grind was open today.

I planned to get a large coffee. Karis Johnson, who along with her husband Hal own The Daily Grind, was there again this morning. Recognizing me, she asked, "Are you going to hang around and read the papers again?" I said I was, so she said, "You know, it's a better deal if you get a mug for here, and then you get a refill for 50 cents."

That sounded like a much better idea since I was going to hang out, read one or two papers, and continue reading a book I brought with me. She gave me my coffee, and I found a booth. I began reading the day's editions of the same two papers I read Monday, *The Republic* from my hometown and *USA Today*, to catch up on the national and international news.

After reading for a while, I decided I was hungry. I went back to the counter and ordered a ham, egg, and cheese croissant for $3.95. To my welcome surprise,

Karis said, "Now that you've ordered something to eat, you get *two free* refills on your coffee."

I thought to myself, "It doesn't get much better'n this." Within a very few minutes, the croissant arrived at the table, and it was most definitely the biggest such morning sandwich I've ever had. The ham, egg, and cheese were spilling out on all sides of the large croissant. Not only have I never had a bigger breakfast croissant, but also I've never had one that tasted so wonderfully delicious. I savored each bite.

As I drank my coffee, ate my breakfast, read the papers, and continued reading a book, I decided this routine for starting my day was the simple, relaxing time I needed to confront the central questions I brought to the woods. Beginning my day with coffee and new friends also resumed my soul's search for answers to my questions. While sitting there, noticing the sun fighting its way through the clouds, I was reminded that I came to the woods to renew the search for my authentic self. In so doing, I felt I could rediscover the clarity with which I saw three of my paths from atop the tower and use that pristine image to find the final path, my direction from the crossroads.

I was confident finding new meaning for myself would give me the courage to let go of an ego that had gone way beyond a sense of self-confidence. My ego had become inflated because my essence, my soul, had not found a way to rein in the pretentious thoughts of myself and create a better blend between my head and my soul.

Because I received a lot of positive feedback for my work as a school administrator, I began to think I could do no wrong in those jobs, and my ego grew in disproportion to my soul. I actually thought I was the best school leader in suburban Chicago, quite an outlandish thought considering the number of school districts in that large metropolitan area. A comforting sense of self-confidence in what I did was important; however, the inner feelings of knowing what I was doing became exaggerated to the point that I felt I could do no wrong. I thought the events causing a situation to become askew had to have been someone else's shortcomings, not mine. But, since I was so afraid of making mistakes, and since I wanted everyone to like me, I probably would have dismissed any criticism to, "They really do not know what I do." At that time in my career, I knew nothing about the critical importance of standing in front of the full length mirror and seeing what I was doing wrong, or right, in any particular situation. When problems occurred in the school setting I was never at fault. I now try to accept my responsibility for the problems as well as (only) my share of the plaudits when my life is moving in positive directions.

In the woods, I experienced that blending of ego and soul every time I enjoyed the wildflowers; looked out into the woods from Tawny Apple's porch and enjoyed their beauty during my hikes; went to The Daily Grind to read, enjoy the folks there, and return to those questions I struggled with every day; heard wonderful stories about this place and the people there; read some ideas that applied directly to me; met good people like Art and Charlie; and reflected on my calling and God's plan for me, now and in the future.

When I finished my coffee and walked out into the inviting sunlight, I broke one of my self-imposed rules for the two weeks: I went to the beautiful, new Nashville Public Library to gain free Internet access to check my e-mails from the office. I went through the library's large doors and walked up a very wide set of stairs to find the main desk. The entire library had a feeling of openness and spaciousness, the same two features symbolizing my hopes for the time here. A gracious lady told me I could certainly use one of their computers to log onto the Internet. All I had to do was complete a very brief form, which she said she would keep on file during my time there. I wasn't surprised, really, to find at my university's website a total of 55 messages waiting for me, which accumulated in two days. I also was not surprised to find a single message requiring any immediate attention on my part. Another lesson in humility – "Ed, you are not as important to others as you think you are!" Maybe I won't go to the library again while I'm here. I have other, more enjoyable activities to anticipate, rather than spending time on the Internet, and I am so enjoying each day's events as they play themselves out in my life.

Every moment, *every single moment*, during my stay in the woods assured me that God wanted me to be right there, right then. I know I've said these words before, but I have to share them with you more than one time to show the impact they had on me. The words I wrote flowed effortlessly, something that has rarely happened during my novice experience as a writer. In order to protect myself from thinking past the two weeks in Brown County, I absorbed every moment of my time there. I cautioned myself from asking, "OK, what's next, God?" My propensity for wanting to know what the future holds has always caused me an interesting combination of anticipation and dread. I vowed not to do that to me while I was there. I owed it to myself to enjoy so much my unstructured time and let the future be waiting for me when I arrived.

A Gift from a Fellow Chicago Cubs Fan

At one point during the day, as I once again sat on the beautiful mezzanine level of the rustic, old Abe Martin Lodge, I ventured outside to sit awhile in the beautiful courtyard. As I closed the heavy, wooden door behind me, I noticed a gentleman sitting in a chair. He was wearing a Chicago Cubs baseball cap, so I asked, "Are you a Cubs fan?"

"Yes, I am," he said.

"I am too." He sat there with his head cupped in his hands, facing downward toward the concrete patio beneath our feet. I sensed he must be deep in thought and didn't want to engage in conversation. So I remained quiet.

He and I sat there a long time in our silence. As he got up to leave, he said, "Boy, it's sure beautiful out here – the flowers, the hummingbirds."

As he went through the door, I agreed, saying, "It surely is." Just as the heavy door solidly closed behind him, I realized something. During all the times I ventured out into the courtyard to rest and to think, I noticed and mentioned those beautiful flowers. Up to the point of my brief conversation with my fellow

Chicago Cubs fan, I had been looking toward the ground, allowing the beauty of those magnificent flowers to flood my eyes.

However, I never looked *up* to see the hummingbirds coming to their feeders right above my head. As I did so, I saw two of these beautiful small birds hovering like tiny helicopters in mid-air and sipping the sugar water put there for them. Thank you, sir, for that unexpected but welcomed gift. Although we didn't talk much, you added a wonderful sense of joy to my day by reminding me to look both up and down in my life. Seems I had already forgotten the experience during my hike! On the hike I savored the beauty both at my feet and toward the pastel, blue sky. Life needs that wonderfully delicate blend of savoring the grace at our feet and delighting in the majesty above us.

Memories from My Childhood

Earlier I made the decision not to go to the pool. I was into my writing and my reading, and, after all, the day started out overcast and rainy, feeble excuses not to experience something I had enjoyed the first two days. I was fine with my decision until about 1:30 that afternoon. Looking out one of the huge twenty-foot mezzanine windows, I noticed the bright, glimmering sun playing a wonderful symphony on the flowers. Why should I *not* go to the pool? Since I didn't have a good answer to that question, I packed up my gear, returned to the cabin, pulled on my trunks, got a book, and headed to the ol' swimmin' hole.

I'm so glad I went. Upon entering the pool area, I overheard some young people playing a water game I enjoyed as a youngster: "Marco Polo." It's a game of pool tag, and I used to play it with friends at Donner Pool in Columbus.

As I lay on my recliner at the pool, soaking up some rays and reading my book, I overheard (within a matter of minutes) two mothers giving two very different messages to their sons, who appeared to be close in age. I instantly recalled a section of Eldredge's book, *Wild at Heart*. In it he describes the importance of mothers beginning the difficult, often painful, process of letting go of their sons, in order that the young boys might move toward their fathers and begin developing and understanding their masculinity.

The first mother watched the boy's father heading towards the diving board. As he bounced on the high board, the mother yelled to her son, "Watch! There goes Daddy, Joey!" From her words I assumed she so wanted her son to see his father doing something requiring skill and courage – and he did, as his father did a flip and creased the water with hardly a splash.

Shortly, the second mother yelled out to her young son in the pool, "You be careful, honey." Believe me, at some point very soon in that young boy's life, he is going to be aching for his mother to do something she may find very difficult – quit calling him "honey" in a public setting. And she has to encourage him, not over protect him. Author Diana Coogle described the task of letting go of her son, Ela: "With a jolt I find myself making adjustments to a boy becoming a man with a man's independent means as well as a man's independent mind… There will be a time when this job of mothering will be over – not the relationship, but the job… And I hope I can give him a hug, congratulate him warmly, and let him go, urging him, 'Yes! Do it! Let go! Walk!'"

I thought of those words I wanted my mom to say to me: "Get out there, Eddie, and explore." I am always amazed where in my life I either learn new lessons or have reinforced for me lessons learned but forgotten. In his book, *Through Many Windows*, Arthur Gordon said, "Every child must go through the phase of rejecting the parent-model, shaking off those inherited values, trying to stand on his or her own feet… Somehow the parent must learn to say, not, 'Be like me,' but, 'Be yourself, and let me help.'" I didn't get from my parents that encouragement to be myself, with an offer to help. I am not sure they knew how to either encourage or help.

I thought back to those early years in Columbus. I did not do a good job of detaching from my mom at the time most boys begin moving toward their fathers. I remained very close to Mom all the way through high school. Because of my own situation, I identified so much with the different interactions between these two mothers and their sons.

After spending time at the pool, I went back to the cabin and read some more. Then I decided I was hungry. Art, who told me about the fried chicken buffet at The Seasons Hotel, also told me about the "Tex-Mex" buffet each Wednesday night. As I drove by the hotel, I decided to turn in and try some Mexican food. Turns out, it was a good choice because of what I experienced there.

Charlie Begins His "Story"

The buffet was from 5:00-8:00, and I arrived around 6:15. I decided to stop in the bar for a drink before enjoying the buffet. To my pleasant surprise, sitting at the bar were Art and Charlie! We traded greetings, and Art insisted on buying me a drink, to which I only mildly objected.

While I learned some of Art's story Monday night at the Hotel Nashville, that night at the Seasons I began learning Charlie's. Art, Charlie, and I talked for a while when Art said he had to leave in a few minutes due to a prior commitment. But for a short time Art, Charlie, and I sat at the bar, and I could sense Charlie was willing to share some of his story with me, and I was more than anxious to hear it.

Charlie told me stories about his motorcycle racing days, during which he became internationally known for his skills. We also talked about Brown County and Nashville where Charlie lived for 45 years. When I reminded him why I came to Brown County, he said, "This is a magical place. And it's good you're here, Ed. I've seen couples walking up and down the streets in Nashville who probably haven't held hands in 40 years, and they're holding hands!"

As if all of the above weren't enough, Charlie then told me about how he bought an *entire town!* for $1 million. There is a little "wide place in the road" just south of here called *Story*, Indiana, a place I've known about since I was a youngster growing up in Columbus but had never visited. I was curious about *why* and *how* someone buys an entire town and wanted to find out more. When my curiosity got the best of me, I asked Charlie, "What are you doing Saturday?"

"No plans," he said.

I suggested, "How about if I pick you up at the hotel at 10:00, and you can show me Story?" Charlie seemed to like the idea a lot! Actually, there was one other place I wanted to visit with Charlie on Saturday, a place that also reminded me of my early years, the annual Bill Monroe Bluegrass Festival.

Growing up in Columbus, I learned to appreciate country/western music. Every single Saturday night, before we owned our first TV, I well remember sitting on the living room floor at home, listening to the Grand Ol' Opry on our huge floor model radio, turning the dial once in a while to retrieve the fading reception. Because of those Saturday nights I became a country/western and bluegrass fan and continue to love that music today.

Bean Blossom, Indiana, (five miles north of Nashville) has been the site of the Bill Monroe Bluegrass Festival for 38 years. During this weeklong event, bluegrass bands and individuals from all over the country come to perform to sold-out, appreciative, foot-stompin', fun-lovin' audiences.

Knowing Charlie had "picked the strings" on the banjo for years, I asked him if he knew Bill Monroe. He said, "Oh, sure. I knew Bill Monroe before he died a couple of years ago. We used to get together for meals and some 'pickin' every time he came to town." Hearing that, I asked him if he'd also like to go to Bean Blossom on Saturday, the last day of the festival. Again, Charlie said, "I don't have any plans. That'd be fine."

Later in the conversation I found out that since the previous February Charlie had been struggling with colon cancer and also a tumor on his back. He said, "I've made my peace with God, and I'm gonna fight this." Charlie then got that smile on his face and said, "I don't think He wants to deal with me. I'd probably get up there and wanna reorganize everything!"

I then asked him how he came to be a permanent resident at the Hotel Nashville. He said, not in a boastful way, "Well, I owned the property the hotel stands on." He and Art have their own suites there, and everyone who works there looks out for Charlie.

His daughter, who has a Ph.D. and teaches at a university in Houston, told her dad, "This is the best example of assisted living I've ever seen!"

Missing the Tex-Mex Was Fine with Me:
I Found More Connections

At 8:15 Charlie had to leave. It was getting dark outside, and since he doesn't see well, he needed to get back to the hotel. Charlie ended our conversation by saying, "I've led sort of a ragtag, wild life." That's all he said – just that simple statement.

As he was leaving, I said, "I'll see you at 10:00 Saturday morning." He asked me to write the day and time on a napkin so he wouldn't forget.

Then he looked at me and said, "We'll have a good time."

As I was settling my tab, the bartender said, "I hope you didn't come for the Tex-Mex tonight." (Remember it was 8:15, and the buffet only went until 8:00.) I told the bartender I knew I had missed the buffet. But I did so intentionally; while listening to Charlie, I looked at my watch, noting the time was fast-approaching the magic 8:00 hour, and I made a conscious decision to stay and listen to his stories. The allure of Charlie's warmth and the magic of his stories were far, far better than a Tex-Mex buffet.

I said above that my ongoing journey to reclaim my lost authentic self, find connections these two weeks, and leave the crossroads did not come only by focusing on those concepts, separate from all my experiences. Rather, that journey happened as I collectively took in all the many events happening around me. As in my life, I was constantly circling back while in the woods, finding those places my journey intersected at the crossroads. When I was hospitalized the first time with clinical depression, my life took a circular path back to my early years, that first crossroads, as I tried to understand the reasons for my depression.

At that point in my journey to the woods I was not completely sure why I had such a tremendous inner desire to spend time with those two guys. But after some thought I began to understand. New friends seem to come into my life just when I need them. Author Sarah Orne Jewett said, "Yes'm, old friends is always best, 'less you can catch a new one that's fit to make an old one out of." I caught a couple of new ones who I was sure would become old ones.

CHAPTER 5

Encouraging Others by Extending Care and Understanding

The New Employee and a Lesson from Katie

I slept in a bit Thursday morning, rolling out of bed at 8:00 rather than 6:30. My first thought was, "Oh, no! I'm almost an hour and a half behind the first three days!" After a couple of minutes of this negative self-talk, it hit me: "Ed, <u>let it go</u>! You're on a retreat schedule, not a work schedule. You came with no expectations for these days. You must have needed the extra sleep, so enjoy the moments of the day from this point on."

I read my daily devotional, got dressed, and headed to The Daily Grind to drink some coffee, read the papers, and listen to the local chatter. The workers at the coffee shop, already recognizing me, had my mug of coffee waiting for me as I arrived at the counter. Chip (the owners' son) asked if I wanted a ham, egg, and cheese croissant, which would enable me to get my two free cups of coffee. I said, "I sure do."

As I watched the employees work, I noticed one young helper who obviously was having his first day on a new job. Chip was very patient with the new young man, showing him the various steps to take and then moving back to let the new kid on the block have a go at it. I also noticed a very important interaction.

When the new worker did something correctly, Chip *always* said something like, "That's great. You got it the first time." At another point, Chip said, "I don't mind helpin' you, but ya gotta think on your own too," thus affirming his belief that the new employee could, and had Chip's permission to, make decisions for himself!

Thinking of the new employee's apprehension and fear on his first day, I was overwhelmed by Chip's response to him. He was encouraging the new worker and helping him gain self-confidence. I continued to watch Chip patiently teach the new employee about his job, aware that what he was giving the young man was exactly what I needed for myself: encouragement and confidence.

Watching the interaction between Chip and the new employee, I remembered something I wrote in *Lessons from the Porch*, a valuable lesson I learned from my golden retriever, Katie: We *all* need encouragement and positive reinforcement in our lives. I learned this lesson one evening when I put Katie on her leash for a walk. Arriving at our favorite park, I took off her leash, as I always did, letting her run free. Immediately, she re-established the parameters of her outer boundaries, sniffing the ground for messages from her friends. She glanced back once in awhile to see if I was still there and to hear me shout, "Go on, Katie; explore!"

Every so often she returned to my side and looked up at me with those beautiful brown eyes and long eye lashes. All she really wanted at those times was a pat on the head, a sweeping wave of my hand, and another, "Go on, Katie, get out there and explore." With that, she ran back into the field and continued exploring, again looking back once in awhile to see if I was still there. When she finished her adventure, she came and sat next to me, panting and looking at me with those brown eyes. If I repeated my usual wish for her and she still sat there, I knew she was ready to continue our walk. As I said earlier, how I wish Mom had given me that encouragement when I was a young boy, the encouragement that new worker got this morning, and the encouragement I gave Katie. I wanted to have adventures, but I was afraid, perhaps because my mother didn't encourage me and help me gain confidence

Encouraging Others by Extending Care and Understanding

I want to share with you a powerful story about a little seed and the encouragement and confidence that allowed it to grow. A friend of mine, Kathi Robinson, wrote this powerful story and gave me permission to share it with you. One day, a very long time ago, a little seed was planted and covered with soil. The hole was dug way too deep; therefore, the seed didn't do as it would be expected to – it didn't sprout as quickly as it should have. The seed was buried so deep in the ground it wasn't getting any sunlight or water. No one knew it was there.

But this seed was special, filled with stories it wanted and needed to share, stories from its heart and its soul. It was determined to keep hanging in there, for the possibilities that were waiting in a place the little seed knew nothing about. This little seed wanted to poke through the ground, discover the unknown, and grow.

One day the seed discovered something was different, for it felt both warmth and the quenching of its thirst. Someone happened to be walking by where this seed had been planted and just sensed there was something special and important buried there. This person seemed to know of the potential that lay beneath the ground.

Each and every day the friend returned to this same spot to sprinkle the seed with water and to spread sunshine on the ground where the seed was trying to grow.

Before long that seed started to feel what was being sent its way and thus began to focus all its efforts on growth. The friend continued to nourish that little plant, and more and more green started pushing through the ground. The plant blossomed and produced the most beautiful flower anyone had ever set eyes on.

The plant was a special gift, and maybe that is why it had been buried so deeply in the ground. Maybe it had to work extra hard to grow, and maybe that work made it more whole and capable of realizing its true potential. Perhaps it needed that someone walking by, believing in the potential of that plant, to help it grow. The seed was crying out from within itself, struggling, working toward birth.

Was that someone, that friend who walked by, God? Am I the seed wanting to blossom and grow, nourished by His unconditional love and caring? "Go on Eddie; get out there and explore!" Like the new employee and Katie, I realized the tiny seed also needed encouragement to grow, and I affirmed again that same need for nurturing my own soul, buried deep within me.

In his book *A Hidden Wholeness*, Parker Palmer adds a rich extension to my story about the little seed: "What seed was planted when you or I arrived on earth with our identities intact? How can we recall and reclaim those birthright gifts and potentials? ... Whom is this meant to feed? Where am I called to give my gifts?" I was the seed planted with my identity intact. My trip to the woods was to reclaim my now impaired identity. Beginning my journey to rediscover my authentic self returned me to wholeness, and this wholeness provided nourishment, not only for myself but also for others.

As if I needed yet another reason for going to The Daily Grind each morning, I was sure I needed to be there to observe these exchanges between a mentor and his protégé. This kind and caring place goes way beyond the good coffee and the ham, egg, and cheese croissants it serves. Chip and the tiny seed reminded me of the reasons I ran to the woods.

An Unexpected Gift

Out of necessity, Friday I went into town to the laundromat, not because I really *wanted* to spend any time in a laundromat during my escape to the woods but because I *needed* clean clothes. I sat outside while waiting for my clothes to dry. A mother and her daughter got out of their car and headed into the laundromat. As they walked past me, the little girl said, "You're the best mommy in the world."

And *immediately* the reply came back, "And you're the best daughter in the world." What an affirming gift I received during my unwanted trip to get clean clothes – a very important affirmation of the love that exists between a mother and her daughter. Is there anything more important to encourage a "tiny seed" than her mother's love and nourishment? The new employee, Katie, the seed, the little girl, and I received the nourishment to grow. I often find this message in unexpected places.

After I returned to the cabin and put away my clean clothes, I thought about those special items I packed in my bag and brought with me: a clear and open mind and an accepting heart; the needed confidence to leave my self-doubt at home; the opportunity to be in a community of new friends I would find in Brown County; and my faith in God. I was certain my time there was influenced by the items God so lovingly encouraged me to pack.

While continuing to reflect on the importance of those five special gifts, I returned to the mezzanine at the lodge. I resumed journaling my experiences and then took a break to visit the beautiful courtyard. While there, I found myself in the middle of a lecture a park ranger was giving to about 20 visitors. She was telling them the names of all the wildflowers and describing the various functions they perform, all to keep this magic ecosystem working as it should.

I eavesdropped on her remarks, finding there was much beyond the outward beauty that captured the importance of these flowers, much work taking place beneath the ground, just like the tiny seed. I couldn't help but realize it's the very same with each of us as we struggle to keep our own ecosystems working as they should. Much of the work is unseen because it's inner work. Like replacing pipes, wiring, and insulation in our homes, this necessary inner work – to keep our homes functioning as systems – also goes unseen.

I finished writing and headed into town. Once again I was reminded of the charming folks in a small town while sitting on the patio at the winery that afternoon; I was listening to a local singer, Robbie Bowden, spin some yarns with his songs. As usual, the chatter at and among tables competed with his words. But his voice rose above the chatter when he sang "Down Home Folks":

Down Home Folks

I was feeling out of place.
The city was no place for me.
So I went back to familiar faces.
It was there they made me see.
Chorus
I'm in love with down home folks.
They really brought me around.
You come see the down home folks.
If city life gets you down.
They've got a way of makin' you feel
Just like you belong.
Sit down here in an open field.
An' play a down home song.

This song told my story. I *was* falling in love with those down home folks who allowed me to see the grace and joy all around me. After Robbie finished singing, I strolled down to the Hotel Nashville.

Dee, the bartender, greeted me with a friendly "Hi, Ed!" By now she knows I'm going to order an Early Times and Coke in a tall glass. She fixed it and placed it in front of me. "Wanna see a menu?" she asked.

"I don't know yet. I'm thirstier than I am hungry right now," I replied. Charlie came in, dressed in his usual blue jeans, bright red suspenders and all, with an Abe Martin Lodge T-shirt on, using his walking stick again as he always did. With his beard, Charlie resembled old Abe, an appropriate resemblance since that year marked the 100th anniversary of the Abe Martin Lodge. The local cable television station had asked Charlie to do a program, sharing some of Abe Martin's famous advice.

Charlie sat down beside me, and as soon as he saw Dee, he asked, "You know this is 'HLD' day, don't you?"

"What's HLD day, Charlie?"

"It's Hug a Lady Day," replied Charlie, with a big grin covering half his face.

Dee said, "I'll be right there, Charlie, as soon as I get this drink fixed." And sure enough, in a couple of minutes, Dee walked around the bar, went up to Charlie, and gave him a HUGE hug and kiss. As she was hugging him, I heard her ask in his good ear (the one in which he has 30% hearing – in the other he's totally deaf), "Are you ok, Charlie?" Charlie said he was great, and again Dee asked, "You sure? I worry about you." I, too, asked Charlie if everything was okay, and he assured me it was.

I came to expect that kind of exchange among friends in Brown County. Dee knew Charlie was going to the doctor yesterday morning to have the hole in his back (where the non-malignant tumor was) unpacked, examined, and repacked. She was concerned, and so was I. In the same way Chip encouraged the new worker, the mother encouraged her daughter, I encouraged Katie, and the friend encouraged the tiny seed, the folks there extended care and understanding to others as they encouraged their friends through both rough and smooth times. As my friends experience difficult times in their lives, I try my best to offer them understanding and empathy. I always encourage others more than myself. At times my insecure self-esteem just isn't open to hearing my own encouragement. By observing the caring and encouraging of others while in the woods, I hoped to learn how to extend the same grace to myself.

The stories I heard in Brown County helped me look inward as I searched for the grace I needed to encourage me to once again stumble upon myself. I knew I so enjoyed spending time with Art and Charlie because they were both excellent storytellers. They talked about their small piece of tranquility, shared its stories, and transmitted the culture of this tiny part of the world. Their stories provided the setting for helping me find the path with the word on the road marker. I went to Brown County to help untangle the mixed feelings I had about the need for change in my life, just as Jon Katz ran to his mountain in upstate New York as he dealt with change in his life. The stories I heard went to my heart and soul because the storytellers were honest and authentic. I needed to find peace and comfort in my life. The culture Art and Charlie described reminded me of the similar environment in which I was raised next door in Columbus. The folks in my hometown shared stories that were similarly real to me as a youngster. Now as an adult, and because the people I met in Brown County shared their stories of times past, I knew what I saw while there was not much different from the place I knew as a young boy.

I love and remember stories told to me just as I'll forever be reminded of the storytellers in Brown County. I may forget some of the specific facts surrounding the place where I heard a story, but I never forget the story I was told while there. Sue Monk Kidd, in her book *The Secret Life of Bees*, said, "Really, it's good for all of us to hear it again …Stories have to be told or they die, and when they die, we can't remember who we are or why we're here."

Having loved the stories I heard, I ended my night at the Hotel Nashville because Charlie got tired. I reminded him we were going to meet Saturday morning to go to Story and Bean Blossom. He pulled out the napkin I gave him and held it up for me to see.

I told him specifically where I would pick him up. Because Charlie doesn't get along too easily with his walking stick, I didn't want him wandering all over the parking lot, trying to find me. After listening to my explicit details of our meeting place, Charlie very casually reminded me, "I know; I live here." I decided I had told Charlie more than he needed to know.

Encouraging Memories as I
Reclaim my Authentic Self

The time flew by my first week in Brown County. I wanted time to slow down a bit because I had such a wonderful few days in the woods while seeking the path that takes me out of the crossroads. The memories of the week and the stories I heard were the reasons some of the clouds drifted higher above the intersecting paths at the crossroads, helping me begin the journey of retrieving the clarity I found at the top of the foursquare tower. I came to the woods to find ways to reclaim my true self. I knew part of that rediscovery would come from the people I would meet and hear their stories. My hope was certainly confirmed over and over throughout the week, and as the clouds floated higher above the crossroads.

I expected even more clarity to follow my second week in the woods. I started my eighth day in my favorite way with a trip into town to The Daily Grind. Finding my mug of coffee on the counter, I started to tell Karis what I wanted to eat when she asked, "Ham, egg, and cheese croissant?"

"Yep." I finished my breakfast and headed back to the park.

Driving back through the park to my cabin, I was flooded with some good memories of my childhood. My family and I came to Brown County for day outings and picnics. I saw the old shelter house where we had many a cookout. The lookout tower along the way seemed ten stories tall when I was a boy, and it took forever to climb, much like the tower I found at the crossroads. I don't do well with heights, so I was always scared when I got to the top. Today that tower seemed very small to me. I got out of the car, climbed the *thirty feet* to the top, and marveled at the beauty in the hills. Because the tower wasn't high enough to see over the beautiful woods, I still could not find the images I vividly saw while looking out the four windows of the crossroads' tower, a sign that I hadn't yet discovered definition for that fourth path.

As I thought about the writing and reading that were awaiting me on this day, I became both excited and anxious for the unknown. What should I read, and what would I write? I never knew the answers until those parts of my day began, always after my trip to the Daily Grind. I realized that some of the books I chose to bring along on this trip were recommended by a very disparate group of people: my therapist, two good friends from Illinois, my dear friend, Dick, from Colorado, and my son and daughter-in-law who live in southern Oregon.

I'm amazed that each of these individuals, mostly unknown to any of the others, recommended a perfect collection of books for my journey to the woods. I believe God had something to do with each of their suggestions.

One book my son, Eric, daughter-in-law, Stacy, and my two-year-old granddaughter sent me as a recent birthday gift is entitled *On Nature: Great Writers on the Great Outdoors.*

Inside the front cover, Stacy wrote a wonderful thought from Emerson, which seemed *so very pertinent for my trip to the woods*:

> In the woods, we return to reason and faith. There I feel nothing can befall me in life – no disgrace, no calamity, (leaving me my eyes), which nature cannot repair. Standing on the bare ground, my head bathed by the blithe air, and uplifted into infinite space, all mean egotism vanishes. I become a transparent eye-ball; I am nothing; I see all; The currents of the universal Being circulate through me; I am part and particle of God.

Eric wrote his own message: "Take deep breaths, and **GET DIRTY!** Hope you find some insights in this book. We thought it was appropriate for your adventure." He was right! Getting dirty reminded me that inner work is messy. Our life is often a mess in the middle as we move through those transitions between an ending and a new beginning.

We have to be willing to live with ambiguity and uncertainty when we're in those transition places. After finishing *Lessons from the Porch* I once again learned to ignore the ambiguity in my life until my inner turmoil wouldn't let me continue to ignore the uncertainty. As I wrote this book I realized the uncertainty was defined as I ignored my authentic self. I can tolerate only a certain amount of time in my transition places, following a path I didn't truly understand and doing what others mapped out for me, taking jobs others thought would further a career over which I gave up my own inner control. For many years the spiritual path I walked was determined by the early set of religious beliefs I internalized. I had not yet learned it was okay to create my own. The personal path I walked was full of the uncertain feelings and memories I clung to from earlier times at home. I felt I wasn't the father I wanted to be for Eric and Tracie because I modeled the path of fatherhood I saw in Dad. I assumed I could not be the father they needed. I gave away to my wife Bonnie much of that responsibility. I was not a good conversationalist when all the family was home. Like Dad I was absent in my presence at home. I did not encourage my kids to come to me with their problems, because I felt I could not help them. I didn't turn to Dad when I encountered difficulties in my early years and did not know how to be present for Eric and Tracie in their early years.

I wanted to change what I experienced along those paths yet didn't know how to do so. Only when the paths became like a maze did I acknowledge the fog surrounding me, reminding me of the fog I encountered as I looked all directions from the crossroads. The fear and uncertainty I felt there reminded me of the blurred images I saw when I entered the hospital ten years ago with clinical depression. While writing *Lessons from the Porch* took me out of that crossroads and back to my authentic self, during the intervening years I once again lost my way. Perhaps I reclaim my authenticity when I write about my struggles. Telling my story is the way I pull from my soul the memories that point me toward an authentic path that allows me to respond to these new challenges, one God wants me to find. And I am finally allowing God to help me face those challenges.

The new adventures on this part of my journey made me happy, relaxed, and so very glad I came. I continued to believe, with greater and greater assurance, God sent me to this place, at this time. There were too many connected events to explain why I took my retreat at this time in my life. I took one day at a time and listened with my heart. The confusion and uncertainty about what I should be doing tomorrow would be resolved in good time. Could I wait? I hoped so. I needed to wait in the silence, while realizing the silence can be deafening at times. I needed to sit and think with my head *and* my heart, hoping to avoid the old saying, "Sometimes I sits and thinks, and sometimes I sits and *thinks* about thinkin'." I said a short prayer: "Lord, help me to wait, realizing that much good can come to me if I have the patience to listen for your messages and your questions, and the wisdom to learn what you want me to learn."

CHAPTER 6
Saturday: My "Travels with Charlie" and Findin' Home

...When we begin our pilgrimage, we want only to return home... We try to find home even when we are somewhere else.
Murray Bodo O.F.M. - *The Place We Call Home: Spiritual Pilgrimage as a Path to God*

Perhaps I am telling this story in an attempt to heal myself, to confront what I do not know, to create a path for myself with the idea that "memory is the only way home."
Terry Tempest Williams - *Refuge: An Unnatural History of Family and Place*

Saturday finally arrived, and I knew I was in for a great time with Charlie! I hoped my day with Charlie would help me, in Williams' words, "attempt to heal myself" and better understand that fourth path leading from the crossroads.

Charlie was outside sittin' on a stump when I arrived at 10:00 a.m. We headed north on Hwy. 135, taking the five-mile drive to Bean Blossom, home this week to the 38th Annual Bill Monroe Blue Grass Festival.

During that five mile drive, Charlie pointed out landmarks on both sides of the road. We were passing through some absolutely breathtaking countryside. Many of the landmarks were actually homes and cabins where Charlie had lived over the years. Charlie knew all the families who lived for generations along the ridge. As I listened to Charlie, I remembered seeing those same landmarks during the time I lived in Nashville 25 years ago. However, those oft-seen places took on new meaning that Saturday morning as Charlie shared their history and his memories of Nashville.

As we entered the bustling town of Bean Blossom, Charlie said, "Let's turn left on Hwy. 45 just ahead and make a stop in Helmsburg." I thought we were going to the Blue Grass Festival, but I didn't say anything. As it turned out, there was an antique truck show Charlie wanted to see.

As we drove into the very tiny, dilapidated hamlet, Charlie laughed as he commented that what this town needed was "a good strong wind" to come along and blow it all down so folks could start anew. We found the antique truck show, down a dirt road in a vacant lot next to an antique store.

Charlie knew all the owners and the details of the twenty trucks that pulled in – the model year and the type of engine under the hood. I remembered seeing those types of trucks growing up in Columbus. I rode in similar trucks on my cousin's farm and visited with the other farmers who lived close by. As I looked around, walked into the middle of a huge field next to the antique shop, remembered all my experiences of the first week, and listened to the chatter among the truck owners, I was hit with such an interesting thought: I had gone home that first week in Brown County. As Terry Tempest Williams said in *Refuge: An Unnatural History of Family and Place*, "I sit on the floor of my study with journals all around me … and I remember the country I come from and how it informs my life." So much of what I saw, thought, and wrote about my first week there was recorded in my journal. The writing brought back the happy memories of my childhood – memories that I saw for the first time.

I have written about some of the unhappy memories of my childhood. There were pleasant memories as well. I had not returned to my actual childhood home but to the new meaning of home I found in Brown County. My new friends, and the stories they told, brought me back to a home I saw for the first time. In his poem "Morning," author Robert Lax put it this way: "Sometimes we go on a search and do not know what we are looking for, until we come home again to our beginning."

Saturday: My "Travels with Charlie" and Findin' Home

I came home to my beginning when I took some time out while writing this section to go through the shoe boxes of pictures I brought home after Mom died. What a wonderful experience. My parents took all the pictures while my sister and I were growing up in Columbus. Such happy memories came flooding into my soul. I saw those pictures through new eyes just as I saw my mother with new eyes that day my granddaughter and I were sitting on her parents' back deck.

So many pictures were of my family, and in almost every picture we all had smiles on our faces. Several pictures were of Mom and Dad. In every single one of those pictures they either had their arms around each other or were holding hands. In one picture, Mom had her head tilted toward Dad with a huge smile on her face, looking like an eighteen-year-old girl in love for the first time. Some pictures of Dad and me showed him holding me when I was only months old, and, again, in every picture he was looking down at me. By the smile on his face and the look in his eyes, I know he held me with love in his heart. In pictures of my dad and me when I was a teenager, we both had smiles on our faces. Another picture, taken outside on that special Christmas we received identical winter coats and hats, highlighted the smug looks on our faces, acknowledging we thought we were pretty cool dudes.

I saw pictures of my son, Eric, and me during his teenage years. We had arms either around our waists or our shoulders. That legacy from Mom and Dad had been passed on to me and as I looked at more recent pictures of Eric and his two daughters, I realized the legacy had continued to be passed along. Recapturing earlier times was perhaps the most salient experience while writing this book. I had focused so much on the negative aspects of home and conveniently erased the happy times.

Because of the love I felt while revisiting those earlier times, and the happy times I had while visiting Brown County, I knew in my heart I had returned to where I began. Despite my desire to forget home, I realized I needed to remember those early experiences in my life. In his book *The Longing for Home,* Frederick Beuchner talked about the importance of finding home through the memories in our lives: "But the tide that carries us farther and farther away from our beginning in time is also the tide that turns and carries us back again…More vividly than ever before…we find ourselves remembering the one particular house that was our childhood home."

The memories allow me to take my home with me wherever I travel. I still miss some aspects of my childhood home, and especially my mother's cooking. My mom was the world-renowned, blue ribbon champion in meatloaf, mustard potato salad, cole slaw, fried chicken, and cherry pies. My wife tried and tried, without success, to replicate the tastes of those delightful and delectable morsels. Still I enjoyed a nice variety of "close to – but not quite" dishes over the years.

I remember Christmas's with special gifts, like my first two-wheeler bike. I vividly remember one Christmas receiving a pair of gray flannel slacks and a silk green shirt from my Grandma Jolly. The holidays were about the only time my extended family gathered. Uncles, aunts, and cousins all came together to exchange gifts and tell stories. But, they were all from my mother's family. My dad had no family to gather at the holidays, or any other time. I still remember some of those stories of my mom's family, relating humorous experiences from when they were growing up on the farm in southern Indiana.

As I considered <u>both</u> meanings for home, the physical place and the portable place I carry in my heart, I realized that my portable home includes the dreams and hopes, the fears and uncertainties I carry with me from 31 S. Gladstone Avenue. As I considered the struggle of remaining comfortable where I am or making changes in my life, I needed something to cling to. The memories, both positive and negative, helped free me from the crossroads, begin the process of rediscovering my authentic path.

My retreat brought those memories flooding back to my mind and my heart; they brought me home. While moving through fancy job titles in very nice upscale communities, I didn't realize how much those early childhood events impacted the happy childhood I had forgotten. Recalling these memories while in the woods once again helped point me toward my authentic self because if my inner self is authentic it will include memories from my past. Only after finding those happy childhood pictures was I able to let go of many of the negative images that I still carried with me from those early years. The old saying "pictures are worth a thousand words" was certainly present with me as I looked at the pictures.

My authentic path does not change over time but I have lost my authentic self over the years. I have strayed from that path that always holds my core values, my basic beliefs, and my dreams. My personal, professional, and spiritual paths have changed over the years because quite often I didn't carry those core values, basic beliefs, and dreams that were part of my authentic self. I wore my masks along those other three paths which didn't let me see the authenticity I needed. Also I lost the connection among those three paths with my authentic self.

Understanding the disruptive feelings in 2004 that dropped me in the middle of the crossroads pointed the way back to my authentic path. I struggled to rediscover my never-changing authentic path because doing so meant looking back to the memories while looking forward to once again reclaim my path. Some of those changes I recognized while others I didn't. I ignored some changes I saw because of my fear of changing those parts of my life in most need of transformation. My personal path evolved as my kids grew and required a different role as their father. My personal path also changed over the years as some of my beliefs and dreams evolved in my marriage. My spiritual path changed as I adapted those early religious beliefs and aligned them to my current life. As Presbyterian minister and author J. Barrie Shepherd asked, "Does there come a time for everyone when looking forward yields to looking back; when fond memory takes over from anticipation and what has been holds pride of place because, somehow, it always will be sealed with the tight retainer amber of the storehouse of the mind?"

After finishing *Lessons from the Porch*, I truly thought I had exhausted all my childhood memories. Fortunately for me I hadn't. For me, findin' home means remembering those old experiences, incorporating them with the current meaning in my life, and finding new ones that add understanding to my world. The authentic path I walked a few years ago was not only to be full of sweet, lingering memories but also to lead me to a path toward a new meaning for God in my life. Author Sue Monk Kidd had this to say about home: "The image of coming home is a powerful, archetypal symbol for returning to one's deepest self, to the soul. To come home is to return to the place of inner origin, that original imprint of God within. Therefore, coming home fills us with a sense of being in the right place, a sense of deep spiritual belonging. We all have this profound longing to come home, whether we recognize it or not." I also recognized that certain conditions have inspired my ability to recall those memories. My time in Brown County was full of those conditions: wonderful people, great stories, peace, and inspiration.

The visit to Helmsburg with Charlie brought with it all those memories of home and its new meaning. We left Helmsburg and backtracked three miles to the intersection of Highways 45 and 135, turned left and went about 30 yards to the entrance of the Bill Monroe Blue Grass Festival. We hung out there for a while, enjoying the music. Once again Charlie saw very few people he didn't know by name.

The Stories at *Story:*
Synchronicity Once Again

After lunch we returned to Highway 135 and headed south on a scenic, winding, 20-mile drive to Story, Indiana, the town Charlie bought for $1 million. He later sold it to two German entrepreneurs who both happened to be there when we visited. What a beautiful place! The Story Inn is famous around this "neck of the woods." A wedding was taking place when we arrived, a big tent set up behind the Inn to hold the reception for 250 people.

The town of Story was founded in 1851 with the grant of a land patent from President Millard Fillmore to Dr. George Story, a medical doctor who hailed from a clan of timber harvesters in southern Ohio and who built many of the structures that distinguish this town today. Story soon became the largest settlement in the area. In its heyday (1880-1929) the village supported two general stores, a nondenominational church, the Inn, a one-room schoolhouse, a grain mill,

Saturday: My "Travels with Charlie" and Findin' Home

a sawmill, a slaughterhouse, a blacksmith's forge, and a post office.

However, Story never recovered from the Great Depression (1929-1933) as families abandoned their hilly, marginal farms in search of work elsewhere. Brown County lost half of its population between 1930 and 1940, this exodus paving the way for the creation of the Brown County State Park and the Hoosier National Forest, the reason this county is 80% forested today. The economic hardship also fostered a cottage industry producing bathtub gin.

As Charlie and I approached the fabled Story Inn, a tall, skinny fella was playing his guitar right outside the Inn, dressed all in black and sounding *very* much like Johnny Cash, another one of my favorite artists. If I closed my eyes, I could picture Johnny standing there singing for us. To my surprise, Charlie did *not* know this guy's name.

We went down into the basement where the bar is. After ordering myself a drink and Charlie his normal glass of Merlot, I headed back upstairs to use the restroom. As I passed the singer, I stopped dead in my tracks. I couldn't believe my ears! He was singing a song – *Will the Circle Be Unbroken* – that Johnny Cash recorded with The Nitty Gritty Dirt Band several years ago. I was so taken with this song when I first heard it I had it played at Mom's funeral three years ago. She loved Johnny Cash, and the song, to this day, reminds me of Mom and the gifts she gave me. I couldn't believe he was singing this particular song when I walked by.

Another of life's connections awaited me a few feet closer to the restroom. Charlie had been talking about a talented songwriter and singer he knew from the area, Barry Johnson, a name that sounded so familiar to me. As I headed toward the restroom, I passed a big, framed picture of a country/western artist. Smaller pictures of local artists surrounded his picture. Two of those smaller pictures were Barry Johnson and Tim Grimm.

Only a few months earlier, I heard about a concert held in an old church in Lombard, Illinois, not far from where I lived. Tim Grimm was the featured artist, someone who is becoming a very well-known folk singer in the Midwest. I was attracted to the concert because Tim is the son of Lloyd Grimm, someone with whom I taught years ago in the social studies department at Columbus High School and whom I greatly admired as an educator.

The concert was spectacular. I met Tim after the concert and made the connection with his dad. Now I'm in Story, Indiana, looking at Tim's picture. When I returned to the bar, I asked Charlie, "Do you know Tim Grimm?"

"Sure I do." I told Charlie about the pictures of Tim and Barry Johnson. Once again I was amazed that there were very few people in Brown County Charlie didn't know. During my experiences that day with Charlie I was amazed at the connections to my life in Columbus. While we sat at the bar, another connection came as Charlie told another story about his bike racing days. I mentioned the name of my brother-in-law, Norman Barr who lives in Columbus and used to enjoy motorcycle racing. Charlie asked, "Is he any relation to Allen Barr?"

"He's Norman's second cousin, why?"

"Because Allen Barr and I used to compete against one another racing cycles." I continued to find connections with the place I grew up and the home I carry in my heart. The connections reminded me of those values, beliefs, and dreams found within my authentic self which slipped away from me over the years. Like that quivering bush in California I mentioned in Chapter 3, when a butterfly flaps its wings in New York City, the flapping has an effect on the wind currents in Tokyo. Too many experiences happened in Brown County to leave that much to chance. The visits to Helmsburg, the Blue Grass Festival, and Story helped me brush away some of the fog I found at the crossroads by bringing back fond memories of my youth and my family.

Around midnight, after a very long and wonderfully enjoyable day, I dropped Charlie off at the Hotel Nashville. Looking at Charlie several times during our travels, I could tell he was having a great day. And so did I! As I got ready to head to bed, the events of my day with Charlie had already found a place in my soul because I was able to bring to the surface, and write about, events in my life that took on new meaning. I discovered some of the memories I needed to remember if I am to recover my authentic self. Findin' home today gave me the courage and resolve to continue looking for my way out of the crossroads and finding the connections of those four paths, just as I found connections with my life and dreams I thought I had forgotten.

God has sent me many dreams, some recognized and some not. I chose to ignore some of the dreams I recognized, those times God was trying to help me find my authentic path. I was either afraid to chase the dream, or I was stuck in the life I had. Those dreams I chose not to pursue, and those I didn't recognize, went away. I will never know the paths they might have taken me down. Several dreams appeared as I tried to find my way out of the second crossroads of young adulthood. I followed my career dream of becoming an educator. I succeeded in my dream of getting married. Bonnie and I dreamed of having children, and we had a son and a daughter. We talked about how great it would be to have grandchildren, and now we are grandparents.

At the fourth crossroads, I wanted to find my way out of depression. Doing so allowed me to find the authentic Ed Poole and eventually write a book. Each dream led to a bigger one. While in the middle of the third crossroads, I found my inner guide, who helped me see that the dreams others saw for me as a superintendent was followed by a bigger dream of finding myself for a moment in time and moving on to bigger dreams with my newly found self. At the fifth crossroads, I tried to find my authentic path once again and see if God wanted me to follow a dream of writing and speaking full time. Although I did not totally recognize it at the time, each of these sequential dreams came from my open heart and a belief that God was carrying out His perfect plan through me.

CHAPTER 7

Oh, No! My Second Week Is <u>Already Here</u>

I drove to my favorite coffee spot at the start of my second week. I experienced both grateful and sad feelings. Going to the Daily Grind, I found myself feeling grateful for this wonderful opportunity to begin each day with new friends, good coffee, and great croissants. The Daily Grind seemed back to its more normal weekday quietness after a very busy tourist weekend in tiny Nashville. The weekend weather was perfect, and I know the local merchants were grateful for the wonderful gift of beautiful days. At the same time I realized half of my retreat had come and gone.

Do You Work Here?

When I finished my coffee, breakfast, and reading, I returned to the cabin, got my laptop, decided which books I would read, and headed to the lodge. Arriving at the mezzanine level, I noticed a father and his son playing a game of Monopoly, a great way to spend time together. While watching them, I lamented the fact Dad and I did not share many times together during my early years.

After doing some writing, I went out into my beautiful courtyard to relax with a cup of coffee. I noticed a wife holding her unsteady husband by the hand as they went around looking at the flowers. They walked a bit, stopped to enjoy the beautiful flowers, and then proceeded around the courtyard. As they approached me, I said, "Beautiful, isn't it?"

The wife said, "It sure is. Wish I had a little cottage right here. I'm getting there, though. I've got some beautiful flowers at home."

The husband, noticing my wrinkled old shorts, Daily Grind T-shirt, and dirty old baseball cap, asked me, "Do you work here?"

"No," I told him. "Just visitin'." Three thoughts came to me: "WOW, I must be fitting in around here." Then I thought, "Ya know, this wouldn't be a bad place at all to work!" Finally, I also realized that, out of necessity for his own safety, the husband looked down at the ground all the time he and his wife held hands and walked around the courtyard. I haven't had nearly as good a reason as this gentleman to look down, but "look down" I've done for most of my life, missing much of life's beauty along the way.

While in the courtyard I saw a woodpecker drilling a huge hole into one of the wooden supports for a bird feeder. After a while, a second woodpecker came along, chased the first woodpecker away, went to that same hole and began its own work. Observing this activity, I realized the second bird was taking the easy way out, going to the work already begun, rather than starting its own hole somewhere else.

So often in my life I have taken the easy way out, to avoid all the work of starting my new hole somewhere else. In high school I took courses I knew would be easy for me rather than struggle through more difficult classes. Many of my friends took those more difficult courses and, as we talked after we all entered college, I found they were much better prepared than I to face the challenges of the work in higher education. Rather than stand still and face the challenges of major issues with my jobs, I took the easy way out of those situations by finding a different job. I took most of the positions because others felt those jobs were right for me at the time. I never stopped to understand what was right for me. I simply followed expectations of others. There were very few job changes where I listened to my heart. I took the high school principal's position in my hometown, because

I wanted to have that experience in the school that held such fond memories for me as a teenager. I left that job because I wanted to apply my leadership skills in a much different kind of organizational setting. I became Education and Training Director for a Fortune 500 company. I was unable and unwilling to face the pressures in that job. I never stuck in there to meet those challenges. Within the context of fight or flight, I always took flight. My tenure as a school administrator was the best example of living up to expectations that were not my own. After I finished writing of the events of the morning and afternoon, I returned to the Hotel Nashville and my new friends.

Two Men with Much in Common
and the Faith I Gained on a Tandem Bike

When I arrived at the hotel, Art was there, and we began another wonderful conversation. He asked me about my day, and I asked him if he had a good day. "It was ok," he said. Art is usually full of life and bubbling over with enthusiasm, so for him to say his day was "ok," I knew it wasn't one of his best.

I asked him to tell me about his day. He said he went to his doctor for a physical, adding, "My daughter will be proud of me." Again, Art's 84 years old, and by his own admission, as well as appearance, he was in excellent physical health. When he worked at Western Electric, he had an annual physical as part of his employment. Since retiring, however, Art had not kept up with those annual physicals. He said he had to return next week for blood work though he assured me the tests were "nothing out of the ordinary."

Getting his physical, remembering his age, and mentioning his daughter prompted Art to talk more about his family. He shared a story about longevity in his family. Both sets of Art's grandparents lived a long time. He had an aunt who was 101 years old as he told me about her, and his dad lived to the ripe old age of 89. Art's dad took a whirlwind trip around the country right before he died to visit relatives spread far and wide. When his dad returned to his home in Springfield,

Missouri, a dear friend, Gaylor, picked him up at the airport. When Gaylor met Art's father, "Mr. Ed" was in a wheelchair. Gaylor asked him what was the matter, and Art's dad said, "Oh, I felt a little dizzy, so they put me in this thing." Gaylor took Mr. Ed home and encouraged him to go to bed and get some rest after a grueling trip.

The next morning when Gaylor went to Mr. Ed's home to check on him, he found he had died in his sleep. After reading the analysis of Mr. Ed's blood work, the coroner confirmed an assumption Art had: Mr. Ed had not taken his heart medicine for several days. Art saw his dad's trip as a "last hurrah" and believed Mr. Ed was ready to die.

I then asked Art a very direct question: "Art, were you able to gain closure with your dad before he died?" Many men might wince at this question but not Art. He described the time he stayed with his father while Mr. Ed was hospitalized. One evening he was sitting with his dad and reading a magazine. Mr. Ed said, "Arthur, come over here."

"Do you need something, Dad?"

"Come closer, Arthur."

"Do you need some water? Is your mouth dry?"

"Come closer and bend down." As Art bent down, his dad grabbed his face between his two hands and kissed him on the lips, saying, "You have been a good son, and you always will be." While he was telling me this story, Art's eyes filled with tears. I could see that, after all those years, that night in the hospital provided the closure Art, a son who never felt close to his father, was seeking. I wish I had been given a similar opportunity to bring closure to my life with Dad before he died.

Art then talked briefly about his early years at home. Over the years he became more subservient to his dad, acquiescing to Mr. Ed's controlling personality. Both Art and I had submitted to our controlling parents. Art's was a more overt submission while mine was more covert. Following my normal pattern, I didn't confront or argue with Mom and Dad about anything. I pushed my feelings deep inside, never bringing them to the surface until I entered the hospital to confront my depression.

While Art saw his father as the dominating figure in his family, I saw my mother in that role. Mom was the financial manager at home, and she made most of the decisions for our family. Dad told me *many* times, "If it wasn't for your mother, we wouldn't have anything." Looking back, I know he was right. Mom also doled out the punishment. I never remember my father punishing me directly for my many misdeeds. What he did was much worse. As young boys, we learn from our fathers that a wound that hurts is shameful, this lesson sometimes causing us to be more submissive to the demands of our parents. Whenever I misbehaved, Dad pulled me back from what he considered immoral behavior by saying, "Don't you know you made your mother cry?" Dad wounded me each time he told me I had made Mom cry, pangs of guilt and shame rushing through me like a knife jammed in the middle of my stomach. Even now I feel sadness whenever I recall Dad's punishment.

Looking back on those parental roles, I realized more and more, as I grew into adulthood, I was driven to reverse those mother-father roles. I handled the finances, and I made the decisions. Both of those dominating roles often brought disastrous results, for I am not one who makes a budget and sticks with it. Bonnie and I got paid twice a month, and I put both checks in the bank and began spending.

As long as we had money to pay the bills, I considered all left-over money expendable cash. I never put excess cash into a savings account. When Eric and Tracie were ready to go to college, Bonnie and I had to do some creative financing to pay their expenses. When I realized Dad's wisdom in letting Mom take responsibility for the finances, I saw my own propensity for financial control as a weakness rather than a strength. Eventually, Bonnie began managing the finances for our family.

Still I maintained control of my family. I made the decisions about where we lived based on what I did professionally, sometimes *dragging* my family kicking and screaming behind me. Some of those professional moves occurred during critical times in the lives of Eric and Tracie. They left good friends behind and went through the uneasiness of finding new ones. They were pulled out of schools they liked and put in schools they knew nothing about. I ignored those critical times if I felt the move was right for me.

Unlike the dominant role I saw in Mom, during all of our conversations, Art never mentioned his mother. He only spoke of the lack of communication and emotional distance between him and his dad. Unfortunately, my entire household was non communicative. No one talked much to *anyone* else about *anything*. My dad worked very hard every day, so when he got home in the afternoon around 3:45, Mom expected my sister and me to be very quiet. Dad was tired and didn't want a lot of confusion, noise, **or** "horsing around." Ironically, Dad loved to talk to most anyone, except those in his own family. I don't think he knew how to talk to us because he didn't talk in his own home, as I discovered during our visits with Grandpa Poole.

To use Robert Bly's term, my dad must have been "wounded" as a young boy. Although Dad and I never talked about this possibility, I just know he was. After Dad died, I found out he never talked to Mom about his early years.

When Dad and his brother Johnny were quite young, their biological parents placed them in an orphanage north of Indianapolis. A family from that city adopted both Dad and his brother. Some short time later the family realized they could not support both boys, so they returned Dad to the orphanage.

How abandoned he must have felt. He must have thought, "Why didn't they keep me too? Why did my brother get to stay and not me?" He must have felt he would be abandoned and orphaned his entire childhood. In *Wild at Heart* Eldredge writes the words Dad must have felt. He said, "Where did all this fear come from? Why do I feel so alone in the world...and so young inside? Why does something in my heart feel orphaned?" In writing about his father, Eldredge went on to say, "But like so many men of his era, my father had never faced the issues of his own wounds." At some point Grandpa and Grandma Poole adopted Dad, and he finally had a home.

Dad's stepparents expected him to work in order to help with the family's finances. Because Dad dropped out of school at the end of 6th grade to help Grandpa Poole with his construction business, he always had to "hop the clods" (work hard) all his adult life. Dad worked for a time on the railroad, leaving Sunday evening and returning Friday evening, going to wherever the railroad was either being built or repaired, never close enough to allow him to return home each night.

Dad's hard, laborious work continued when he drove a milk truck for a local dairy, picking up milk from farmers and delivering it to the dairy for processing. He worked for the local Farmers' Co-op, lugging big bags of grain. He worked for a moving company and made long-distance drives, another job keeping him away from home. He spent his last 25 years at Cummins Engine Company, the Columbus-based manufacturer of diesel engines. He always worked hard at what he did and always returned home bone-tired every afternoon.

Even when Dad was "present" in our house, he was "absent" in his conversation, his time to play with me, and any guidance he might have given me. During my time in the woods, I've come to realize that I must be asking God to give me the guidance I never received from my own dad.

John Eldredge added another pertinent thought: "Despite a man's past and the failures of his own father to initiate him, God could ... provide what was missing." At another point Eldredge said, "The gift was perfectly timed, for I knew it was time to allow God to father me." My gift for taking that critical retreat was perfectly timed as well. For the first time, I allowed God to begin fathering me, continuing to guide me toward my authentic way out of the crossroads.

Earlier I stated that I didn't experience closure with Dad while he was alive. I came the closest to finding closure one night on my friend's 36-foot Hunter sailboat. Dave sailed *Messenger* on a big lake close to the Twin Cities. He invited me for a long weekend of sailing, explaining that we were devoting one of those nights to a Native American healing ceremony. We were all instructed to bring something with us, anything we wanted to "give back to the water."

As my gift back to the water, I wrote a letter to Dad. In it, among other thoughts, I told my dad what a good job he did fulfilling what he saw as a father's greatest responsibilities: to be a provider for and a protector of his family. I told him he did those jobs so very well. As far back as I can remember, Dad told me I was going to get a good education. He never had that opportunity, and he wanted to make sure I did. Dad's high expectations for my education were a gift and a legacy. I truly believe that because of those expectations I chose education as my life-long profession. I shared these beliefs with Dad in my letter. I told him many other thoughts that were in my heart at the time, and I said at the end, "Good-bye, Dad. I love you," and signed it Eddie.

Some participants brought flowers to throw on the water. Others brought family pictures and various treasured family mementos to give back to friends and family, current and past. At the appropriate time, I put Dad's letter in a beautiful silver bowl, lit a match, and watched the letter burn to ashes. I took those ashes and spread them out over the lake. The ceremony provided much needed healing, but it wasn't the same as having Dad around so I could read my letter to him and give him a hug and kiss as Art's father did for him that night in the hospital.

I said "I love you" at the end of the letter for a specific reason: Mom and Dad never said those three words to me. Never! And, as I wrote in Chapter 2, they seldom showed any affection to one another. They were both very private, never threw their arms around me with a big hug, and never even embraced each other in front of my sister and me. However, I saw their affection for one another in those old family pictures I returned to. As a father, I wanted to break the cycle I just described. I always hug and kiss Eric and Tracie every time we get together. Doing so is important to me. I do not want them to experience the lack of love I felt growing up.

Sometime before he died, I wrote Dad a letter, signing it, "I love you." A few weeks later I received a return letter from Dad, and at the end he wrote, "And I love you too," the only time he expressed those words to me. I know my dad loved me; he just never told me. Receiving that letter is the closest I came to knowing Art's feelings of having his dad kiss him on his lips and tell him he was a good son.

As I've grown older, I often take opportunities to revisit my relationship with Dad and Mom. I now realize that because Dad probably felt inadequate in his role as a father, he knowingly gave that role to Mom. I did exactly the same when Eric and Tracie were young. If I had an inkling a difficult situation was brewing at home – an issue concerning discipline or times I anticipated I would not be able to assume the role of father I thought I should, I thought of any excuse I could to get out of the house. I did not know how to have conversations with my kids when they were living at home. I never had a meaningful father-son talk with my dad. I was home, but I wasn't there in terms of helping Eric, Tracie, or Bonnie. I was clueless. Therefore, I always saw Bonnie as the more capable parent in interacting with Eric and Tracie, and to this day I attribute to their mother much of who Eric and Tracie are as adults. As with me, Dad surely missed out on those crucial, early years of bonding with a father because he didn't have one. I had my dad, but I believe he was unsure of his ability to be a father.

My parents' struggles were many. However, in their own ways, they left me lasting legacies, most notably my frustrations with and lack of understanding of my early years, just as Dad surely had with those years in his own early life. Does that sentence sound strange? These unclear understandings about my roles as a husband and a father have created this tremendous internal struggle to bring greater clarity to my own journey, to stumble upon my authentic path. Some have said, "But, Ed, you can't *change* those events in your life." I know this statement is true, but I can continue to *understand* those early years as I struggle to find my way out of the crossroads. As I do so, I am better able to accept those early years without anger and bitterness.

I may never know the complete meaning to my reflections about my parents, but inviting the reflections allows me to ponder these ideas that continue to be so important. I'm convinced my mom and my dad did the very best they could as a father and a mother, especially considering the experiences they brought to those two roles. I am also doing the best I can as I take what I received from my parents and try to better the lives of my family.

My Religious Beliefs

Like many others, I was given my set of religious beliefs long before I was ready to understand them. Many adults remain steadfast in those childhood beliefs, and they internalize them as their understanding evolves. The foundations of their faith have provided sharper focus as they mature and see their beliefs as appropriate in today's world. My sister and brother-in-law, for example, continue to attend, and are very active in, the church in which we all three were raised. The world makes sense to them, and their faith has seen them through many difficult times, including the loss, due to leukemia, of their three-year-old daughter in 1965.

The family environment in which I grew up was surrounded by strong Christian beliefs. However, this early grounding was built on a vengeful, angry, "I'm gonna getcha" God, a God that gets even with all on this earth who sin. That church not only scared hell *out of* me but also, at the same time, scared hell *into* me. In that church, I learned the world is always black and white. A person is either "fer" God or "agin 'im." Each time I did something wrong, I was surely "going to hell," according to my church, my mom, and my dad. I was afraid every time I went to church on Sunday, but I was more afraid <u>not</u> to go to church on Sunday. At those times I saw God as my observer and my judge, who kept track of all I did wrong so He would know whether I deserved heaven or hell when I die.

Because of my fear, I have followed a different path than my sister and brother-in-law. For many years I did not embrace those early beliefs because I did not believe them within the context of my adult years. For a long time I did not attend church; I found no meaning there. I have adjusted those beliefs over the years to match my current meaning of life, and my beliefs will continue to take on new meaning throughout my life. In the book *Father Joe: The Man Who Saved My Soul*, author Tony Hendra describes how Father Joe rarely spoke of God without using the word love. Father Joe's relationship with God is beautifully stated as Hendra said, "Father Joe didn't appear to need the clerical metal ruler of do-it-or-I'll-tell-your-father. The 'he' of his God was gentle, generous, endlessly creative, musical, artistic, an engineer and architect of genius, a 'he' who felt his joy and your joy deeply, who could be hurt just as deeply but would never give up on you, who showered you with gifts and opportunities whether you acknowledged them or not, who sent you tasks but didn't abandon you if you failed them..." The beliefs and feelings Hendra ascribed to Father Joe were the opposite of mine until ten years ago. Every word Hendra used was the opposite of a word I would choose. My God was not gentle or generous. He could give up on me if I left the "right" side of the page with that line down the middle and drifted to the "wrong" side of that page.

While continuing to internalize my beliefs during my retreats, I tried to connect them to what God wanted me to do with my life. I felt God wanted me to reflect, be in the moment, and not give up on my questions or let anyone take them away from me. Perhaps God said, "Ya know, Ed, you and I sorta got off on the wrong foot. Why don't we spend some time together so we can get reacquainted?" I did spend some time with God so I could find out more about Him as He rediscovered me and I rediscovered Him.

For much of my adult life I didn't want to spend time with God. Because of my individual choices, God and I were in our separate rooms. I was in a prison of despair and hopelessness. Because of my decisions, not God's, I couldn't feel His presence in the room. God was in the cabin with me, I just couldn't feel His presence. I did not know He was waiting patiently for me to open my door allowing us to get reacquainted.

Because I didn't open my door, God opened it for me, breaking my silence during my last three struggles at the crossroads, and inviting us to spend time together, get out of our separate rooms, and get better acquainted.

I truly believe my willingness to accept God's invitation to spend more time together resulted in shortened time spans between the last three crossroads experiences. Twenty-five years passed between the first and second time spent in the crossroads. Only a total of sixteen years elapsed between the third, fourth, and fifth times I landed in the crossroads. Of those experiences, my time as a superintendent had the greatest impact. I vividly remember sitting alone in the dark one night, trying to understand my thoughts and feelings. I thought I should be able to do this job well, but I wasn't. I was very unhappy in this role as the leader of an entire district. Each day I faced unpleasant challenges with the local teachers' union, unhappy parents, and disgruntled faculty members. Finally, when the understanding wasn't coming from all other reflections, I realized I had only one choice left. I said to God, "I cannot do this by myself, Lord. I need your help. Please help me find my way." The words were precise because my soul felt so lost and afraid. The second time I accepted God's invitation to spend time together was at my fourth crossroads, my first battle with depression. And the third time I recognized God's presence was my time in the wilderness as I once again tried to find those images at the crossroads.

While sitting in the middle of this crossroads, I saw an image I had never seen before. I pictured God and me riding a tandem bike. When I wanted to be in control, I put God on the back seat while I was in front, determining both the speeds and the directions we traveled. I'm sure He was thinking, as He allowed me free choice over my direction in life, "Okay, Ed, I will leave you in control until you realize we should change places." Those realizations only came when I struggled so much from the front seat I couldn't make one more push on my pedals. I had guided God and me smack into the middle of the crossroads.

When I finally allowed God to be the front seat driver and guide for our journey, my life changed. He knew delightful shortcuts up mountains and through rocky places as we pedaled at breakneck speeds. Even though it looked at times like madness, He kept saying, "Pedal!"

I got worried about our wild and unpredictable journey. "Where are you taking me?" I asked. He just laughed and didn't answer. Fortunately, I learned to trust.

God took me to people with gifts that I needed, gifts of healing, acceptance, and joy. The individuals I saw during our ride were friends, colleagues, religious leaders, and folks I didn't know. They gave me their gifts to take on my journey. Then we were off again.

At first I thought God would wreck my life. But He knows bike secrets – how to make it bend to take sharp curves, how to jump over rocks along the way, and how to fly through scary passages. I am learning to shut up and pedal in the strangest places and to relax and enjoy the cool breeze on my face. And when I am sure I just cannot do anymore, He just smiles and says…,"Pedal!"

In his writing author Stephen Sondheim captures the essence of working with God along our journeys. In *Into the Woods* he said, "It takes two. I thought one was enough, it's not true. It takes two of us. You came through when the journey was rough. It took you. It took two of us. It takes care, it takes patience and fear and despair to change. Though you swear to change, who can tell if you do? It takes two."

CHAPTER 8
Finding the Hole in My Sidewalk

With what I learned from my first week in Brown County, I was ready to confront the events that plopped me into that fifth crossroads but, at the same time, also provided me additional direction toward the path I sought at that time in my life.

I began my day at the Daily Grind. I got my coffee, paid my bill, and went to my favorite table to wait for the croissant. Once my croissant arrived, I secured a couple of the daily papers, always kept in the same spot in the center of the room.

While reading my hometown paper, *The Republic*, I noticed an article written by the paper's associate editor, Harry McCawley. When I lived in Columbus, Harry was the sports editor for this paper. He and I often had an opportunity to talk as he covered all the sporting events at the high school where I was principal.

Today Harry's article was titled "Senior Citizens' Oral History Eye-opener for Scout Troop." My eyes riveted on the title containing the words "oral history."

Turns out, the article highlighted a local Boy Scout, Kyle Louder. In order to obtain his Eagle Scout badge, Kyle had to complete a significant project, in my view one of the most unusual attempted by a sixteen-year-old. He asked 50 of Bartholomew County's senior citizens to talk about themselves.

The beginning of McCawley's article reminded me again of memories with Dad when he revealed that his own dad died when he was 16, writing, "I really didn't know that much about him, especially that part of his life when he was a young boy and later a young man… We didn't have a whole lot in common, and he wasn't exactly the sharing kind." McCawley went on to say, "I don't even know some of the most basic things about who he was or what he thought or dreamed, such things as: What was the house like in which he grew up? Who were his best friends as a child? What did he hate doing when he was a child? What did he love doing? What's the smartest thing he ever did in his life? What's the luckiest?"

Then McCawley described Louder's project. Louder asked his 50 senior citizens these same questions, as well as others. How I wish he had done his Eagle Scout project while Dad was still alive because I might have taken the opportunity to ask him those same questions. In defining the smartest thing they ever did, many of those interviewed said the smartest thing was marrying their spouses. I'm sure my dad would have said the same thing.

Upon completing the project, Kyle explained what he had learned from his work. His answer: "I learned that it's not so bad growing old." What a wonderful experience for a young man.

Reading the article, I could identify so readily with what McCawley said about his dad. Earlier I shared some of my issues with my dad, and, just as with Harry, I still have so many unanswered questions about his life. I knew very little about Dad. I didn't get to know him as a father. His childhood was a mystery my ancestral heritage from Dad's side a blank page. I thought about McCawley's article all day. I know I would be amazed if I knew how many men have shared boyhoods similar to Art's, Harry's, and mine. Far too many!

After making this meaningful trip to The Daily Grind and reflecting more about my dad, I plunged headfirst into my writing and reading. Throughout the afternoon the mezzanine, the courtyard, my cabin, and a hike through the woods served as familiar settings for my words and thoughts.

The result of those words and thoughts are reflected in the stories I heard in Brown County. Some may appear connected, and some may not. There were two connections for me. The stories all came from the hearts of those sharing them with me. Secondly, because the stories were all connected with the questions I took to Brown County they helped me learn something about myself. I became more aware of my inner desire to pursue writing and speaking. At that time I didn't know if I could follow that desire and remain in education. I realized that writing *Lessons from the Porch* was not an isolated experience. I wrote and reflected that first week in the woods, leading me to the conclusion that I still had thoughts and feelings within me that needed to be released and put on paper. Amidst the hills of Brown County and my new friends, I felt the best I have in a long time.

I described my own lived experience while in the woods while trying to find my way out of the crossroads. Events in our lives don't just happen. Each of us is a tiny speck in a gigantic community, a community that God oversees with love and compassion. The more authentic connections we find, the better we become at sharing our stories and learning from the stories of others. We are not where we are without some God-given reason for being there.

Providential Grace:
My Hole in the Sidewalk

There are no mistakes, no coincidences. All events are blessings, given to us to learn from.

Elisabeth Kubler-Ross

As I reflected on my experiences in Brown County, I realized my time was part of God's creative design for me and not a set of coincidental and unrelated events. I was absolutely certain the stories would continue to grow in their connections. God's the "master planner," and though God has a plan, I make choices that can either draw me closer to His plan or alienate me from it.

God has loved me so unconditionally during my life, and He has allowed me to make choices, some not in my best interest. Some of those choices took me down paths that led me into the wilderness. I've had to learn to stand still and let those desert times hurt. God gives me the choice of learning the lessons to be found there. But He is always hoping, beyond hope, that I will learn them.

I Couldn't Write Fast Enough: The Five-Chapter Autobiography that Grabbed My Heart and Won't Let Go

As I entered the Daily Grind the next morning, Karis asked, "A mug?"

"Yep," I said, "and a HEC," the code for ordering a *h*am, *e*gg, and *c*heese croissant.

She looked at me and smiled. I got my mug, and soon Karis delivered my HEC to my table. I was fully prepared to drink my coffee, devour my croissant, glance through two newspapers, and continue reading one of my books. But for some reason, *this* particular morning, thoughts, feelings, and words were flying out of me with the speed of those racing motorcycles I've heard about from Charlie so many times.

I read for a few moments and then put aside whatever I was reading to jot a note. I was at the coffee shop for almost four hours, longer than my stay all the other times. Why that morning, I do not know. Perhaps those moments, thoughts, and decisions about what notes to take were an example of a series of events coming together at one time, giving them new meaning.

Returning to the Hospital

While enjoying my coffee, I reflected on my second hospitalization with clinical depression, a life-altering experience leading to the fifth crossroads that took me to the woods. Returning to the Linden Oaks psychiatric care unit for a two-week stay in late February and early March, 2004, I knew I had forgotten some lessons from my first four crossroad experiences.

You see, I thought I had learned it all after *Lessons from the Porch* was published. Silly me! I should have known better! I will always be learning throughout my entire life and finding the happiness from that learning.

I remember exactly when my depression resurfaced, in July 2003, almost seven months before I was hospitalized. I was in the middle of teaching one of my graduate classes that afternoon. With the speed of an oncoming train, the bottom fell out, and my depression took a southward nosedive. My students knew about my depression and told me later they could "see it in my face."

I told them I just could not continue. I gathered up my books and papers, put them in my office, locked the door, and went home, retreating like Jon Katz when he realized he was not doing what he wanted in his life. I was unable to function. As the afternoon went on, I knew I would not be able to meet my class the next day. Phoning my secretary, I asked her to send an email to my students simply telling them there would be no class tomorrow.

Fearful of those all-too-familiar self-destructive thoughts I was having, I called my daughter and asked if she could come spend the night with me. Though I had a restless night with little sleep, I felt comforted, supported, and protected knowing Tracie was there. She wanted to do more to help me, but she also knows enough about my depression to know I have to do the work myself. Still, her presence meant so much.

The next day I remember sitting outside, looking off toward faraway places I didn't recognize. Tracie and I didn't talk much. She let me have the space I needed to work through my depressed state. I'm not sure why, but by the middle of the afternoon, I had the thought, "I can handle this." Like the flip of a switch, I seemed like my old self. Some swings with my depression do happen that fast. I handled those swings for the next seven months.

However, in February the depression hit hard again. This time I could not find my way out of the darkness by myself. I talked with my doctor, and he arranged an evaluation session with one of the clinicians at my local hospital. The clinician felt I needed to be hospitalized.

As I went into Linden Oaks Hospital that day in February and sat in those group therapy sessions, I was angry. Even though I admitted myself to the hospital, I was surprised I was there. Why was I not able to control my depression? I was doing just fine (or so I thought) until seven months ago. I remained quiet the first two days, finding myself asking, "Now, God, why is it, *exactly*, I'm here?"

The third day, I knew the answer: I *had* forgotten many of those valuable lessons I discovered while writing my first book. You see, I had once again retreated to my usual pattern of getting immersed in my work and forgetting about me.

I knew the moment, *the exact moment*, I understood the reason I returned to the hospital. Our group was given a page to read, taken from Portia Nelson's book, *There's a Hole in My Sidewalk*. The title of this piece is "Autobiography in Five Short Chapters." The message in this brief autobiography impacted me like few others have in my life.

Chapter 1

I walk down the street.
There is a deep hole in the sidewalk.
I fall in.
I am lost ---I am hopeless.
It isn't *my* responsibility.
It takes forever to find a way out.

Chapter 2

I walk down the same street.
There is a deep hole in the sidewalk.
I pretend I don't see it.
I fall in again.
I can't believe I'm in the same place.

But it isn't *my* responsibility.
It still takes a long time to get out.

Chapter 3

I walk down the same street.
There is a deep hole in the sidewalk.
I see it is there.
I still fall in… it's a habit.
My eyes are open now – I know where I am.
It *is* my responsibility.
I get out immediately.

Chapter 4

I walk down the same street.
There is a deep hole in the sidewalk.
I walk around it.

Chapter 5

I walk down *another* street.

That day in the hospital, Portia Nelson's story caused my face to turn blank and my eyes to fall toward the floor as a feeling of absolute failure and unrelenting sadness surrounded me. I was absolutely certain *I* was the hole that I had fallen into again, that I was responsible for my depression's return. I knew then why I was back in the hospital. "Here we go again," went through my mind as I lamented the fact that I was back on that same street, unable to avoid the hole.

The responsibility for finding my way out was mine! Initially, though, during both hospitalizations, I thought the therapists were supposed to find my way out of the hole. As my time in the hospital progressed, I knew the therapists could guide me, but getting better was completely my responsibility. After writing my first book, I forgot about the work I had to do to climb out of the dark hole I had fallen into with my depression. I also lost the path that led me out of that crossroads. The twenty-two lessons in my first book put me back on my authentic path. They were my lessons and I saw them clearly because I believed I had described all of my thoughts and feelings I discovered when I left my first hospitalization.

During this second time in the hospital I asked myself some tough questions: How long will I continue to fall into that same hole? Will I ever be able to walk around it? Will I eventually find that other street to walk down? I thought about Chapter 3 in that short autobiography, which does, by the way, show amazing parallels to my current autobiography. I took jobs in new locations to try and leave my professional problems behind. My personal problems at those times contributed to making professional decisions to leave. The pressures of being a good husband and parent were manifested in the inordinate amount of time I worked on my professional life. That time on the job exacerbated the problems in my personal life.

Each time those same problems of lack of self-confidence, an ill-defined sense of self, and an inability to live up to others' expectations kept finding me. Will my eyes be opened after I leave the hospital this time? Will I know where I am? Will I assume my responsibility? If I fall again, can I climb out immediately?

An article in *The Chicago Tribune* titled "Hawking Backs Off Black Hole Theory," made me think immediately of the story of the hole in my sidewalk. Stephen Hawking is considered the world's foremost theoretical physicist, an expert on black holes, whose intention is to unify quantum mechanics with Einstein's general theory of relativity, forming a single scientific theory to explain the origin (and end) of the universe.

In part, the article said, "After almost 30 years of arguing that a black hole *swallows up* everything that falls into it…the world famous author…said he and other scientists had gotten it wrong: The galactic traps may in fact allow information *to escape*…'I've been thinking about this problem for the last 30 years and I think I now have the answer to it…A black hole only appears to form but later opens up and *releases* information about what fell inside. So we can be sure of the past and predict the future.'" This skilled scientist and researcher was willing to admit his mistake, thus allowing his human fallibility to show.

As I said above, initially I thought I was that black hole in my sidewalk, into which I continued to fall. My black hole sucked me to its dark, dank bottom to remind me of all my fears, guilt, shame, and lack of faith in God and myself.

Am I ready, like Hawking, to let go of my own black hole theory and replace it with a new one, one that sees my deep hole in the sidewalk not as an enemy but as a friend? While there, will I release into the heavens those same demons I thought were hounding me and keeping me from escaping?

Also while in the hospital, I was reminded each and every day to "take care of me." How could I do this in a productive and healing way? As I said earlier, many of my decisions in life have been strictly "to take care of Ed." However, most of them came from a very selfish part of me. I assumed if something was good for me, it was good for everyone close to me. Because I forgot much of what I learned while writing *Lessons from the Porch*, I reverted to my old tendency to take care of myself in ways that didn't continue my healing process. Much of life, once again, centered around Ed Poole. I kept my secrets. I would go on a spending binge and hide the receipts. I began gambling and built up close to $70,000 in credit card debt. I hid this addiction and debt from Bonnie for a long time; however, she figured out my passwords and was absolutely dumfounded by my actions. She was livid and I understood her anger. I began to drink heavily. Bonnie never knew just how much I drank but, she too, was aware my drinking had increased dramatically. The gambling and drinking are two ways my addictive personality manifested itself at that time in my life. I also made significant professional decisions without consulting Bonnie and informed her of these decisions after the fact. I began to feel my soul shrinking.

Author Timothy Johnson's words (*Finding God in the Questions*) came to mind: "When we make important life choices based on purely selfish considerations, we eventually find ourselves 'rewarded' for such choices…Even though there may be no immediate consequences of each individual choice we make, there will be an ultimate and cumulative effect from the many choices we make in our lives."

How could I take care of myself and not be selfish in doing so? How could I make choices that would not bring harm to others but would also heal me? I have to be open, in both heart and mind, to God's guidance each and every day.

While in the hospital, I wrote four statements to help me take care of myself: I can think about what I need and not bring harm to others. It's good for me to take time for myself and address the unfinished business in my life. I don't have to be perfect to be loved. I am open to receiving support from others.

Taking care of myself is not a selfish act if done for the right reasons. Unfortunately, for much of my adult life I have taken care of me without any consideration of how my decisions would affect others. I've written about my selfish professional and personal decisions. Whenever I felt a need to get out of the house, I thought of any excuse to do so which left Bonnie to deal with many issues with our kids. If the impact was negative, I really didn't care. Life was all about me. Taking care of me without harming others is, I now know, being a good steward of the gift of my life. If I don't take care of myself in a selfless way, I turn that responsibility over to others as I have done in past years. If I don't take care of my life, I will not find my way out of the crossroads.

As I learn to take care of my life in ways that do not bring harm to others, I realize one way to do so is by serving others. But before I can help others along their journeys, I need to have a better understanding of my own journey. For much of my life, I've expected to be served by others, rather than being of service to them. I thought about all the people I met during my retreats. I thought of words I could use to describe these folks. They were selfless in helping others. They were honest, caring individuals. They were willing to share their stories, doing so from their hearts, not their egos. They were humble, down home folks. Somehow all of these characteristics, when taken collectively, revealed their desire to have a blend between self and others.

These attributes identify my struggle to help myself by helping others. The words also embrace the questions I took with me and those important items I packed in my suitcase as I began my journey. I use the word blend, and not balance, in seeking to help others and myself. When I think about the word balance I always see a balance scale. One tiny addition to one side of the scale can bring it out of balance. To have a balance always means a zero sum accomplishment.

When I have a blend in my life I think of a recipe. To have the product be as good as possible, the blending of the ingredients must be right. Sometimes in my life I have to re-arrange the blend because the ingredients have become out of proportion. The ingredients must be the same to have the same cake every time. My authentic self has to have the right balance so my life can continue down my authentic path. The path doesn't change; however when the blending is no longer allowing me to move down that path I must do some adjusting. Serving others and self requires the blend of my outer and inner self. For much of my adult life my main goal was telling others of my many accomplishments. They had little chance to talk. I monopolized the conversation, because life was all about me. I've learned to do more listening than talking. I want the other person to tell me his or her story and then I want to respond in ways that will help them. During these conversations I've become pretty adept at helping others reveal some of their true selves. I only give advice or offer suggestions when invited to do so. I ask a lot more questions rather than make statements. Doing so helps me as well because as I listen to the stories of others I learn more about my own story.

My New Diagnosis: Another Gift

My second visit to the hospital came as I struggled in the middle of my fourth crossroads. For eight years, I took medication for clinical depression. This medication works on the principle that those "down times" need to be elevated. For some time, my meds were doing just that. During several conversations I had with my psychiatrist while in the hospital that second time, he began to realize I may not be clinically depressed but rather BiPolar2, different from a regular BiPolar diagnosis.

BiPolar is the newer term for manic depression. This illness can bring about violent mood swings between some high point (manic phase) and a corresponding low point (depressive state). Medication helps smooth out and blend the highs and lows. Without medication, an individual is always traveling between the two extreme points of the cycle. My mother-in-law struggled with this illness most of her adult life, and I saw her many mood swings over the years. As she grew older, the swings became more violent and moved closer together.

BiPolar2 has the same mood swings as BiPolar though not as extreme. My medication for clinical depression was bringing up the low times but was not recognizing the high times. Today I'm on a completely different regimen of medications, intended to help blend my shift in moods between high and low points. The difference in medications recognizes the need to reduce the more manic phases I experience. Like the gifts that allowed me to find my authentic path at the end of my first hospitalization with depression, this second time I sought help also brought the gift of a new diagnosis. I am still in this fifth crossroads, but the medication is clearing my head and heart as I stand at the crossroads.

Uneven Numbers, Flat Stones, Straws, and
"Is that picture crooked?"

Also during my stay at Linden Oaks, my psychiatrist recognized in me what he termed characteristics of Obsessive Compulsive Disorder (OCD). OCD manifests itself in different ways and with varying degrees in those of us who exhibit these tendencies. For example, in the movie *As Good as It Gets* Jack Nicholson's character has OCD, with more of the stereotypical manifestations.

Nicholson avoids stepping on all cracks *anywhere*. He either jumps over or walks around his "hole in the sidewalk." Every day he eats at the same restaurant, orders the same food, and always brings his own (wrapped) eating utensils along with his own plate. Relentlessly, he washes and dries his hands a certain number of times. Once inside his apartment, he locks and unlocks the door a certain number of times, and he always turns the lights on and off the same exact number of times.

Many people have the milder version of what I saw in the film, including me; however, regardless of the ways the characteristics manifest themselves, differences exist between OCD and what I call "rituals." I have certain rituals I perform every day. I go through my rituals at the beginning and ending of each day. When the Midwestern weather is nice, I begin each day sitting alone on the back patio. In the fall, when the morning sky is clear, one brilliant star just peeks over the rooftop as I sit down. I have made this star mine, and I always get a big smile on my face and say "good morning" when I see it in the blue sky.

While looking at my star, I go through my morning prayers. I thank God for seeing me through the night, and I always return to those questions I took to the woods, asking God for His continued guidance that day, to allow me to move toward a greater understanding those questions hold for me.

As I dry off after my shower each morning, I ask God to look over my eight "kids" that day – daughter, son, their spouses, and my four granddaughters. My requests differ for each of the eight, but I always end by thanking God for the gifts of those individuals in my life.

I have another ritual I follow each night before falling asleep. As I lay my head on the pillow, I thank God for seeing me through that day, ask Him to help me through the night, and end my ritual by saying, "And please let me have a peaceful sleep."

During the day, my OCD tendencies visit me – uneven numbers, flat stones, triangles, and crooked pictures. Everything I count, *everything*, has to end with an uneven number. For example, the thermostats at home and in my car are always set at uneven numbers, 69, 71, 73, and never 70, 72, or 74. If I count a group of objects and the total is an uneven number, I let it alone, for a while. I often return to those objects and count them again, just to be sure they continue to total an uneven number. If I count a group of objects and the total is an even number, I find some way in my mind to make the total uneven. I'll count the "parts" of the objects until I find unevenness or quickly sweep my eyes over the entire group of objects, using that final, sweeping glance to create the uneven total. Each day, I count many, many objects, always finding unevenness. I live on the third floor of a condominium with a thirty-foot balcony over looking a lake. Across the lake is a high-rise condominium. Every night I sit on my balcony and count the lights that are on in the high-rise. I always count the lights until I find an uneven combination, and I count those lights tens of times. As fall arrives the leaves from the trees surrounding the lake drift lazily down onto the lake. I count those leave until, once again, I find an uneven combination and then I repeat that counting over and over again.

    I also seek uneven numbers with my flat stone. I love to walk the beach, looking for flat stones. On a recent trip to Ashland, Oregon, to visit my son and his family, we went to the Oregon coast for four days. While walking up and down the beach, inspecting hundreds of flat stones with my eyes, I found the perfect stone for me. It's beautiful – a deep purple, with gray and black streaks running through it. One side of the stone is smooth, the other rough. As soon as I picked it up, it became my special stone. I attached to the smooth side those parts of my days I hope will go well. Knowing all my days will very seldom be smooth sailing, I count on the rough side to remind me of the rough spots that may present themselves on any given day.

    This stone has become an integral part of my life. Each day I transfer the stone to a new trouser pocket for that day. Many times during the day, I reach my hand into that pocket and rub both sides of the stone. I always rub each side an uneven number of times, the smooth side more times than the rough side. The more times I rub each side indicates the relative ratio I might expect between the smooth and rough parts of my day – for example, 7 smooth and 5 rough (71% ratio);

Finding the Hole in My Sidewalk

11 smooth and 9 rough (81% ratio); 23 smooth and 21 rough (91% ratio). Each of the ratios is, of course, an uneven number. When I use a public restroom, I always push the towel dispenser an uneven number of times – 3, 5, or 7 – depending on how wet my hands are.

On a recent Sunday morning, I walked around the vestibule at church prior to entering the sanctuary for the worship service. I walked around the vestibule reading the various postings and as I did so, my right hand went deep into my trouser pocket to find the flat stone, my fingers rubbing both the smooth and rough sides. I finally entered the sanctuary. After the service, I walked back out into the vestibule. In a few seconds, I looked down to the floor and saw a familiar-looking object. I moved closer, thinking, "That looks like my flat stone." I bent over, picked it up, inspected both sides, reached into my right trouser pocket, and found no stone. It <u>was</u> my stone, which had accidentally worked its way out of my pocket as I walked and rubbed before church. I had several questions: Why did I choose to exit the sanctuary and return to the vestibule? I could have taken several other exits. Why did I retrace some of my earlier steps, instead of heading the other direction toward my intended destination? Why did my eyes look to the floor at precisely that moment? Why did I look downward at all, instead of straight ahead or up toward the ceiling? Why did my eyes see the object on the floor, and why did I choose to move toward it and inspect it? As I put it back in my pocket, I said, "Thank you, Lord, for guiding me as you do."

Recently I attended a university-wide faculty meeting. The meeting lasted one and one-half hours, way beyond my level of endurance and concentration. The meeting's topic was fairly innocuous, way beyond my level of interest. As I sat down, I noticed a number of lights straight ahead of my seat. Without exaggerating I counted those uneven lights 100 times during that meeting. One way I counted them, there were five. Another viewing created seven lights. I counted and counted, which greatly interrupted my ability to pay any attention to the topic of the meeting.

Another OCD tendency is making triangles out of my drinking straws. Every time I have any kind of drink served with a straw, I take the straw out and make it into a triangle. With multiple drinks, I always link the straws together. The triangles represent a sense of connectedness, for my life and with others. Then I twirl the triangle(s) five times around my left index finger. Finally, I put the straws on the counter and flip them with my finger until I see the straws making several rotations in the air before they land back on the counter or on the floor. I think about the flip-flops along my life's journey. I'm never sure where I'll land. Sometimes I land on the floor and sometimes at a crossroads. If the waitperson doesn't bring me a straw with each new drink, I always ask for one. If that person knows me, he or she knows never to take the straws away as part of the trash picked up around me. When the server doesn't know me, I give him or her a huge scowl, which means, "Leave my straws alone!"

Finally, I straighten pictures hanging crooked on the wall. I very seldom walk past a picture without noticing if it is straight. If it isn't, I will always give a tug on one of the corners. Two small pictures of sailboats hang by the door of my office. Closing the door each day causes the pictures to hang on a slant the next morning. I always straighten those pictures before beginning my day.

Though both my rituals and OCD behaviors occur routinely, they have a different impact on my life. My rituals do not interrupt my day; they give it more meaning. My OCD tendencies, on the other hand, most always interrupt my day. No matter what I am doing in any part of my life, at home, at work, at church, in social activities, I will stop what I am doing and thinking to count objects, rub my flat stone, make triangles (when I can), or straighten a picture. My attentiveness in conversations is diverted when I need to count something, straighten a picture, or count the number of times I touch the smooth and rough sides on my stone.

Because these OCD behaviors can consume large amounts of time, they also interrupt the search for my authentic self, causing the same lack of attention to the search and to why I'm on the journey. These mindless tendencies block out my desire to continue the journey. To regain my authentic path I've had to drastically lessen the number of objects I count, the number of straws I make into triangles, and the number of pictures I straighten.

CHAPTER 9

Back to a (true? or false?) Sense of Reality

While enjoying my mug of coffee that morning at the Daily Grind, I had an insight: I rediscovered and redefined my faith while in the woods of Brown County. Many times in *Lessons from the Porch* I conveniently skirted around my faith and my beliefs, perhaps because I just wasn't ready to understand what my faith means to me. In that earlier writing I was embarrassed to let my readers know of my faith in God. I made only general references to a Supreme Being so I wouldn't offend potential readers. The scarcity of discussion about my faith was an avoidance technique, but it also meant I was not ready to talk about my faith. Now I am finding the readiness I did not have ten years ago.

If my trip to the woods was an opportunity to redefine my faith and come upon my authentic self, I wondered if the retreat would end up being a life-changing experience for me. Was I ready for a life-changing experience? Was I afraid? Had I been so fearful of change that I settled for the life I had? Was I blind to the possibilities my life has to offer? Could I really put my life in God's hands and let Him give me the direction from the front seat I so desperately needed?

Though I crave spiritual guidance, I was unwilling to embrace a new life because I didn't feel safe enough to do so. There have been times in my life I've settled for the status quo. I stayed in a marriage that had lost much of its meaning for both Bonnie and me. We went down separate paths long before we realized the journeys had separated. We were the epitome of a co-dependent marriage. We were full of judgments toward the other person. We stopped having fun. At times I became obsessed with the need to travel the path of self-discovery, and then the need would disappear, and the journey ended. I didn't have enough faith to leave the security of where I was at the time. I convinced myself that I had everything I needed right there, at that moment. I also adamantly held onto the belief that any other relationship would have its problems, so why not just stay where I was? I knew the problems and had to learn, in either healthy or unhealthy ways, how to deal with those issues.

Then one day I got an unexpected and surprising feeling coming from deep inside. The pain of not making some changes in my life became greater than beginning the journey toward a renewed and reinvented Ed Poole. I wanted to leave the field of education and move into a new phase of my life as an entrepreneur. I wanted to move down my own path, on my own, alone. "Where did that come from?" I didn't ask for this discomfort in my heart; it just appeared out of nowhere, like my poem *How Dare You*. After a while I got over it and breathed a deep sigh of relief. "Whew! I weathered *that* storm, again. Why should I put myself through all that misery of seeking another job, another place to live, another spouse, a different church, a new car, or a new calling? I knew where I was and what I was doing. I coped with most of my problems. Why would I give all that up?" But that unsettled feeling kept resurfacing.

This Time I Did Say Good-bye

Although my first retreat to the woods in Brown County had brought some peace to my soul, the unsettled feelings were still there. One person, above all others, who helped bring me some inner peace was Charlie. Charlie and I made plans to have breakfast my last day in the woods. I wanted one last opportunity to say good-bye to my friend. Lots of folks were concerned Charlie might not be around much longer.

I shared their concerns, at the same time hoping we were all wrong!

When I got to the Hotel Nashville, Charlie wasn't waiting outside for me as he usually did. I looked all around and went into the lobby to find him. No Charlie. I went to his suite and knocked on the door. In a bit, he answered. He was dressed, so I asked, "Ready to go to breakfast?"

"I can't go this morning, Ed. I had a seizure last night. How about we go sit on the deck?" Behind the hotel is a beautiful, large deck. We walked slowly down the stairs and sat. I positioned myself on Charlie's right side so he could hear.

We sat, surrounded by the beautifully landscaped grounds at the hotel. I could see that Charlie's arms and hands were still shaking from his seizure at 3:00 that morning. Because he didn't feel well, we didn't talk much.

I sat and watched Charlie in silence, his and mine. In our silence, the memories of those two weeks with him came speeding through my heart and mind. In a few short minutes I recalled all our fun and meaningful times together and all the honesty, genuineness, and laughter. I thought of Parker Palmer's words in *A Hidden Wholeness: The Journey Toward an Undivided Life:* "It takes good friends to sustain silence and laughter because both make us vulnerable... We can share silence and laughter only when we trust each other – and the more often we share them, the deeper our trust grows." I knew Charlie and I trusted one another. We shared too much for it to be otherwise.

Both Charlie and Art knew about my struggles with depression and the gifts of self-understanding and courage to face my demons that came as a result of the depression. My demons were still inside me, and Charlie carried his own list of demons. He had been a wild man, drinking too much at times, going through money like water running through a sieve. He was gone a lot from home, and his wife had the major responsibility of raising their son and daughter. I could duplicate Charlie's list of demons as my own. The contexts were different, but the problems were very similar. I carried these problems because, as an adult, I did not know how to release the guilt and shame I felt from those early religious beliefs I was given as a child.

As Charlie and I sat on the deck I realized he had helped me ease some of the struggles I brought to that first retreat. Charlie was such a dear man. We shared the good moments in our lives, and we shared the desert experiences. We did so because we quickly learned to let each other into our deepest souls. Palmer describes the relationship we had, writing, "Perhaps this is why we have yet another name for people who can share silence and laughter with equal ease: we call them soul mates."

I gave Charlie a copy of *Lessons from the Porch*. I wrote a note on the inside cover for both Art and him. I asked Charlie to share the book with Art when he finished it. Both men, at some earlier point, said they would like to read it.

When it was time for me to push off, Charlie and I stood and gave each other a big hug and pats on the back. "You call me, Ed."

"I will, Charlie."

"You have a safe trip back."

"Thanks, I will."

Needing rest, Charlie said, "I think I'll go upstairs, sit in my recliner, and start this book." With that, we said good-bye, and I headed back to Brown County State Park to prepare to leave. Because Charlie and I didn't have breakfast, I was hungry. I decided to make one more trip to the Daily Grind. I also wanted to say good-bye to the friends I made during my daily trips there.

I said my good-byes and headed back to my cabin. As I drove along Highway 46, I realized, with a great sense of relief, that the heart leads the mind and by doing so becomes a way of knowing. I realized that for so much of my life I've operated in the reverse manner. I've used my mind to lead my heart, and I've always needed to know something before I was able to do anything, and yet action didn't always follow knowledge. I thought of the words of Kidd who, in her book *The Secret Life of Bees*, shared a conversation between two of the book's characters, August and Lily, which illustrates the difficulty of acting on what a person knows. August says to Lily, "Lifting a person's heart – now *that* matters. The whole problem with people is… they *know* what matters, but they don't *choose* it. You know how hard that is, Lily? The hardest thing in the world is choosing what matters."

People can choose what matters only if they trust themselves. For a long time I lacked this self-trust. While writing *Lessons from the Porch*, I sought out the thoughts of many other writers. Their thoughts became my thoughts. I did not have enough confidence in my own writing abilities to allow my own thoughts and feelings to evolve. Often I sat back in my chair, wondering if anything I wrote would be of interest to others. As I refined each draft of *Lessons from the Porch* and gained more confidence in myself, I deleted the thoughts of other writers. However, I still used my own writing to support what I learned from other authors. In *Lessons from the Crossroads*, my confidence as a writer increased to the level that I used the words of others to support my own writing. My goal in writing this book was to tell my own story and not the stories of other authors. As I wrote in the very beginning of *Lessons from the Crossroads*, other writers always challenge my own thinking; however, I have woven into my own thoughts the supporting ideas that others have expressed to extend my own reflections.

As my knowledge and confidence in writing grew while completing *Lessons from the Porch*, I didn't always act relative to that knowledge and confidence. I know why the action didn't follow the knowledge. I still didn't *believe* I could write, so I couldn't *see* myself as a writer. While writing this book, I grew in the belief that I could write; therefore, I saw myself as writer. Being able to do so helped me gain confidence that I could write and would love writing. Since my ability to write full-time was a struggle I took with me to Brown County, I used my heart to continue to ponder my ability to act on what I saw happening as my writing unfolded.

Returning to the state park, I sat for awhile on the porch at Tawny Apple #1, continuing to reflect on my inability to act on my beliefs. I remembered a character from Edgar Lee Masters' book, *Spoon River Anthology*, a fictional account of the Spoon River Cemetery in west-central Illinois where over 200 people are buried. All those buried there had the magical ability to look back from their graves to read the epitaphs on their tombstones and reflect on their lives. The following is what George Gray found on his tombstone:

> I have studied many times
> The marble which was chiseled for me –
> A boat with a furled sail at rest in the harbor.
> In truth it pictures not my destination but my life.
> For love was offered me and I shrank from its disillusionment;
> Sorrow knocked at my door, but I was afraid;
> Ambition called to me, but I dreaded the chances.
> Yet all the while I hungered for meaning in my life.
> And now I know that we must lift the sail and catch the winds of destiny,
> Wherever they drive the boat.
> To put meaning in one's life may end in madness,
> But life without meaning is the torture
> Of restlessness and vague desire –
> It is a boat longing for the sea and yet afraid.

For over twenty years, that time when I've allowed God and me to be in our separate cabin rooms, I've been tortured with the idea that I'll be lying on my deathbed, looking back over my life, and forced to echo George's lament: "And now I know that we must lift the sail and catch the winds of destiny, wherever they drive the boat...It is a boat longing for the sea and yet afraid." George Gray describes my life. I have been afraid to raise my sails, let them catch the wind, and get out there and see what life is all about. I may not like what I find, but I am convinced I will lift those sails and savor both the disappointments and joy that await me. Fear has kept me in the harbor far too long. I will join those other brave souls who have left their porches and lived life to the fullest. While spending time getting reacquainted with God, did I find new eyes through which I saw how I might address change in my life? While in the woods of Brown County did I begin coming alive instead of just thinking about my desire to no longer be a sideline cheerleader about living my life to its fullest?

Unlocking the Mysteries

I know that living with the questions and searching for the answers will be unlocking some of the mysteries of my life. Albert Einstein said, "The most beautiful thing we can experience is the mysterious. It is the source of all true art and science. He to whom this emotion is a stranger, who can no longer pause to wonder and stand rapt in awe, is as good as dead: his eyes are closed." Unlocking the mysterious provides guiding lights, helping us find our way, the light in our hand and the light in our eyes. Through the words of Lily, Sue Monk Kidd said, "I realized it for the first time in my life: there is nothing but mystery in the world, how it hides behind the fabric of our poor, browbeat days, shining brightly, and we don't even know it." For much of my adult life I have been numb to or unaware of the hope gushing forth from the mysteries that surrounded me every day. Those mysteries had everything to do with the paths I saw leading from the crossroads: my struggles with leaving a career spanning more than three decades; my confusion about aligning my spiritual life with the beliefs I held about a loving, forgiving God; and my ambivalence toward either working on my marriage to make it better or striking out on my personal path by myself.

I thought a lot about Charlie's constant comment, "I'm not done yet." From the deepest part of my heart, I knew the same thought applied to the time I spent at my first retreat. Emotionally and spiritually I was not ready to leave. I knew in my heart I would return to my cabin in the woods. I couldn't do otherwise. God had unfinished business yet to do with me there, and I had unfinished business yet to do with Him.

I knew neither the questions nor the decisions that awaited me back in Naperville, Illinois. I was not supposed to know them, but whatever they were, I had to find out and face them. If I am going to become who God wants me to become, I must find my happiness and life's connections from within, and that is what I hoped to do while continuing to find the questions (and perhaps some answers) as I moved along my journey. Author Robert Persig said, "The place to improve the world is first in one's own heart and head and hands, and then work outward from there."

I packed my bag, lugged my arm load of books and my laptop to the car, checked the room to make sure I didn't leave anything (except a big part of me), and went to the front desk in the lodge to check out.

As I passed the guard gate one last time and drove through Aaron Wolf's covered bridge, I knew a flood of emotions awaited me on my drive home north on Interstate 65.

That flood of memories did overtake me as I drove the four and a half hours to Naperville. I could not help but remember the people and events that blessed me while in Brown County.

CHAPTER 10
And the Beat Goes On

Getting out of bed my first day back from Brown County, I realized I really did not want to go to work. While making the 25-minute drive to my university office, I felt my neck and shoulders stiffen and begin to hurt. For weeks before my trip to the woods, my neck and shoulders routinely became stiff and sore, not at all uncommon for some of us who don't deal with our stress but allow it to accumulate inside. During my run to the woods, my neck and shoulders did not bother me *once!* I knew there was a message there.

Driving to the office, I recalled my happy memories of Indiana's state song, "Back Home Again in Indiana":

> Back home again in Indiana, and it seems that I can see.
> The gleaming candlelight, still shining bright,
> through the sycamores for me.
> The new-mown hay, sends all its fragrance,
> through the fields I used to roam.
> As I dream about the moonlight on the Wabash,
> I long for my Indiana home.

What were you telling me, God? Did I really go home? Did I smell that new-mown hay? Did I walk through those fields I used to roam? Did I see the moonlight on the Wabash? Am I longing for my home?

Each day I returned to my normal routines in life, I constantly compared my experiences at home to those that sustained me while in the woods. I heard a saying years ago that helped me be patient while considering the questions in the above paragraph. Its message took on a sense of renewed importance.

> I am the place that God shines through.
> He and I are one, not two.
> He wants me where and as I am;
> I need not fret, will, nor plan.
> If I'll but be relaxed and free,
> He'll carry out His plan through me.

I saw a paradox between what I just wrote and how I defined faith as going out not knowing. Maybe the faith I needed was not going out right now but living with the questions long enough to allow God to carry out His perfect plans through me. Could I actually allow myself not to fret, will, or plan? Could I change seats with God on our tandem bike? Was I afraid of the answers to these questions? The questions are all about abandoning self-will and surrendering fully to God. I've never been good at that kind of abandonment.

During the almost constant reflecting I did after leaving the woods, two songs, which have become an important part of my journey, came to mind. The songs of Brown County, just as these two, have had a major impact on my life.

Several artists recorded the first song titled "I Wish I Knew How..." The context for the lyrics comes from the immensely important and courageous civil rights struggle in this country. I first heard this song in the late 1990's on the soundtrack from the movie *Ghosts of Mississippi*.

And the Beat Goes On

Without detracting from or minimizing in any way the importance of the civil rights movement, I listened to those same words as they applied to Ed Poole, one human being struggling on a personal level with these very same words:

I wish I knew how it would feel to be free.
I wish I could break all the chains holdin' me.
I wish I could say all the things that I should say.
Say 'em loud, say 'em clear, for the whole round world to hear.
I wish I could share all the love that's in my heart.
Remove all the bars that keep us apart.
I wish you could know what it means to be me.
Then you'd see and agree that every man should be free.
I wish I could give all I'm longin' to give.
I wish I could live like I'm longin' to live.
I wish I could do all the things that I can do.
Though I'm way overdue, I'd be startin' anew.
I wish I could be like a bird in the sky.
How sweet it would be if I found I could fly.
I'd soar to the sun and look down at the sea.
Then I'd sing 'cause I know how it feels to be free.

The words truly reflect the dreams of an entire population in our country. The beautiful, inspiring words gave me pause to reflect on my own struggles. What if I found I can fly? When I first heard this song after I left the hospital in 1997, I could not go to sleep at night without listening to these powerful words, another ritual I performed. Every night I sat in my study, playing this song over and over again with my head resting on the back of the chair, my eyes closed, and my heart trying to open to the words I heard.

Recently I was having coffee and writing at a Naperville coffee shop. Coming through the overhead speakers was Nina Simone singing this song. As soon as I heard her voice, I stopped writing, took a deep breath, and felt peaceful as I quietly sang those familiar and meaningful words.

The second song is the wonderful *Desperado,* first recorded by The Eagles. Without repeating all the words, here are the ones that speak so directly to me:

> These things that are pleasin' you can hurt you somehow.
> Desperado, oh, you ain't getting' no younger.
> Your pain and your hunger are drivin' you home.
> And freedom, oh, freedom; that's just some people talkin'.
> Your prison is walkin' through this world all alone.
> Don't your feet get cold in the winter time?
> The sky won't snow and the sun won't shine.
> It's hard to tell the night time from the day.
> You're losin' all your highs and lows.
> Ain't it funny how the feelin' goes away.
> Desperado, why don't you come to your senses.
> Come down from your fences, open the gate.
> It may be rainin', but there's a rainbow above you.
> You better let somebody love you, before it's too late.

For much of my adult life, I've been ridin' the fence rail, afraid to jump to either side – back toward my past to help me better understand who I had become or forward toward my future where I could follow my heart. I know sometimes in my indecision I jumped in both directions, not realizing that leaving the fence requires a willingness to see the two directions as both/and, not either/or. Until I began writing *Lessons from the Crossroads,* I had internalized the thought that fence-jumping had to be in only one direction. As I wrote this section of the book, jumping off the fence became a metaphor, just as the porch, for inviting and accepting change into my life. I couldn't straddle the fence, and I couldn't stay on the porch and once again catch a glimpse of my true self.

Sometimes, when my depression was particularly crippling, I couldn't see both backward and forward. Instead I lost my highs and was left with the lows, finding it hard to separate night from day. I wanted to regain my equilibrium, see the rainbow above, and let myself love me before it was too late. The person I most wanted to love me was me. I believed doing so would lead me toward that authentic path and a greater sense of wholeness in my life. I have to love myself first before I accept the love others have for me. Because of the relatively sterile and emotionless environment in which I was raised, I'm afraid I do not know how to love someone or let someone really love me. I did not understand the meaning of love as I grew up. Those times I said to a girl, both in high school or college, "I love you," I usually said the words for selfish reasons, and many times those reasons were physical. Although I didn't realize my motives at the time, I latched onto girls to find the affection I didn't feel at home. I used them for my own selfish ends, to fill a void.

The love I was given at home brought along with it conditions and judgments. Therefore, for many years, I attached my own conditions and judgments to those I loved. From the day I was born, I wanted more than anything to feel love. I never felt I was being corrected and loved at the same time. And most of the correcting I received from Mom and Dad related to their religious beliefs. Several times Mom or Dad would say, "Eddie, if you don't stop that, you are going to hell." Believe me, at least for awhile, that statement struck fear in my heart. As a boy I had learned to keep secrets in order to get around the stringent rules from Mom and Dad. I did not know someone might love me just for who I am. Because I was self-serving, I didn't know that love is best expressed by helping others. I wish the love my parents had for me would have been shared in a way that suggested that, although I often did not conduct my life in ways that mirrored their lives, they could honor the good in me and want the very best for me. Now I realize they did just that.

For me unconditional love means regardless of what I do or say people will love me fully and without reservations, without expecting anything in return. But in my life I struggle to accept my own definition of unconditional love, especially in giving myself permission to fail. Intellectually I know I learn from my failures. But in my heart when I fail, those thoughts of guilt return. My need for perfection often denies me the right to fail. As an adult I have come to understand that I am solely responsible for the choices I make.

The love from my parents had an enormous impact on my life. Mom and Dad loved me in the best ways they knew how to love. They gave me the best love they had, and I now know they did not understand unconditional love as I do. They could not possibly have given me something they didn't have. I am responsible for changing my concept of loving others and myself.

Understanding how to love unconditionally took me to a place where I could feel trust and support. After returning from Brown County, I went to our community's Riverwalk, a multi-block piece of serenity in our town that serves as an oasis for my soul.

Arriving at the Riverwalk with a book to read, I knew exactly where I wanted to sit. I picked a shaded bench right next to the labyrinth, created in the heart of this beautiful landscape.

A labyrinth is an ancient symbol that relates to our journeys toward wholeness. It combines the imagery of the circle and the spiral into a meandering but purposeful path. At its most basic level, the labyrinth represents the journey toward the center of our deepest self and back out again into the world. We can walk it, which I have done before while visiting this spot. Joseph Campbell, author of *The Hero of a Thousand Faces,* said a labyrinth is "where we had thought to travel outward, we will come to the center of our own existence." It is a metaphor for life's journey, a symbol that creates a sacred space and place and takes us out of our ego to that which is within.

I was drawn to this particular spot on the Riverwalk because I was struggling with finding the path out of the crossroads and into my deepest self. I wanted to understand more about me and those questions I carried with me to Brown County and continued to hold in my soul.

Sitting close to the labyrinth, I recalled the beautiful words of author Caroline Adams:

> Your life is a sacred journey. And it is about change, growth, discovery, movement, transformation, continuously expanding your vision of what is possible, stretching your soul, learning to see clearly and deeply, listening to your intuition, taking courageous challenges at every step along the way. You are on a path...exactly where you are meant to be right now. And from here, you can only go forward, shaping your life story into a magnificent tale of triumph, of healing, of courage, of beauty, of wisdom, of power,
> of dignity, and of love.

As I reflected on Adams' words, I decided if I remembered what she said, I could continue along my path of bringing new meaning and happiness to the struggles I took with me to my woods.

While remembering Adams' thoughts, I asked myself more questions: Was it the place, Brown County, that allowed the thoughts and feelings to flow freely from my heart, or was it the writing itself? Was I writing more clearly because God allowed me to see I was ready to write and that my writing would bring clarity to those questions in my life? While in the woods writing, was I leading the life I felt I wanted to lead? What parts of me were not yet finished with those beautiful, inviting woods? Could the various parts of me become one? Should I try writing elsewhere and see what my feelings were in different locations? Why was I so *driven* with getting my thoughts and feelings onto paper? Could I rediscover those four paths at the top of the tower while standing on the ground?

I wrote this chapter after my first trip to the woods of Brown County. I struggled with being back home, once again getting caught up in the daily tasks of my life and my work. Almost on a daily basis, I compared how I spent my time on the retreat with how I spent my time in my real life. I realized that my journey toward both wholeness and my authentic self is never-ending, that my life is going to be imperfect. I had no answers for the questions I listed at the end of this chapter when I wrote them. I hoped to find the answers as I walked my way out of the crossroads.

CHAPTER 11
A Tug-of-War to Relocate My Authentic Path

Why is there such a tug-of-war over breaking through this Comfort Zone in my life?
Bruce Wilkinson - *The Dream Giver*

As I reflected on the questions I just listed, I felt like I was in a **tug-of-war** with myself. During the eleven years I was principal at Naperville Central High School, the junior and senior classes always ended the year competing in a fierce tug of war. The seniors wanted to win to preserve their supremacy over the other three classes. The juniors wanted to win to prove they were ready to assume their rite of passage of becoming seniors, just as I was seeking my own rite of passage from the crossroads.

The local fire department was always there, exploding a steady stream of ice-cold water in the middle of the two classes. As I stood directly in front of the two classes, looking down the two long lines of willing participants, I could not see the last person. That person was always a very large male, serving as the anchor, around whose waist was tied one end of the large tugging rope.

The battle began, with each class desperately and unrelentingly trying to break the inertia and begin dragging the opposing group through the stream of water. Each class had a captain who, like Chip at the Daily Grind, ran up and down the line yelling encouragement to his or her classmates. As the first person in each group neared the water, a surge of power and teamwork pulled that team away from the water and that ever-present line in the sand which neither group wanted to cross. With their reputations on the line, the two classes pulled and pulled with everything inside them, often calling on strength they never realized existed. The crowds in the stands screamed encouragement to their respective teams, hoping beyond hope the team they represented would have a greater commitment to winning than the other.

When the strength of one class overtook the other, the first person on the opposing side went through the stream of water. Once that barrier was broken, the chance to draw back vanished. The commitment, and the mud created by the water, allowed the winning class to begin the happy task of pulling the remainder of their ever-weakening, disheveled, and disheartened opponents through the water and mud.

The tug of war represented my comfort zone through which I *hoped* to pass (unlike the losing team in the tug of war). It symbolized the difficult decision I faced of whether to return to my Hills of Brown in southern Indiana or to stay away from my forest oasis. If I chose the latter, I might forget all that running to the woods represented for me.

I knew I could actually win by losing as I became committed to breaking through my dry comfort zone, getting wet, going through the mud holding my struggles, and emerging on the other side, a place I could not see because the steady stream of water blocked my view. I imagined I was at the front of a long line of valiant warriors, going through the steady stream of water first. As I felt the pressure from that unrelenting, piercing, frigid, watery blast and got to the other side, I was certain my internal tug of war was over.

The water stung as it hit my body, like the stinging of our souls as we question God's wisdom in sending us off for new adventures. The loss, which was my much-hoped-for victory, made my decision crystal clear: I knew I was going to return to the woods of Brown County. I didn't know when, but I had to go back.

The day I won my tug of war, I started taking care of me. As I went through the water and got to the other side, I was sure my victory would ultimately lead me back to Brown County, and I was sure I had jumped off the fence and was seeking freedom outside my comfort zone. Stepping across that line in the sand was, for me, a message that my work in Brown County wasn't finished, and I knew more insights were there waiting for me.

Getting past the forceful stream of water was symbolic, powerfully telling me my trip to the woods and my return home were opportunities to reclaim my freedom from those whose expectations imprisoned me. By the choices I made I hoped to find my own happiness. I sought freedom from a life of guilt, shame, inadequate self-esteem, fear of change, and lack of an internal guidance system. I know I'm forgiven for all past, present, and future transgressions. This forgiveness comes from God, those who love me, as well as from myself. But I struggled to let go of those feelings of guilt and shame and realize how holding on to those feelings prevented me from a true inner journey, a journey toward the freedom I hoped to find along my still undefined path out of the crossroads. The guilt and shame I carried with me before that initial retreat were greatly diminished while I was in the beautiful woods of my oasis in southern Indiana.

Like George Gray, will I look back over my life with despair for how I spent my time? Will I still be struggling with regrets? Will I be tormented by a nagging conscience for what could have been? Facing these questions is crucial. I've talked a good game, both with others and with myself, about the questions but rarely faced them head on or searched for the answers.

Letting go of my fears and doubts is illustrated in an ancient fable about three men. Two were struggling to take back their freedom and find their happiness. The third, however, was well on his way toward the freedom and happiness I sought. Together these sojourners walked everywhere they went. Each man carried two old, weather-beaten sacks, one hung in front of him and the other across his back. When the first traveler was asked what was in his sacks, he said, "In the sack on my back are all the good things I've done. Carrying these good deeds on my back hides them from view. In the front sack are all the decisions in my life that I regret. Every now and then I stop, open the front sack and take out those regrets and that sadness. I look at them and feel so much shame for what I did – to myself and others." He often stopped to look at all his guilt, shame, and regrets. His pace slow, he didn't get very far in life.

The second man also explained his two sacks to those who asked: "In the front sack are all the many blessings and good fortune in my life. I take them out a lot so I can remember them and tell others about all my joys. I keep all my mistakes and regrets in the back sack, but they're always with me, weighing me down, and reminding me I am not as free as I could be. The sack on my back is so big and heavy my walking is slow. I just can't seem to put it aside."

The third man had a different explanation for his two sacks: "The sack in front carries all my good deeds and all the joys and freedoms I've experienced in my life. I also keep all the wonderful gifts others have given me – time, love, and compassion – all wonderful memories. The front sack is heavy, but it keeps me moving forward. The sack on my back is empty and doesn't slow me down. You see I cut a big hole in the bottom of that sack. All my regrets, shame, and guilt go right in the top and fall right out the bottom."

If I traveled with those three men, I would walk somewhere between those first two travelers. My sack full of regrets, shame, and guilt is in front, and it is very heavy. I inspect those regrets all the time. They just keep adding to those already in the sack. I regret not being around as much as I should have been when Eric and Tracie were growing up. Bonnie did a wonderful job in my absence. I was afraid I did not know how to be a good father. I was like my own father in that respect. I regret making much of my adult life all about me. As a young boy I felt guilt and shame about my self-centered decisions. I was raised on guilt. Most times, even as an adult, when I stepped into my shadow side I remembered the vengeful, unforgiving God I discovered as a young boy. Then the guilty feelings flooded over me.

Keeping secrets was also an unfortunate habit I learned as a young boy and brought with me into adulthood. As a youngster I kept secrets from Mom and Dad, secrets about some of my behavior about which I knew they would disapprove and probably tell me once again I was going straight to hell. In addition to keeping secrets, being selfish was also learned as a youngster. Because of my unrelenting need to be popular and accepted, I directed most of my decisions toward accomplishing the recognition I so craved.

My selfishness was at the forefront in most decisions I made as an adult. Because of my self-centeredness, I denied my family the opportunity of participating in many life decisions that impacted their lives as well.

As I wrote earlier, these decisions focused on my personal and professional life. I continued this secretive behavior as an adult. I made up stories or withheld information about where I was going and what I was doing so Bonnie wouldn't know about my shadow side. For example, I bought new, expensive clothes and then sneaked them into the house so Bonnie didn't see my new purchases. Doing so prevented me from having to feel Bonnie's frustration and anger when she told me, rightfully so, that I already had too many clothes in my closet.

Until recently I viewed guilt and shame as one in the same in terms of their meaning. I used the words interchangeably, sometimes using the word guilt and other times speaking of my shame. When I feel guilty I now understand I am *doing* something wrong. Shame works on me at a deeper level of guilt. I feel ashamed when I feel I am actually *being* wrong. For example all the times I took Bonnie for granted and took advantage of her love and forgiveness I was being wrong. For many years I tried to rid myself of these unwanted feelings by projecting onto others: colleagues at work, my family, and my friends. I now understand why I created these victim stories for myself. If I could blame others for my behavior and see them as causing my problems, I felt better. Doing so did a great injustice to both them and me. Whoever was on the receiving end of my anger and frustration didn't deserve what I pushed out of me and onto them. In most instances Bonnie was on the receiving end of these feelings of frustration and anger. Many of these feelings were to relieve the shame I felt for how I was treating her as a human being and a marriage partner. Also, when I felt better by projecting my behavior onto others, I no longer had to try and understand where the real problem was – with me.

My sack of joy, happiness, and sense of freedom doesn't fill up as quickly as the other, and I do not look at those blessings often enough. My greatest joy is my family. As they say in southern Indiana, Eric and Tracie "cleaned up good," mostly because of the parenting they received from Bonnie. Good people attract good people, and my belief about this attraction is certainly true with the spouses my kids brought into their lives. And now I have four wonderful granddaughters. Bonnie has been the rock and foundation of our family, as well as the knitting that has kept us together. Even with this having been said, I can't yet cut a hole in my regret and shame sack to lighten my load. If I gain a healthier perspective, I'll find a pair of scissors and make that hole.

Part of my freedom will come when I no longer talk a good game about my wishes, dreams, and desires but actually pursue them so I can reach my bliss. Recently I received an email from a former college professor who has been my mentor for forty years. As I shared some of my struggles with Bob, he ended his note by saying, "Ed, it's time to stop thinking and start living." And, in my heart, I know he was right on with his advice.

I wanted to rediscover all my highs and lows so I could celebrate the highs, confront the lows, knowing I could face them, learn from them, and release them from their dark hole. As author Lynn Grabhorn said, "So we have choices; lots and lots of choices offering us not only the opportunities to live and enjoy whatever is in this bountiful world we desire, but also to find out just how much torture and deprivation we're willing to put ourselves through before permitting those desires into our lives." When I eliminate the amount of torture I'm willing to endure, I will accept the gifts that come from my journey and remind myself of my blessings and dreams.

I Wasn't Done Yet

Remembering the lessons from my tug-of-war, I knew Brown County was my best hope for finding some answers, so I packed a bag, my books, my laptop, my hikin' boots, climbed into my convertible, put the top down, and headed south on Interstate 65. I had made a second reservation at the State Park in Brown County. I took vacation days from the university and prepared myself for another wonderful adventure.

Exactly fourteen days after leaving, I was back in my serene, peaceful setting. I returned to good friends, great stories, and smooth Merlot. Once again I was in the woods of Brown County State Park.

Before leaving home, I thought a lot about my return to the woods, and in my heart I was prepared for this trip to be different from the first. Even in this brief window of time, the people had changed; more importantly, I had changed, and I viewed my return with different eyes. During those fourteen days I thought a lot about those questions I took with me to the woods. I felt better about myself, because I knew I so badly wanted to become the person God wanted me to become. Therefore, I knew this trip to the woods was going to be refreshing in its newness.

I have Bill Bryson, author of *Rediscovering America on the Appalachian Trail*, to thank for this accepting attitude. When he and his hiking companion Stephen Katz got to a particular point on their hike along the Appalachian Trail, they had to part company. Both men had commitments during the upcoming months, but they agreed to meet again the end of July to continue their hike.

Bryson, like me, could not stay away from the woods. He began taking one, two, and three-day hikes into parts of the Appalachian Trail he and Katz hadn't traveled. Bryson expected these shorter trips to be exactly like the much longer hike. When he compared his feelings about the two different time frames for hiking the trail, he was sorely disappointed with the shorter hikes. But once he realized the shorter trips carried their own magic, he was happy he had returned to hike the trail. I was also happy I returned to the woods. Though my stay was shorter, only one week, the magic was out of sight!

Although only a two-week interval, a time span that seemed like months, separated my visits, I felt so very happy to be there again. I wanted and needed to get back to Brown County as quickly as possible. My wonderful feelings after the first trip were still so fresh in my mind, heart, and soul that I longed for a second foray in the woods. As I said earlier, I was afraid that if I didn't return within a relatively short time period, I would lose my positive thoughts and feelings. Whether or not the diminishing effect really would have occurred, I didn't want to take that risk.

Wandering and Wondering in Our Lives

Before going to the state park to check in, I walked around Nashville. During my walk, I returned to the "Life is Good" T-shirt shop where I bought the shirt that says, "Do what you like. Like what you do." This time I found one with the following message written on the front: "Not all who wander are lost" – with a pair of hiking boots above the words. I thought of Bill Bryson's trek along the Appalachian Trail, the wandering he and Katz did, the times they relied on maps to keep from getting lost, and the hiking boots they relied on so much.

For most of my life, I have *wandered* before I *wondered* about where I was going and why I wanted to go there. I accepted this job, that job, *any* job, if I thought it would further that climb up the (now unsuited) ladder of success. And those job changes were prompted by expectations from others that making a move would continue my climb up that ladder I now know I didn't even want to be on. Because I wandered before I wondered, I had a lot of false starts and stops. On two different occasions I actually accepted a new job in a new location and later backed out. On one of those two occasions, my wife and I had placed a down payment on a new home in that community. My ego was fed by receiving offers I didn't really want. I kept finding the hole in the sidewalk and losing hope about finding my way out. Because I spent no time wondering about who Ed Poole really is, I had no internal guide for my decision-making. I fell into the hole and rescued myself by writing. Getting *Lessons from the Porch* out of me and onto paper, I thought I had done all the wondering I needed in my life.

I was wrong. I returned to the woods in part to do more wondering about who I am and what happiness means to me. I also wanted to wander some more amidst the beauty here. Should I continue teaching full time? Should I write and speak full time? Was this anxiety over happiness and my calling in life one of those "either/or" times, or could it be "both/and?"

Returning to the woods felt like coming home and I knew feeling at home again would help me answer the questions I brought with me. Though I couldn't return to Tawny Apple #1, I felt as much at home in Emma Moots #1, for much was the same: the rough-cut lumber, porch, picnic table, and the trees on the outside; the pea-green chairs, absence of phone and television, tiny bathroom, and the same wonderful musty smell on the inside. Also, I knew I would find peace in the events of each day and the conversations I would once again have with my friends.

After doing some writing, I drove into town and settled in at the winery with a good glass of merlot. Charlie usually showed up each day between 4:00 and 4:30. Sure enough, in about five minutes, he walked through the door, gave me a big grin, and hugged me. "Glad to see ya back, Ed," Charlie greeted me.

Seeing My New Friends Again
and Headin' Back to Helmsburg

Charlie had to take a friend to see about repairing the bumper on her car, so I told him I'd meet him back at the Hotel Nashville later on. As I entered the bar at the Hotel, Dee screamed, "Ed," and gave me a big hug. "Want that Early Times and coke?"

"I sure do." In a few minutes, Mike, Sue, and Jim drifted in, and a short time later, Charlie slowly and carefully came through the door, assisted by his walking stick. We all laughed and laughed at the stories going 'round the bar. A new guy, McGinley, a jovial, round-faced, ruddy-looking Irishman, was full of jokes.

LESSONS FROM THE CROSSROADS

Charlie told me he enjoyed his early reading of *Lessons from the Porch*. At one point, he stopped reading and gave the book to Art to read for a while. Just as he told me this, Art entered the bar, walked over to me, shook my hand, and said, "We will have to have a long conversation about Chapter 1." I knew Art was talking about my book, but I wasn't sure what conversation he wanted to have about Chapter 1. I told him I would love to talk with him.

Charlie and I were deciding what we wanted to do for the evening. The Figtree Gallery and Coffee Shop in Helmsburg is open only on Thursday. On that night it becomes a musical venue. Since it was Thursday, Charlie suggested we go. A musical group Charlie knew (of course) was playing there. After a short drive, we were trying to find a parking spot behind the Figtree. The lot was almost full! Once inside, I saw close to 200 people sandwiched together in a room built to accommodate at the most 75. If the Fire Marshal came in, he or she would not be at all pleased! But, as far as I knew, the Fire Marshal could be sittin' in the audience, enjoying the show.

As soon as Charlie and I came through the door, we saw at least a dozen women standing together and dancin' a hoedown to the music. One of them grabbed my arm and pulled me in. Another grabbed Charlie, and he too joined the dancers. We gladly became a part of their enlarged circle, laughin', stompin', and clappin' to the beat of the song. I sensed in his day Charlie was one helluva dancer. These days, however, his unsteady stature forces him to move ever so gently to the music.

As we moved further into the room, with all the tables taken, we had no choice but to stand. Seeing his walking stick, one lady got up and offered Charlie her chair and urged me to move closer to Charlie so I didn't have a partial wall obstructing my view of the band.

After being inside awhile, Charlie and I needed some fresh air, so we went out back and sat on the patio. Charlie told me a little bit about his time growing up around here. An only child, he grew up in Nashville and Southport, just about 45 minutes from Nashville. As Charlie described his father, I knew the work ethic

Charlie exhibited throughout his life came from his dad. As I watched my own dad work hard, I know I inherited the same ethic from him.

When we went back inside, the band was playing "Workin' Man Blues." The locals readily identify with the words because they work hard, take care of their families, and enjoy life. Folks around here that I've met are protectors and providers, the same two roles so important to my parents. As I assumed those roles with my kids, I have come to appreciate those gifts from Mom and Dad.

The band played 'til 10:00. After Charlie and I said good night to some of the crowd and went outside, we headed back to Nashville, and I dropped off Charlie at the hotel.

The Stories and Connections Just Keep Comin'!

After delivering Charlie to the hotel, I drove back to the park, thinking about all the wonderful stories I heard that night. I can honestly say never before in my life have I had such strong and unrelenting affirmation of that statement I made earlier: The story of any one of us is, in part, the story of all of us. Without exception, this statement was driven deeper and deeper into my heart and soul during all the days I spent in Brown County.

The connection of all those stories is with *my* journey, *my* life, and *me* as a person. I found so much happiness in the stories I heard. That happiness is because, in some part, I <u>am</u> in those stories, in my memories, in my quest for who I am on my journey toward wholeness. After moving in 1980 to a very upscale, suburban Chicago community, I think I reinvented myself into a very sophisticated person. I didn't want to be known as this southern Indiana hillbilly who made it to the big city. I became someone, as with most of my life, who wanted to fit in and be accepted. I enjoyed the prominence of my job and the interaction with the movers and shakers in the community. I forgot my roots, but the trips to Brown County brought them back to me, and I was grateful.

Storytellers often have the same goal as they tell their stories: They hope the listeners will not only identify a part of themselves in those stories but also, eventually, internalize the stories, making them their own. As I listened to the songs and stories and reflected on their meaning in my life, Brown County became more and more a part of what defines Ed Poole.

Not only did those memories I put to rest after I finished *Lessons from the Porch* take on new meaning, but the never-before-discovered memories of my childhood opened new windows through which I viewed myself and the world around me. Why did I realize all those stories were mine as well? As an adult I have led a self-serving, pretentious life, full of suburbia, busyness, an out of control ego, and the expectation I would receive recognition for what I did. As Parker Palmer said, "There is a great gulf between the way my ego wants to identify me, with its protective masks and self-serving fictions, and my true self." All that pretentious behavior and all those protective masks were stripped away in Brown County. Sue Monk Kidd asked, "How do we fashion an environment in which we become stripped and stilled, in which the ego patterns of a lifetime begin to move away from the center and our innermost spiritual life is reconstellated?"

I found Kidd's environment in Brown County because folks only knew me as "the guy writing a book" who grew up next door in Columbus. I could relax and be Ed Poole, wearing grungy, baggy shorts, crinkled, coffee-stained T-shirts, and shoes that were falling apart. The Ed Poole I found there was the person I'm trying to become, leading an authentic life found along that path out of the crossroads.

Dreams that Uncover Our Authentic Self

As I began my second day back in Brown County, I was overwhelmed with more memories and dreams I hoped would lead me out of the crossroads and lift the weight of uncertainty from my heart. I rolled out of bed at 6:45, after staying up 'til 1:15 writing and thinking. I threw on my clothes and raced into town for some coffee at the Daily Grind, a place I greatly missed during my time away. Because I could not wait to get there, I arrived at 7:50, ten minutes before opening time. I sat in the magnificent courtyard, enjoying the sun beaming down on the fields of wildflowers. Rosemary, who takes such loving care of that masterpiece, was smiling as she patiently tended the flowers.

At 8:00 sharp, Karis opened the massive door and turned the CLOSED sign over to OPEN. She saw me and with a smile said, "Thought you left us. You might just as well move down here, you love it so much."

I enjoyed seeing all the smiling faces again. I ordered my usual, a mug of coffee (with two free refills) and a HEC. I grabbed the local papers to read. I also had Bill Bryson's book.

I savored every bite of my croissant, happy to have the thinly sliced ham and melted cheese again. After I finished eating, drinking my coffee, reading the papers, and enjoying Bryson's book, I opened the door to leave, and my body was completely overtaken by that good ol' southern Indiana humidity. It had been raining when I awoke. But as I left, the sun was blazing overhead, a perfect combination for a sticky, humid day.

Before going to the Lodge, I fought the heat and humidity to hike around Lake Ogle, a five-mile jaunt. The lake was pristine, and the trees reflected on the water as I hiked. The sunlight shimmered on the still, blue lake. The freedom I felt was nearly palpable as I once again hiked the paths of the state park.

After my glorious hike, I got reacquainted with my peaceful mezzanine in the Lodge. I had a wonderful time writing more of my story and reading the thoughts of others that continued to challenge my thinking. I read Sue Monk Kidd's book, *When the Heart Waits: Spiritual Direction for Life's Sacred Questions*. Not only did the book's title speak to me, but also Kidd's writing reminded me of those dreams and memories I was uncovering as I searched for the signpost on that fourth path leading from the crossroads.

While moving to the courtyard for a break from my writing, I thought back to the differences between this trip and the first. The blooms on the flowers were bigger, and the stalks were taller. The hummingbirds still hovered in front of their sugar water, but they had grown during the past two weeks. I worked into the early evening and then decided once again it was time to find my solitude in the community of others.

Little Eddie Won't Let Me Grow Up Without Dreams to Pursue

When I saw Charlie at the winery, he was wearing a T-shirt that said, "I may grow older, but I refuse to grow up." I love that thought, and it resonated all the way to my soul. Charlie's T-shirt spoke so directly to me because part of my journey's quest has been to find "Little Eddie," that inner child in all of us, buried so deeply inside me for too long. He never found the light of day when I was a little boy. I found my inner child for a few waning moments when I wrote my earlier book. But Little Eddie and I got separated in my forgetfulness. Little Eddie is that young boy inside me representing all the feelings, fears, and emotions I had when I was that age. I had to learn to listen to him, listen to his heart, and recognize the signposts he put before me, that part of me I was trying to find.

But, like the little seed, I now have an inner someone encouraging me to grow so my dreams can become a reality. Our inner child is both the *keeper* and the *giver* of our dreams and our aspirations. If Little Eddie is never allowed to laugh and play, to keep my dreams alive, to rejoice with me, to encourage me when times are tough, and to help God light my path through life, we are doomed to a life of lost dreams, lost aspirations, little encouragement to follow those dreams, without any light along our paths. I like the following thought by author Colin McCarthy because my way will be easier to find if I can truly believe McCarthy's words so that I can see my way out of the crossroads along my authentic path.

Keeping Our Dreams Alive

If we don't keep our dreams alive we won't have
our dreams any longer. But . . .
If we can take a chance now and then, seek and
search, discover and dream, grow and go through
each day with the knowledge that . . .
We can only take as much as we give, and

> we can only get as much out of life
> as we allow ourselves to live . . .
> Then . . . we can truly be happy.
> We can realize a dream or two
> along the way, and
> we can make a habit of
> reaching out for rainbows and
> coloring our lives with wonderful days.

Keeping our dreams alive is the theme in a children's book, *The Polar Express*. The book became an adult book as I reread it within the context of my current struggles. The story describes a little boy who still believed in Santa Claus with all his heart even though a friend told him, "There *is* no Santa." One Christmas Eve the boy lay quietly in his bed, listening for the sounds of the ringing bells on Santa's sleigh. Instead of bells, the little boy heard the hissing sound of steam and squeaking metal. He looked out his window and saw a train in front of his house.

The little boy got on the train and went to the North Pole to see Santa Claus. While there Santa gave him a tiny, silver bell. The boy heard the bell because he believed in Santa with all his heart.

As the boy grew into a man, he was still in touch with that little boy and those childhood beliefs inside. He still heard that tiny bell ring every Christmas, because he held onto his belief about Santa.

When I was a little boy, Dad would take my sister and me for a ride on Christmas Eve to see the beautiful holiday lights in Columbus. What Mary Belle and I didn't know was that while we were riding with Dad, Mom was placing all our Christmas presents under the tree. When we returned home, Santa had been there. I always considered Christmas Eve was one of the most wonderful days of the year.

After I married, our family followed the tradition of opening presents on Christmas morning. What a joy it was to see the happy faces on Eric and Tracie as they ran down the stairs to see what Santa had left for them. They had that same belief in Santa that I still have. I'm sure they heard the ringing of that tiny silver bell. Now, as their daughters' eyes come alive on Christmas morning, I'm certain they hear that tiny bell ringing, the same bell the little boy received from Santa as he took that ride on the Polar Express.

Each of my life's experiences provides enough light to help me find the path toward my dreams, just as the trip to the North Pole helped the little boy find the path toward his dream of believing in Santa Claus because he got to *see* Santa Claus. If I still believe, Little Eddie, my dream keeper and giver, will help me see my dreams become reality somewhere along the way. I don't know where my path will lead, and I don't know where the light started. But if I continue to have faith and trust and follow my heart, God will provide the light and the paths when He is ready.

I came to the woods in part to find my inner child and invite him to help me in my struggle to find answers to the questions I took with me and to help me find the word on that fourth sign. I hoped beyond all hope Little Eddie was emerging as I wrote, encouraging me to leave the crossroads. Little Eddie both keeps my dreams and gives me those dreams at just the right time in my life.

No one in any of our lives is as important as the keeper of the dream. Our dream keeper helps us maintain our hope and vision. Doing so, he shows us how to shed gently critical and negative thinking and does so in an understanding, non judgmental way. We sometimes have a funny way of looking for the worst and bogging down the dreams we have inside.

Every person ought to believe that dreams exist. We should know that our dream keeper is positively working within us to assure the pursuit of our dreams. Our keeper of the dreams recognizes our needs and lifts up our journeys. I hope I am becoming better at recognizing my dreams when they come along. More importantly, I hope I can pursue those dreams as God wants me to. I had a dream when I started writing this book: I wanted to find answers to the questions I had at the beginning of that journey and doing so, reclaim my authentic self. Now I have a bigger dream. I want to remember that dream, but beyond remembering, I want to live my life according to the lessons I learned as I wrote. I thought I continued to live the lessons I learned in *Lessons from the Porch*; however, after a few years, the dreams escaped my soul. I vowed never to let that happen again.

    I started the next day with another wonderful visit to The Daily Grind. Hal had a hoot about the Daily Grind T-shirt I was wearing. He wasn't in the coffee shop when I wore it during my earlier visit. He said, "Yer gonna have ta beat them girls off with a stick today. Maybe I oughta start sellin' a big stick along with those shirts." Hal is the quintessential model for that southern Indiana twang I heard, and used, all my life, a twang I resurrected the minute I returned to this neck of the woods.

    As I drank my coffee and ate my HEC, I realized something about the word wandering that I had not internalized until now. I remembered the T-shirt I bought two days ago, the words, "Not all who wander are lost" scripted on the front, with a pair of hiking boots right above the words. I also thought about my hike around Lake Ogle.

    Earlier I wrote about the relationship of "wondering" to "wandering" in our lives. If I allow my heart and soul to join my mind, I can wander to unexplored places with more than my hiking boots. I always wandered with only my boots on my feet because my compass was there or in my hand but not in my heart and soul. I allowed my heart and soul to join my mind and feet to wander from place to place, wondering about all the mystery and magic that awaited me out there. Wandering is good, if we have thought about why we want to wander and if those thoughts include God's plan for us. Perhaps you've heard someone say, "Ah, the wonder of it all." With my new thoughts about the value of wandering, I can now say, "Ah, the wander of it all."

    I view the two concepts, wondering and wandering, as interconnected, circular journeys. As my heart and soul wander, I can then wonder about where my heart and soul seem to want me to go.

    I realized my heart and soul had never joined my mind because I didn't wonder enough about the importance of celebrating the necessary connections these three parts have in my life. I never let my heart and soul, Little Eddie's keeper and giver of my dreams, do their job of leading my feet.

I thought about my granddaughters. They wander throughout their homes and sometimes out into their neighborhoods. They don't have to wonder about why they're walking all over the place. They just know it is fun! Unfortunately, in my case, these two concepts became separated as I moved from childhood toward adulthood.

Later in the day, as I wandered out into the courtyard off the lodge's mezzanine, to rest, refresh, and reflect, I discovered a previously unnoticed swing. Sitting in that swing, lazily pushing back and forth, I closed my eyes and saw so clearly that old, inviting swing on my porch at home where I would sit dreaming of the adventures awaiting me if I could only allow myself to get out of the swing and off the porch to enjoy them.

I sat in the swing for a long time, alone with my thoughts. As a child, most of the time when I sat in the swing at home, I was also alone. Mom and Dad were always too busy to join me. Swings are wonderful places to tell our stories, but I neither heard nor told stories in my swing because no one was there but me.

Art's Tragic Story and His Courage in Telling Me

I finished my writing and headed to Nashville. I met up with Charlie at the winery. Robbie Bowden, whom we saw Thursday night at the Figtree, was performing solo tonight. Both Charlie and I appreciated and identified with his music. The songs he writes speak with such a resounding chord about who he is and what he values along his journey. Robbie lived in the southwest for many years before returning to his roots in Brown County. He talked to me of doing manual labor each August in the heat of the Arizona desert. I thought of Mom and Dad and all the hard, manual work they performed throughout their lives to make my life better.

I enjoyed all of Robbie's songs, but the one I latched onto was "In These Hills," the song written by Charlie's friend Slats Klug, the one he wants sung at his memorial service. All the lyrics were meaningful, but one single line put its arms around me: "The simple path you gotta get lost in to find." I was lost when I came to the woods, and I fervently searched for my authentic path I had lost. I have been on the same authentic path all my life; however, as I view those other three paths differently the authentic path looks different in my eyes. That path doesn't change but, as my journey changes along my other three paths, I view my authentic self with new eyes. Robbie's words affirmed the journey I was on in the woods of Brown County.

Charlie was not feeling well again, after having stood for four and one-half hours today in the blazing sun and humidity, taking money from those who wanted to park in one of the pay lots in downtown Nashville. The temperature today was in the mid-80s, but as Charlie sat in the very small, enclosed shelter to rest, the temperature on the thermometer said 94 degrees. I offered to drive Charlie back to the hotel, but he said he was okay to drive.

After leaving the winery, I went to the hotel to check on Charlie. Jim, Sue, and Dick were there, and I had a wonderful opportunity to talk with them and get to know them better. Art came into the bar right about the time I finished my conversations with my new friends. It was time for Art and me to have that talk about Chapter 1 in *Lessons from the Porch*. As our conversation began, I again had affirmed a thought I shared earlier: As I open myself to others, they more than meet me halfway with their own stories, revealing their true selves. Art was certainly ready to open a very sad chapter in his life.

In the first chapter of *Lessons from the Porch* I wrote about my depression in the fall of 1996. I thought a lot that fall about committing suicide. As Art began his story, I knew he could relate to my thoughts years ago. Art's son was a neurosurgeon/radiologist in New Mexico, his profession allowing him to amass a level of financial security few individuals his age acquire. His son struggled with manic-depression, which, even though a physician, he would not address with medication. I thought about my mother-in-law who, for different reasons, did not seek medical help for her manic-depression. The up-and-down cycles between Art's son's manic state and his depressed state were very far apart. Therefore, most everyone knew Art's son only through his highs, never seeing him at one of his low points.

One day, Art's daughter-in-law came home to find her husband had committed suicide by hanging himself. Then I knew why Art was able to share that story with me after he read the first chapter in my book where I described my own flirtations with suicide. The thought struck me that when Art and I shared stories of our kids, at the end of that very first full day in the woods, he only talked about his daughter, not his son.

What a tragedy for a father, his daughter, and his daughter-in-law to endure. Facing an abundance of unanswered questions, Art found absolutely no immediate answers to provide even a modicum of comfort. As Art shared his story, more than once tears welled up in his eyes, so intense was his grief from six years ago. When parents outlive their children, they struggle to understand why the sequence was reversed.

Art, his daughter, and his daughter-in-law were forced to move through the wilderness, attempting to answer the multitude of questions family members ask at these times. Why didn't we notice any signs? Why didn't he ask for help? Didn't *any* of his co-workers notice differences in his behavior and demeanor? If they did, why didn't they share that with us? And then the biggest, most heart-wrenching question of all: What did I do to cause this to happen? Strangely, out of such tragedies we often find gifts. For Art and his family the memorial service held for his son was one of those gifts. Art said that service was so very special, allowing his family to move toward closure after this tragedy. He has an audiotape of the service celebrating his son's life, which he wanted me to hear.

When I listened to the tape, I agreed with Art: The memorial service was special. Everyone who spoke at the service told wonderful stories of Bob, as a young boy, a brother, a husband, a son, and a colleague in research. The stories helped those in attendance laugh under very difficult circumstances.

The opening remarks by the minister touched my soul so deeply because they reminded me of my own strong thoughts of suicide a few years ago. I want to repeat a good portion of them here because she set the tone and climate for the entire service. At the same time, Reverend Harms gave me much to ponder about my own thoughts of suicide.

> It is an unusual occasion, so I have a statement I would like to make before we begin our worship. It occurred to me that there are usually two ways in which one addresses the subject of suicide. One of those ways is total denial. We pretend it didn't happen. We do not speak of it. We do not say the "s" word. The second way is to heap judgments upon the deceased, call it a mortal sin, and say that one is doomed for all time. Today we will do neither of those things... Robert Janke walked a lonesome valley. Depression, my friends, is an illness. It is a fatal illness, if it is not treated. If it is treated, sometimes, but not always, it can be helped, and sometimes, but not always, prevented. Those who have suffered depression, and I count myself among them, know how difficult it is. Sometimes it is impossible to pull yourself out of it. And when the person is caught in the cycle of depression, and when that person is determined to end his life, there is not much any of us can do to prevent it, short of locking the person off, and even that does not always work, my friends. Depression is excruciatingly painful. The person feels as if there is no way out, and some of you here today may feel partly responsible. You may experience guilt or torment, and be asking yourselves the questions: 'What might I have done? What could I have done to prevent this?' You could not prevent it. For depression is a disease, and we need to acknowledge it as such. You did all

you could to help, and so now it is for you to forgive yourself, as God has already forgiven you. We cannot make a judgment call on Robert Jahnke's choices. We have not walked in his moccasins. We do not know what it was to be him… The God who empowers us to go on – it is that God who receives and blesses, and protects, and redeems, and lifts up Robert Jahnke… Nothing can separate us from God's love. Nothing! Bob Jahnke – Dr. Bob – is safe in the arms of a God who restores wholeness to all situations. There are no exceptions. We who are yet alive are given an invitation. We are invited to let go of guilt and anxiety and fear and resistance, because God is here. The power of God's spirit carries us through, and we are not alone. God weeps with us when we weep and holds us when we need to be held. And Bob is not alone. In life and death, we belong to God. Whether we live, or whether we die, we are the Lord's.

When I allowed Reverend Harmes' thoughts inside me, I found so much of myself in them: contemplating suicide, feeling guilt and shame from some of my decisions, needing to be reminded of God's love, care, and forgiveness, denying those events in my life I wanted to forget, ignoring the light God puts before me, accepting blame for events out of my control, and walking a lonesome valley at times in my life. Although I did not know Reverend Harmes when she began this worship service, her words embraced so much of my journey. She spoke of a God I'm trying to understand and love as I grow older.

A short time before writing this chapter I called Las Placitas Presbyterian Church, hoping to speak with Reverend Harmes. To my surprise, she answered the phone with, "Hi, this is Jane." That friendly greeting assured me I was in for a wonderful conversation, and it was! I made the connection with her and the Jahnke memorial service. We talked for 45 minutes. She and I emailed a few times. I sent her a copy of *Lessons*, and she sent me information about her church and its many activities. She also told me about a beautiful monastic retreat center in the New Mexico desert. I hoped to spend time there at the point the winter in Chicago becomes too cold and dreary.

As difficult as the minister's reflections were to deliver, Art's challenge must have been so much harder. Yet he was able to speak from the heart.

> I have a question. What does one say at a time like this? What does a father say when he's lost a brilliant son in the prime of his life? I never really gave it much thought, because I, like most parents, assumed that I would certainly predecease my children. But obviously that hasn't been the case. So where am I? I've had a chance to reflect on this for a couple of days. I'm saying to myself, and this may sound strange to you people, "How well did we know each other?" One thing I knew of a certainty was Bob realized how much pride his dad had in his accomplishments, and how much bragging rights his old dad had as a result of those accomplishments. What I'm not sure of is if he realized how much I loved him. The reverend mentioned we should not suffer from guilt, but I'm afraid maybe I should be guilty, probably because of my conduct or my lack of statements that would convince him that maybe he didn't realize how much I loved him. I hope he did.

Art's story reflected the fragile, two-word question I've asked many times in my life: *What if?* What if this horrible event had happened differently? What if this senseless sequence of events really made sense after all? I knew this two-word question was of no help to Art and his family. And the question has most often been of little comfort to me. However, Art's words, and especially his questions, have such meaning for me. I have asked those same questions, and wrestled with those same thoughts, so many times in my life concerning Dad. Did I know him? Did he know me? I know he loved me, and I hope he knew I loved him. Art told me of a quote he is going to have framed which reads, "Do not judge a man by how he died, but by how he lived." A wonderful thought to help Art and me through our journeys.

The minister concluded the service with these words: "We've heard many wonderful things, a lot to give thought to. And the one thing I'm going to take home with me, and I would encourage you to take home, is the question that was raised by Art: How well do we know each other? Who do we have to say 'I love you' to, that we haven't said it to in awhile? You've challenged us in all our relationships, so I thank you for that gift."

As Art and I talked about the minister's final thought, he shared with me a wonderful story. After the service, a lady approached Art and the minister. She had a sister with whom she had not talked in twenty years. She said she was going right home, call her sister, and tell her she loved her. I told Art if the service held no meaning to anyone else in attendance, the celebration of Bob's life was worth it to have this one lady contact a long lost sister. That is powerful!

Art was so honest in his feelings when he shared with me he felt he had always been closer to, and perhaps less strict, with his daughter, Susie, than Bob. I immediately thought of Art's description of his relationship with his dad, Mr. Ed, and his perception of his father's closeness to Art's sisters. The questions Art asked were soul searching and may never be answered.

I also realized this service touched me as it did for these reasons: I wondered how close I am to my own two children. How well do I know them? Did I duck my responsibilities *and* my opportunities as a father, avoiding difficult situations at home and leaving Bonnie to deal with them? Secondly, because of my own thoughts about suicide, the words of the minister comforted me. How strong must she have been to share her struggle with depression? What a wonderful way to place her true self into the midst of this service.

Art and I talked a long time about depression. I shared with him some of what I have learned about this illness, and he gave me new information from the research he did. Art gave me a gift that day. It was not the tragic story itself, for I gained absolutely no sense of peace from his son's story and others like it I have heard the past few years. Instead, the true gift was Art's willingness to share his story with me. He didn't have to tell me about that part of his journey, but he did. His gift to me allowed me to revisit my own thoughts about suicide and to realize how fortunate I was to seek help instead of following through with those thoughts. I also had reaffirmed the desire for transparency and authenticity in my life as I heard Art's story and saw in his eyes the emotion of unanswered questions.

As I was returning to my cabin after Art and I finished our conversation, I noticed the big open field adjacent to the swimming pool. As I drove through the guard gate for the last time during this visit and headed toward my cabin, something drew my eyes toward that field. I parked my car and walked smack into the middle of the field where hay was growing to feed the animals during the winter. Even though it was past midnight and the hay was blanketed with a thin layer of dew, I lay down.

I immediately noticed the absence of those gaudy, looming lights of a major metropolitan area, lights that invade the dark sky and diminish the brilliant stars above. Here the sky is black and mysterious, as if God flicked all the stars off the end of his brush. The stars, in all their courses and perfectly planned journeys across the sky, magnified the beauty above me.

The stars were brilliant, much grander than a glorious fireworks display on the 4th of July. My eyes roamed the millions of stars overhead, and I thought of the line from an Eagles song, "You can stare up at the stars and still not see the light." I also remembered some lines from another of Brown County's endearing songs: "Run through the forest. Run through the sky. The light in your hands, and the light in your eyes."

The stars captivated me. I had two thoughts as I lay in the field. I hoped my trips to the woods were allowing my heart the opportunity to experience the more difficult part of that line, seeing the light as well. I strongly felt the light was unfolding before me and, as I suggested earlier, providing the illumination necessary to make enough progress down my path until I find that next ray of gentle radiance already waiting for me.

Secondly, I felt as though I was in a great space of possibility, in a field of openness, with a free and unlimited imagination for exposing my authentic path. Poet and author E.E. Cummings referred to this imagination as walking inside "the ragged meadow of my soul."

Magically, the tall trees surrounding the field seemed to disappear. I saw nothing but unlimited expanse and limitless possibilities because the stars were twinkling like millions of diamonds spread over a soft, black, velvet cloth. At that moment, I knew my path was beckoning and God would light my way toward realizing my dreams. "Go on, Eddie; get out there and explore." The Irish singer, Enya, put it so well:

On My Way Home

I have been given
One moment from heaven
As I am walking
Surrounded by night,
Stars high above me
Make a wish under moonlight.

Chorus

On my way home
I remember
Only good days.
On my way home
I remember
All the best days.
On my way home
I can remember

A Tug-of-War to Relocate My Authentic Path

> Every new day
> I move in silence
> With each step taken,
> Snow falling round me
> My angels in flight,
> Far in the distance
> Is my wish under moonlight.

The stars were high above me in all their brilliance. The runs to the woods allowed me to discover new thoughts and feelings about home and its meaning to me. I moved in silence in the woods, looking for my angels in flight and making my wish under moonlight. Enya's words so directly spoke to me as I gazed into the black sky, bathed in all those twinkling stars. The poet, Rumi (*Open Secrets: Versions of Rumi*) chose his words so well: "Out beyond ideas of wrongdoing and rightdoing, there is a field. I'll meet you there. When the soul lies down in that grass, the world is too full to talk about." When I finally got to my feet, the backs of my shorts and shirt were soaked. I couldn't have cared less.

I realized that one part of the big field I lay in that night was my journey toward finding wholeness, finding home. I did not believe God would grant His permission to continue my journey toward wholeness until, and unless, I learned how to focus on the needs of my fellow journeymen and my ability to serve them on their journeys. Doing so meant I must stop focusing on what I wanted and start focusing on others.

The next morning I checked out, said good-bye to Emma Moots, and once again headed home, not knowing what was waiting for me. My second trip to Brown County continued to point me toward the path out of the crossroads. I had time to reflect upon my personal, professional, and spiritual life and began making the necessary connections to my authentic path. I drove home with more answers as well as more questions.

CHAPTER 12

The Hero's Journey: Providential Moments

We have not to risk the adventure alone, for the heroes of all time have gone before us. The labyrinth is thoroughly known. We have only to follow the thread of the heroic path, and where we had thought to find an abomination, we shall find a god. And where we had thought to slay another, we shall slay ourselves. Where we had thought to travel outward, we will come to the center of our own existence. And where we had thought to be alone, we will be with all the world.

Joseph Campbell - *The Hero With a Thousand Faces*

In order to help me understand the questions I raised and answers I hoped to find I spent several months reflecting on my first two trips to the woods and their similarity to a term coined by Joseph Campbell, "the hero's journey." During my lifetime, I've gone down many paths without knowing why. I was driven by priorities that I selfishly chose or others chose for me, having dismissed God as a guide. Often the choices did not reflect God's plan for my life, my work, my family, and my religious beliefs. I took the jobs I wanted, with little regard for the needs of my family. I managed the family finances, barely making it through some months even though my wife and I made good salaries. I rejected the God I knew growing up and didn't seek a new understanding of Him in my life.

Every journey I took, for whatever reasons, followed a similar plan, a plan I did not recognize until recently. The journeys – graduating from high school, going to college when I was eighteen, getting married, securing my first teaching job, having a family, obtaining my master's and doctorate degrees, serving as a public school administrator, teaching in higher education – all followed the same pattern Campbell describes as the journey of the hero. Going into the hospital both times with depression gave me insights toward understanding this pattern, but I didn't fully recognize the process until I read Joseph Campbell's most famous book, *The Hero with a Thousand Faces*. My trips to the woods of Brown County followed Campbell's steps of the hero's journey.

In the book Campbell describes the archetypal hero's journey as a series of interconnecting phases. Campbell explained that the hero's story always begins with an imaginary "Everyman" just living his humdrum life. Suddenly and unexpectedly Everyman is either pulled out of his ordinary life or chooses to leave that life, moving on to a great adventure, whose ending he cannot know at the beginning. He goes out on faith, not knowing.

The adventure then goes through several phases, always the same for each adventure. The hero journeys into the dark world where he meets various forces or entities he has to confront. Along the way he encounters a guide who offers him help in the new skills needed to be successful in achieving his goal, still perhaps unknown. The decision to spend time by myself and for myself demanded I face the forces and entities within. During my time in the woods, many guides came along to help point the way to my authentic path.

Striving toward his goal, the hero, like me, is challenged to his limit. He endures tests, trials, and initiations. During this phase Campbell said, "Heavy winds blow…" In his book *New Seeds of Contemplation*, Thomas Merton used these words to describe these heavy winds, while at the same time suggesting the hope from the winds: "This is where so many holy people break down… As soon as they reach the point where they can no longer see the way and guide themselves by their own light, they refuse to go any further… It is in this darkness that we find true liberty. It is in this abandonment that we are made strong. This is the night that empties us."

These challenges reach a peak in what Campbell calls "a supreme ordeal." Remembering what he learned from his guide, surviving the ordeal, and staying the course toward his goal, the hero survives the journey and returns home, successful in his quest. Because his beliefs have changed during the journey, he sees a different world when he returns home, and he sees it clearly for the first time.

The best example of my own hero's journey comes from my marriage, an example of the archetypal hero's journey as a series of interconnecting phases. After forty years of being married, I left home fifteen months ago. Like "Everyman," I was jerked out of the life I knew to begin an unknown adventure. I knew I could not find my next adventure while still living at home. One day while Bonnie was not home, I put down my convertible top, threw some clothes in the back seat, and went to stay with my friend, Doug. I left Bonnie a note which she read when she returned home. Unfortunately, I convinced myself that leaving this way would be better than talking to her face-to-face because I knew I would not remember all the thoughts I wanted to share with her if we talked.

Shortly after leaving, however, I realized I had once again taken the coward's way out rather than facing the issue and talking with Bonnie about it. My decision, the way I handled that decision, was once again all about me and my needs with total disregard for my family's needs and questions as they tried to understand. Unfortunately, typical behavior for me. I took myself out of my normal life and had no idea where my journey would lead. I very quickly became my own example of practicing my own definition of faith: I was truly going out not knowing where I was to go.

Leaving my personal comfort zone of a forty-year marriage was by far the most difficult decision I have ever made. I did not just wake up one morning and say, "This is the day I'm leaving home." I thought about the decision a long time; however, as per my normal pattern, I did not talk with Bonnie about what I thought I needed to do. Bonnie would readily agree that we were the classic case study in co-dependency and procrastination. During my initial four-month hospitalization with clinical depression, I was introduced to the healing thoughts of twelve-step programs. After leaving the hospital I read a book by Melody Beattie, *Codependents' Guide to the Twelve Steps*. In her book she said, "As many others have said about themselves, I wasn't me. I was whoever people wanted me to be. And I felt quite victimized and used up by it all. After years of practicing hard-line codependency, the unmanageability in my life was overwhelming." Beattie reflected my feelings to a tee. I was not only who I thought Bonnie wanted me to be but what anyone else thought I should be.

After leaving home, like the hero, I had to confront the issues I encountered. I didn't talk with Bonnie or my kids for three weeks, which only caused their anger, frustrations, and questions to multiply. I didn't know what to say to any of them. I was afraid of hearing Bonnie's frustration and pain at that time. I was too concerned with my own. I repeated my pattern of taking flight rather than standing in the midst of the struggle and working through my reasons for leaving. The hero takes flight to find a new adventure. I did the same, full of the same fear and uncertainty the hero feels. At the time of leaving the hero doesn't know why it is critical to move out of the comfort zone. Not being able to rediscover my authentic self at home was the only concrete reason, at that time, I knew for moving out of my comfort zone and once again beginning the search to regain my authentic self.

One day I saw Bonnie in downtown Naperville. I was going into Starbucks to read and write, and she was leaving a session with her therapist, whom she began seeing after I left home. We sat on a bench and talked. Bonnie didn't understand at all why I left, and, at that time, I didn't understand the reasons either.

I did find many friends and guides as I ventured forth. The most important ones were Doug, my friend with whom I was staying, Nancy, my therapist, and yes, Bonnie.

Doug is an affirmation of my belief that friends and guides come into our lives at just the very time we need them. He offered me a place to stay when I needed one. He made me feel welcome, and we quickly developed a friendship that, I'm convinced, will last a lifetime. Doug and I had many conversations on his back deck. He struggles with depression, had been divorced, and was in such a critical point with his live-in significant other that he considered asking her to leave. Very few friends and guides have come into my life that I have connected with as quickly as Doug. We laughed together, we cried together, we were, and will be, there for each other, and we both realized the story of any one of us is, in part, the story of all of us.

Above all else, Doug is a survivor and has had his own wilderness journeys. He knew he would survive them, and he did. When he got to the other side he tried to understand what he learned from those experiences. Like me, Doug worries about his contributions and his legacies. I know in my heart they will be many. When Doug was 17 he moved out of his home and into an apartment. He had little connection with his father and his mother was verbally abusive, constantly telling Doug he would never amount to much. He worked throughout the remainder of his high school career and for a few years after graduating. He saved enough money to pay his own way through college. He had an older brother who died of aids.

Despite his many trials and wilderness journeys, Doug's son and daughter have been kept upper-most in his heart. I could not have had a better role model during the time I was experiencing the most difficult wilderness journey in my life. He reinforced for me the importance of surviving wilderness journeys rather than perishing in them. As I observed Doug interact with his son and daughter I remembered the importance of Eric and Tracie in my life. He left his wife and shared that story with me. He went out not knowing but knew he could not stay where he was. I was in the midst of making that same decision.

My therapist was another guide who came along when I most needed her. About six weeks after I left, Eric flew in from Oregon. He, Tracie, Bonnie, and I had a four-way session with Nancy, the first time my entire family had been together since I left home. Nancy created a wonderful environment, allowing each family member to share his or her anger and frustrations and to ask the questions that had accumulated in six weeks. The two fundamental questions from all three focused on why I left home and, more specifically, why I left as I did after forty years. I did my best to respond while still having a long way to go towards my own understanding. Toward the end of the hour session, Tracie summarized all of our thinking when, while looking at me, she said, "Dad, it seems like you and Mom have been going down separate paths these last few years. The two of you have different interests and friends and seem to have less in common." Wow! She hit the nail right on the head. Bonnie and I had already talked about the thought Tracie shared. We realized the separate paths we had been traveling. I told her I just couldn't remain true to what I was writing in this book and search for my authentic path while at home. By that time all three members of my family better understood what I had just said. The session ended, and the four of us went out for ice cream after the session and continued our conversation.

    I want to mention the special friend Bonnie was to me during the process of leaving home. Earlier I wrote that Bonnie is the solid rock and foundation for our family. She has always supported all three of us in our desires to change directions in our lives. I cannot imagine the love and courage it took for her to write this note on the inside of a birthday card she gave me five weeks after I left home. She said, "Ed, Hope this birthday card is the start of a meaningful year for you as you try to find your authentic self. Remember to listen to your heart as the answers are there. I will give you the freedom you feel you need for your quest and wish you 'peace' in the journey. May this star remind you of your goal and to pray for others as well as yourself." A bright, beautiful, blue star was also on the inside of the card and on it, in big letters, was the word PEACE. She signed it Love, B.A. The tears poured from my eyes as I read her note, and they continue to flow each time I reread her words to me.

    Campbell's "heavy winds" blew for me the next several months. I was caught in the paradox of feeling right about my decision to leave home while at the same time finding myself questioning that decision. I was caught in my own desire to find hope in the winds that blew. After a year living with Doug I leased a condo, and for the very first time in my 64 years I was truly on my own, alone. I lived at home before going to college, went to college, got married, minimally helped raise our kids, and then when I left home, I moved in with a friend. Being on my own was a tremendous adjustment for me. I recalled the thought I had in Brown County: I valued my alone time, but at times I needed to be in community with others. I went out with friends to ballgames and concerts. I returned to my favorite bar where I always knew I would find some of my friends. This latter search for community, however, put me back into a situation where I was drinking. Alcohol negates, or dramatically reduces, the work of my medications for depression. Knowing of this negative relationship, however, didn't keep me from going to bars and drinking. I spent many nights alone with my own thoughts and feelings. I prayed that God would lead me toward the right path. The Alcoholics Anonymous thought, "God show me your plan for my life and help me find the courage to follow it," became an important part of my morning prayer mantra.

    Needing more community than my solitary life provided, I also considered finding it by reconciling with Bonnie. For forty years she had been a large part of my community. For the last few years before I left neither she nor I felt the community we had earlier in our marriage. Bonnie and I talked for a time about going to a counselor for our codependency and other issues in our marriage, and then getting back together to see if we could improve on our marriage. However, we both engaged in our typical approach-avoidance behavior. We talked about seeking help but didn't follow through with those conversations. At other times we both said we became better friends after I left home than while I was there. We both wondered if reconciliation would diminish the strong friendship we both felt after I left.

    Searching for more guidance as I struggled to make sense of the changes in my life, I turned to Bruce Wilkinson's book, *The Dream Giver*. In it he shares a fable that mirrors this process of change in our lives. The book includes a fable about a Nobody named Ordinary, who lived in the Land of Familiar and reported each day to his Usual Job. Not much happened in Familiar. Most of those who lived there were comfortable with their lives.

One day Ordinary woke up with a Big Dream, a dream he felt but could not describe with any detail. In order to pursue his dream, Ordinary knew he had to leave Familiar, to get out of his comfort zone. Most of his friends tried to discourage him, citing the unknown, the struggles, and the fear for his safety. In reality they didn't want Ordinary to leave Familiar because they remained there, unwilling to follow their own dreams.

Despite his friends' protests, Ordinary did leave, and along his path he experienced the continuation of Campbell's description of the hero's journey. He had a guide. He felt the "heavy winds blow," and he found many stops along the path where he wanted to give up and return to the Land of Familiar; but he didn't. He stayed the course and found his dream – although not the dream he *thought* he would see. Once he found his initial dream, which led him to his Big Dream, he knew he was a hero and had arrived home, seeing it for the first time.

When I first thought about the word "hero," I was concerned. I did not see myself as a hero. Campbell's use of the word does not mean becoming a superstar. A hero begins to trust his or her life, its purpose and its direction. A hero is always in a transformation process. The hero is willing to learn from all situations and all people. To understand their calling in life, heroes have to listen to the inner self. Campbell offers a symbolic way of helping me understand my current journey within the context of increased understanding of life. Now this is the kind of hero I want to become.

The phases of the hero's journey are identical to the change process I described in Chapter 1: an ending, a neutral zone, and finally a new beginning. In the hero's journey the ending is in essence the call to action, the start of the new adventure. For the hero, he or she is saying good-bye to the known and going out on faith, not knowing where the journey will lead. As you already read, endings and beginnings get murky, making it difficult to know the ending from the beginning of the new adventure.

I better understood my call to action, my new beginning, as I found myself dropped into the crossroads. The crossroads gained additional clarity after I read about Jon Katz's call to run to the mountain. He took his pilgrimage in part to fill a spiritual need he felt in his life. As I continued to understand my current stop along the way, I saw myself sitting right smack dab in the middle of that crossroads, not knowing which way to turn, a primary invitation to begin a new adventure. This invitation carries with it the call to a new passage in this spiritual journey – confronting the masks of a false identity as we search for our true self.

The innocence and naivety I felt believing I had answered all my life's questions while writing *Lessons from the Porch* were shattered in the winter of 2004. The resulting breakdown instigated my second trip to the hospital with depression. Although I did not realize it at the time, this trip began my fifth experience in the middle of a crossroads. Out of that fifth crossroads experience I found a sense of calmness and greater clarity to find my path. The breakdown was a breakthrough as I came to understand my need to venture forth.

The call, my request to God, was in part for Him to become my guide and lend a hand with my dreams as I ran to the woods with those questions in my heart. The call came from deep within me. The quietness and beauty I found in Brown County were significant gifts, helping me find harmony amidst my personal disharmony. However, the call to adventure did not end in Brown County; it only began there. The journey is a quest for healing and spiritual guidance and won't cease. Have you ever pressed your fingernails into a chalkboard and scratched across the surface? Parts of my life were feeling and sounding just that way. I was walking through the chaos in my life to find the tranquility I hoped was there because I know out of chaos comes order and peace and a return home, a return I experienced in Brown County.

Although unaware at the beginning of my current journey, I was also being called to renew a kinship with my parents. I needed to return to my roots to better understand and celebrate the many gifts that led me to this calling. Renowned psychiatrist Carl Jung said, "To regain our souls we need to pay attention to our ancestors, who often have much to teach us about our own vocation and identity, especially when we reach the second half of life." Because I think of them so often, Mom and Dad are teaching me more now than they did in my early years and more than I learned from them through writing *Lessons from the Porch*. Much of the frustration with what I *didn't* experience in my son-parent relationship has been replaced with the gifts I *did* receive from Mom and Dad. The more they enter my heart, the more I realize how fortunate I was to have them as my parents. They gave me the gift of uncertainty about my young life. This lack of understanding resulted in my first book and, now, this second one. I used to think I was being a much better parent for my kids than they were for me. I have tried to improve my relationship with Eric and Tracie in ways I thought were missing in my own childhood. I have also realized, however, that I tried to emulate my parent's amazing roles as a provider and protector for my sister and me.

Letting go, letting faith triumph over fear, and beginning the change process are followed by a neutral zone, that space where we feel the "the heavy winds blow." We endure the tests, trials, and tribulations of the hero. The sojourner enters the wilderness, just as Moses spent 40 years in the desert waiting for God to show His people the way. While in the wilderness the traveler may encounter a wide range of feelings: excitement for the journey yet fear of the future. We are betwixt and between. In her book *The Aquarian Conspiracy*, Marilyn Ferguson describes these identical feelings of excitement and fear as the trapeze artist letting go of one swinging bar and turning to meet the oncoming bar that has not yet arrived. This feeling of tenuousness is what Terry Tempest Williams described in the Introduction to her book – that feeling "in the pit of our stomach."

What happens during the journey to recognize a new beginning and continue the change within us will vary for each of us. However, the end is always the same: the journey toward finding our current understanding of true self is the culmination of many life-changing events, bringing us face to face with the best and the worst of who we are. Although initially we may not like what we see, a transformation takes place along the way, and we find a person who is stronger from the trials and tribulations. Central to this notion is not necessarily that the change took place within the individual. Rather, it is the journey itself and our willingness to take the journey, which speaks volumes about us as human beings.

When Jon Katz decided to return to New Jersey, he was recharged, ready to face whatever was ahead of him. He wrote, "Sometimes you go away so that you can come home or find out what home really means. The mountain helped with this. Change is clarifying, like getting a new pair of glasses with a better prescription. The journeys of faith and change help us all see more clearly."

Like Katz, as we experience journey, we are all heroes immersed in a quest to help our personal world respond to an increasingly complex environment. Old answers are no longer viable for the new questions we are confronting. We are all both individual and collaborative journeymen and women, finding solitude within ourselves while in community with others. The object of our quest is the capacity to initiate, support, and sustain meaningful change in our lives and in our work.

To Campbell, the end of the hero's journey is "not the aggrandizement of the hero… The ultimate aim of the quest must be neither release nor ecstasy for oneself, but the wisdom and the power to serve others." One of the many distinctions between the celebrity and the hero, he said, is that one lives only for self while the other acts to redeem society.

As I was finishing this chapter on the hero's journey, I received another unexpected yet perfectly timed gift from my son. Eric had no idea whatsoever that I had spent much of that summer working on this chapter. The gift was in the form of a poem by Mary Oliver, titled "The Journey." Her words so gracefully summarize what I just wrote, but beyond that, the gift from Eric represented his love for his dad and his desire that I continue my own journey.

LESSONS FROM THE CROSSROADS

The Journey

One day you finally knew
what you had to do, and began,
though the voices around you
kept shouting
their bad advice –
though the whole house
began to tremble
and you felt the old tug
at your ankles.
"Mend my life!"
each voice cried.
But you didn't stop.
You knew what you had to do,
though the wind pried
with its stiff fingers
at the very foundations,
though their melancholy
was terrible.
It was already late
enough, and a wild night,
and the road full of fallen
branches and stones.
But little by little,
as you left their voices behind,
the stars began to burn
through the sheets of clouds,
and there was a new voice
which you slowly

recognized as your own,
that kept you company
as you strode deeper and deeper
into the world,
determined to do
the only thing you could do –
determined to save
the only life you could save.

The New Fall Term Begins

When I finished the story of the hero's journey, summer drew to an end, and fall was just around the next curve in the road. I played more than I worked that summer, a rare but welcomed change for me. Right after my second trip to the woods I taught a two-week graduate class. Then I left for North Carolina. I went to New Orleans for a business trip, and upon my return the entire clan went to Jackson Hole, Wyoming, for my nephew's wedding – "Nice work if you can get it, and you can get it if you try" – as the old song lyrics go.

The day after returning very late from Wyoming, my week long university and college meetings began in preparation for the start of fall semester. During this week of meetings, I had an interesting conversation with my dean, who knew I was struggling with my calling and the way I wanted to spend my time.

The Dean and I talked about a process of phasing out of full-time teaching and moving toward a part-time teaching load, giving me more time to read, write, and speak. At the end of our meeting I suggested we both think about our conversation.

As I walked out of her office, my head, heart, and soul exploded with questions bouncing around inside me like steel balls in a lively pinball machine. The feelings rattling around inside me were, in some ways, paradoxical, yet I felt at peace. My feelings collapsed into six questions: What allowed the Dean to enter into a conversation with me about a workload that allows more time to move toward a calling to read, write, and speak? Can I see our discussion as a gift, happening at the *perfect point* along my journey, a guide showing up at just the right time? God, were you working *toward* me *through* the Dean? What do You want me to do with this new information? How can I keep this conversation in my heart so I can carry out Your perfect plan through me? Is the discussion with the Dean a providential moment in my life, an intersecting of my dreams with the accumulation of all the individual choices I've made since joining the university eight years ago?

That week I added a new prayer to my morning mantra: "God, please help me see *Your* perfect plan in all this, and not mine. You know I can easily take the conversation with the Dean and use it for *my* own benefit, and not Yours. You also know I can run 'hell bent for election,' racin' down the path I found in Brown County. You'll certainly give me that choice. Please help me stand still long enough to think and pray so I can see my path only after I believe it's the one You want me to travel."

CHAPTER 13

My Ongoing Pilgrimage Toward My Authentic Path

We are pilgrims on the earth and strangers; we have come from afar and we are going far.
Vincent van Gogh

Pilgrims are persons in motion – passing through territories not their own – seeking something we might call completion.
Richard Neibuhr

A pilgrim who yearns for authenticity realizes the work is hard. The search for authenticity means looking below the surface to understand who we are. Author Kenneth Ruge said, "It means being honest about our desires, fears, and confusions."

As with the hero's journey, my return from Brown County provided me with my next new adventure, my next pilgrimage. My classes were in full swing. The preparations for classes, the class time itself, my other daily tasks, and the endless (mostly unnecessary) meetings filled my days and nights. My work almost replaced the peaceful, unscheduled times I enjoyed in Brown County.

The questions that were burned into my soul as I left that meeting with the Dean remained but became increasingly insistent, begging for my attention. My soul cried out to spend time with me again, the kind of time we valued on our pilgrimages to the woods. I so missed the solitude and sense of community I found in Brown County. I felt this sense of community with my students, but the community I experienced with my classes was totally different and did not replace the community of friends I found in Brown County. Once the new school term began, I did not find time during my days to connect with God and to listen to the messages and questions He was sending me. Just as I thought, life had become "daily." I was back on a schedule of attending meetings and teaching my classes. Instead of interacting with myself and with God about who I am, I was talking with my colleagues at the university about student learning outcomes and the measuring devises we needed to create to measure that learning. The world I once again found at work was so very different from the world that had embraced me during the summer. Frustrated, *I* cried out to my soul with assurance that we *will* find that time to be together. And we did – at a retreat center near my home.

The Cenacle Spirituality and Retreat Center sits on its 40-acre site, offering an oasis in the midst of the never-ending hustle and bustle of the Chicago suburbs. I went there to recapture the solitude, aloneness, silence, and peace I discovered at Brown County State Park. As I took the fifteen-minute drive from my home to the Cenacle in Warrenville, Illinois, my heart and soul became aware that we once again were about to find time for ourselves and get reacquainted. We anticipated the grace awaiting us those next two days.

Immediately upon passing through the beautiful yet simple entrance to the Cenacle, I drove down a winding path back into the grounds of this retreat center. The trees on both sides of the path touched each other at their tops, once again forming an archway through which I drove. The trees, beautiful flowers, and a sense of reverence surrounded me like the arms of a loving and caring parent when we are cradled as a child.

I parked in the lot and walked across a beautiful wooden bridge that traverses the DuPage River. I noticed the leaves on the many willow trees that lined both sides of the river falling out over the water and dancing lazily with the breeze moving past them. The Cenacle was not an unfamiliar place. I had attended two weekend retreats at the Cenacle as I recovered from my first hospitalization with clinical depression. I needed the Cenacle then, and I needed it that fall as my spiritual journey continued. Both times I was there I knew I wanted time to reflect on my experiences, my depression and now my retreats to Brown County.

As in Brown County, I began each day with the same prayer. I asked God to empty my mind of all outside thoughts, fears, and worries. I asked Him to allow me to be in the precious presence, grace, and beauty that engulfed me. Finally, I asked God to direct my thoughts and actions so my heart could be open to His messages and plans for me while there. As in the woods of Brown County, I had no expectations for my days. I just wanted the time and events to be filled with whatever awaited me.

I spent some time each day walking the grounds. As with other recent journeys, I read and wrote inside, but after a time I needed to get away and reflect. On my walks I was aware of the feelings that entered my heart and soul. I was grateful for finding another setting where I could read, reflect, and write. I recalled my trips to Brown County and the writing I did there. I reflect on the questions I took to Brown County and brought with me to The Cenacle. I felt I was approaching a decision to write and speak full time. I felt I was continuing on a journey God planned for me long before I began.

Only squawking of a flock of geese and the grinding engine of a lawnmower driven by one of the groundskeepers interrupted the silence. The groundskeepers also tended the gorgeous flowers and bushes artistically sprinkled with great care throughout the acreage, just as Rosemary tended her treasures in front of the Daily Grind. Each day I saw a blue heron gliding effortlessly close to the surface of the river.

Lunch was served at 12:30. Those of us on private retreats ate in a small dining room around two large, rectangular tables with room for eight around each table. A beautiful painting hangs on one wall. The artwork shows several sail boats, their sails down, silent and still in the harbor. I wondered if those sailboats, like Edgar Lee Masters' character George Gray in *Spoon River Anthology*, were longing for the sea and yet afraid to venture forth.

I ate lunch each day with three other fellow travelers. A sign at each table read, "Silence is the gift you give to those gathered here." The four of us sat as silent strangers. I wondered if each of us was asking an unspoken, similar question: What are all the struggles that brought us together in this place at this time in our lives? That question was perhaps the synergy that bonded us on our common, silent, internal pilgrimages. We nodded and smiled as we ate.

The Cenacle has a labyrinth setting in the middle of a clump of beautiful shade trees. The one here is much bigger than the one along the Riverwalk in Naperville. However, that same DuPage River I crossed to enter the building winds its way along the labyrinth in Naperville, another connection, like the woods of Brown County, providing comfort for my ongoing journey into the unknown. Both labyrinths share a common purpose: to take a time out from our busy lives, leaving stress and schedules behind.

As I entered the labyrinth both days, I asked myself to remember I was entering a sacred space. I wanted to walk the circular path with reverence, asking God to help me find the grace awaiting me as I wound my way toward the center and back out again.

All labyrinths start along an inner path. While traveling this inner path, I was led outward and then back toward the center. After reaching the center, I retraced my paths to the outer part of the labyrinth. The path of this sacred journey represents our hope for life itself – the magical and mysterious synchronicity we seek between our inner and outer self.

As I arrived at the center, an old tree stump greeted me. A small fallen tree lay close to the stump. The rings of a tree provide a good indication of its age and history. The growing edge of a tree, its membrane, is the most alive part of the tree, not its center. Yet, without the strength and inflexibility of the center, the tree's firm foundation, the outer growing edge could not do its work of allowing new life to occur. The inner strength and outer growth of a tree are symbolic of the labyrinth itself, that combination of inner and outer connections that allow life to continue. My own work, the center of my being, is intrinsically connected to my outer work, closest to my growing edge. I sat alone on that stump, in my silence, writing in my journal and using all five of my senses to drink in the beauty of this place. As I sat amidst the beauty surrounding me, I returned to the question of why I came to the Cenacle at this point in my quest to find my authentic path.

As I sat on that old tree stump, I wrote in my journal those thoughts and feelings that found their way into my heart: I made notes in my journal about the questions I took to Brown County that continued to find their place in my soul: Should I leave the field of education to write and speak full time? How would I feel if I seized the opportunity to live these two callings? Can I remember the excitement, joy, sense of fulfillment, and inner peace I experienced as I wrote my first book, *Lessons from the Porch?* Was that writing a one-time experience, from one who still does not consider himself a writer? Had I forgotten the opportunities to speak to groups about my journey and my enjoyment of those opportunities? When do I feel my best? Do I feel good about the way I am living my life? Can I believe in myself as much as others believe in me?

I thought about my meeting with the Dean and the messages for me in that meeting. At the time of the meeting I still didn't know my way toward my rediscovered authentic path out of the crossroads. I knew it was there but still hidden from view. I didn't know what I would see when I found it. I also did not know if I would like what I saw. I wrote in my journal that I was more definitively considering leaving education to write and speak full time. I came to realize I could not do justice to all three: writing, speaking, and teaching. I didn't want to divide my time among those activities.

I knew God would once again help me recognize my authentic path. I also believed there would be no guarantees the path would be free of wilderness journeys. I never thought about this reality until I began writing *Lessons from the Crossroads*, but I should have. I now understand the authentic path I've been walking will, at times, be full of new holes in the sidewalk. God will continue to give me free choice about how and when I choose to climb out of the holes. When the desert times become too overwhelming, and the pain of not rediscovering my authentic path becomes greater than the struggle of where I am, I will again be at the crossroads searching for my path and my next adventure.

I believe the Dean and I had that particular conversation, at the specific time it occurred, for a reason: I needed guidance, and I felt Joshua there, helping me both during the conversation and afterward as I wrote the questions. I needed a guide. God was working through both Joshua and me. Without that conversation with the Dean, I likely would not have focused on those specific questions I asked after our meeting, and I realized those questions were an extension of the ones I took to the woods. As I sat on the stump, I continued to ask myself: What am I to learn from that conversation with the Dean? Even though time flew by after I met with her, I continued the struggle of trying to bring clarity to those questions I asked after leaving her office. Why did they stay with me so long?

She may have seen desires in me more clearly at this time than I saw in myself. Her insights may have been her way of helping me break through some of the clouds at the crossroads and move toward a new calling. This call had the potential of forcing me once again out of my personal and spiritual comfort zones and into another life-changing pilgrimage.

The discussion with the Dean came as a gift just when I needed it. I truly believe God was working through the Dean as we discussed opportunities to pursue my dream of writing and speaking. God planned the meeting before I went to the Cenacle so I could use my time there to put our conversation into a perspective of helping me find my way out of the crossroads.

While sitting on the stump, I also remembered the joy and sense of fulfillment I felt while writing *Lessons from the Porch*. At that moment I knew that writing was not a one-time experience. If my first book was to be my only writing, God wouldn't have laid before me an authentic path I no longer recognized. He would not have created the uneasiness within that sent me off on my various sojourns to rediscover that path. I had the strong feeling that my journey held other opportunities to be off by myself until I recognized that newly defined path. Before going to The Cenacle, I had opportunities to speak about my journey. I so loved and looked forward to those speaking engagements. God arranged those opportunities to remind me that people want and need to hear my story.

I thought about when I felt my best and knew the answer was when I was writing and speaking. I still enjoyed teaching, but the enjoyment was dissipating and being replaced with my writing and speaking. I was beginning to understand that I felt best about how I was living my life when I was working on my book and talking with others about my journey. Also at those times I believed in myself and God's gentle insistence that I find the authentic path I lost somewhere along the way.

Carrying these thoughts with me, I left the labyrinth feeling my time there helped me find some connections between my inward and outward journeys. I left the Cenacle after my second day with understandings I didn't have before I arrived. I experienced a different place where I could read, write, find the peace and grace to reflect, and just be in the moments that came to me. I, like Bill Bryson during his treks along the Appalachian Trail, had a different journey with God than during my runs to the woods in Brown County. The physical surroundings of each place satisfied my inner needs even though their settings were different. While at the Cenacle I held tightly to my soul's invitation to write. God helped me find both places. God's guidance brought me more clarity to the questions I took to Brown County and the questions I brought with me from my meeting with the Dean. Although the fifteen-minute drive home from the Cenacle didn't compare to the five-hour drive from Brown County, my heart filled with the same sense of gratitude for the place I visited. The conversation with the Dean was frightening for a while because it forced me to consider really breaking through the comfort zone I was in, rediscovering my authentic path leading from the crossroads, and moving on to territory unknown.

My experience at The Cenacle whetted my appetite for another trip to Brown County. As I enjoyed the solitude at the Retreat Center, I was reminded of the peaceful setting in those woods in southern Indiana.

CHAPTER 14
Is the Third Time the Charm?

Sometimes, rare times, we can mark a change of seasons with such a perfect ritual that the satisfaction in the closure of one season is equal to the anticipation of the season to come.
Diana Coogle - *Living with All My Senses*

What a beautiful October day to be driving south on Interstate 65! The temperature was in the mid-70s, the sun was out, and I had my convertible top down headin' back to Brown County State Park. Three months had gone by since my last visit with Emma Moots. I looked forward to getting back to southern Indiana.

October is the month all Nashville business owners love. Nashville and Brown County are packed with wall-to-wall people soaking in the fall colors and, to the delight of the businesses in the area, helping them reach their annual quotas. The fall trees danced with color as they pulled energy to their centers in preparation for winter and cold. Early dusks and late dawns wrapped me snugly, slowed me down and invited me inward. Fall's opportunity is of an inner nature. If I could take a moment in the cooling air, I would feel a nourishment deep within, each moment an opportunity to experience life more fully.

Being back in Brown County in the fall held special meaning for me. The bright colors God splashed on the trees with His paintbrush gave me a sense of peace, a reminder of His love, and another opportunity to invite His grace into my soul.

Returning again to Brown County reminded me of fall seasons I experienced as a boy. Each fall Dad raked all the fallen leaves from our many trees into one huge pile. My sister and I got the tall stepladder out of the garage, climbed to the highest step, and jumped into the center of those inviting leaves, laughing and clapping as we fell all the way down. Dad patiently recreated the pile, and we climbed to that top step, poised for the dive down, and jumped! Again and again, Dad raked, and we floated on air all the way down.

These thoughts of my childhood reminded me of the reason I returned to Brown County. The trips brought back those happy memories from my early years I could never find. This place also helped me feel my outer self pulling my energy inward as I prepared for the winter months ahead. During those long, dark winter months, my soul warms to provide much-needed protection from the outer cold pushing against my skin, trying to find its way through. When trees drop their leaves in fall, they remind us to give in to the change, to give in to nature's way, cherishing what we have, knowing we will pass into spring. During my more inward, winter journeys, I become more contemplative. Like the little seed, I bask in the extra love and care my soul provides, and I feel excited for the green leaves returning in the spring, following their own winter of anticipation. I always hope the new spring growth I see in nature is accompanied by the new growth I feel in my soul. During the winter, I hunker down within my soul.

All these feelings and memories stayed with me as I drove through the gate and headed toward the lodge. I passed the field where I saw both the stars and the light last time as I lay there looking toward the sky. The hay growing there on my last visit was now freshly cut. I stopped my car and smelled the sweet aroma of the new-mown hay, just like the theme song for Indiana says, "The new mown hay, with all its fragrance, through the fields I used to roam." I had returned to roam the fields, hills, and hollers of Brown County, already anticipating winter's arrival.

My cabin was Professor Alexander Tansey's, another of Abe Martin's neighbors. Professor Tansey is the triplet of Tawny Apple and Emma Moots, the same on the outside, with slight differences inside. Again I was smack in the middle of a grouping of tall trees. The underbrush was untended, providing its own evidence of the coming of fall. After unpacking and settling into the Professor's place, I went to the BCI to enjoy the music.

As I awoke the next morning, The Daily Grind was calling my name. I drove into town and found Karis and Chip working hard at 8:00 sharp! We caught each other up on the past three months. I thought about my earlier statement that old friends are best unless you can take new friends and make 'em old ones. This thought reflects my feelings toward my friends at The Daily Grind. I found *The Republic* and *USA Today* on the same center table. I was so delighted to catch up on the hometown news from Columbus.

The Hummingbirds (thankfully) Headed to Warmer Climates

Finishing my coffee and breakfast and reading the papers, I returned to the state park and went to the mezzanine to write. I looked out at the beautiful fall flowers in the courtyard. Their brilliance was irresistible, so I put aside my work and went outside to relax. I noticed a big change. My tiny, beautiful, hovering helicopters, the hummingbirds, were gone, bird feeders replacing their sugar water feeders; I missed them. I saw Burt and asked him about the hummingbird feeders. He said, "Well, if we keep putting sugar water in the feeders, the hummingbirds will stay around, and it's not good for them to be here in the winter. When it gets real cold, the water will freeze, and the birds will die because there are no flowers to help provide nourishment. As soon as we take down their food supply, the birds head south for warmer weather and the food they need to survive the winter." With that explanation, I was very thankful my little friends were no longer around.

In their place, many different varieties of birds were swarming around those feeders. Like me, I discovered birds enter those big feeders in different ways. Some hopped right in and started eating. Others landed on the ledge outside the feeder, as if waiting for an invitation to the feast from a friend already eating. Some landed on the roof, running back and forth, peeking below the roof to see who was there. My life was a mirror image of the three different behaviors I observed in the birds. Sometimes I jumped right into a new job. Other times I accepted a new position and later rescinded the acceptance. My head told me to accept the position, but later my heart told me to stay where I was. I refused other offers when I peeked below the roof and didn't like who was there.

"Ed, you sound like you're from around here."

I immersed myself in another peaceful afternoon of reading and writing. I spent hours working on my laptop, refining previous writing and adding new thoughts reflecting the joy I felt in being back in Brown County at that particular season of the year. I noticed an easy, peaceful feeling surrounded me once again. The afternoon sped like wild fire through a dry forest. Later I went to the wine tasting party at the winery. A young couple from Lafayette, Indiana, sat at the table next to mine. They were visiting for the weekend and asked some advice on where to shop, eat, and drink. Those with me at the table, all locals, named their favorite places in town. I joined in by giving my own thoughts. By the time the couple had all the information they could absorb, my friend Cheryl laughed and said, "Ed, you sound like you're from around here." That comment once again made me feel at home among my new friends. I smiled after Cheryl said I could pass as someone from around there.

I ended my day at the BCI, singin' to the music of Slats and Robbie. My first full day back home was like the rest, unstructured, full of writing, reading, thinking, praying, continuing to make new friends old ones, laughing, and sharing a conversation with Cheryl about our common struggles with spirituality and our faith. She was raised in a religious environment very similar to mine. Cheryl was searching for comfort in her religious and spiritual life while holding on to many of those early religious experiences that have meaning in her current life. She had been through desert times in her life, especially a difficult divorce and financial struggles because of the divorce. She lived in a trailer on the outskirts of Nashville and barely made enough money to meet her monthly expenses. She survived those experiences and did not perish in them. I admired and respected who she was even more, knowing the story of how she got to her present stop along her journey. Her struggles weren't mine; therefore, the struggles we each had in the wilderness carried their own kind of pain. Talking to Cheryl reminded me that when we share our stories and use another to help lighten our paths, the days are brighter, and the holes in our sidewalk are not so deep. My path was lightened because I was reminded that the story of any one of us is, in part, the story of all of us. Like me, Cheryl did not perish in the wilderness but survived and got to the other side.

    I left the BCI and returned to my cabin where I found Professor Tansey waiting to hear about my day. In the peace and quiet of this secluded place, I felt a warm glow while recounting the events of the day. I was truly blessed and went to sleep thanking God for His love and grace.

    The alarm clock went off the next morning at 7:50 sharp, not in my cabin but in the one next to mine. All the laughing and chatter made it seem like 100 people were herded together next door in a cabin the same size as Professor Tansey's. I thought of the '60s when records were made and later broken by people cramming themselves into a tiny VW Beetle. Through the walls I heard visitors making plans for their Saturday adventures in Brown County. "The van's leavin' at 8:00 if you wanna go," someone announced. There didn't seem to be much opportunity next door for solitude but ample time to be in community with one another. I threw on a jacket, went out on the porch, and marveled at the swarms of people moving in and out of the cabin next door. After the 8:00 van left for destinations unknown, quiet returned. I read my daily devotion and thanked God for another beautiful day in Brown County. I went inside, got dressed, and headed for my morning coffee.

Tending to Our Souls

Each region of the country has special fall getaways where visitors come in droves to enjoy the beauty and, for a while, leave behind their daily lives. In Indiana, one such place is Brown County. At 8:30 Saturday morning bumper-to-bumper cars were already streaming into town, reminding me of the pace lap at the Indy 500. I drove around several blocks before finding a parking place five blocks from the Daily Grind.

For the first time during my three trips to the woods, a line had already formed out the front door at The Daily Grind as customers eagerly waited to be the next in line for their coffee and breakfast. How could all these strangers be descending on my coffee shop? The familiar chatter became a hearty din of animated conversations.

Hal was calling on all his ten years' experience owning this place, as coffee and specialty drinks came flying from behind the counter like baseballs spit out of the pitching machine when a player is taking batting practice. But Hal's distinctive, booming southern Indiana drawl resonated above the crowd as he yelled to every departing customer, "You have a great day!" The packed house didn't deter Hal from his ever-present, friendly demeanor. Hal has never met a stranger. A lot of visitors were having their morning coffee "jump start," and Hal smiled through it all.

I left the coffee shop and lingered in the courtyard. With a great deal of love, Rosemary was tending to her beautiful flowers this morning in the courtyard. Some of the summer beauties were joined by new friends, especially the beautiful fall colors of the chrysanthemums, with their lavender, maroon, yellow, red, orange, and white blending with the rainbow of colors in the trees above. I talked with her for the first time and asked, "How much time do you spend each day taking care of the flowers?"

"Well, it depends on the time of year, sometimes all day, sometimes a half-day, and sometimes an hour." Tending to our souls can also vary during the different seasons of the year – winter, spring, summer, and fall. We have to trust that, during the winter months, our soul, like the tiny seed, may need extra nourishment as we lie dormant. We need extra guides, lots of folks like Rosemary, to encourage our souls.

After ending my conversation with Rosemary, I returned to the park to write. When I got to my favorite spot in the lodge, it was virtually empty. All the weekend guests were out enjoying their days. Wafting up and over the mezzanine railing was a conversation from the chairs below. A young couple, three youngsters, and four older ladies were clustered in one area, telling their stories. One asked, "What do you remember about that?"

The answer began, "I remember when…"

Another said, "My earliest memory is…"

"He was a plumber," was another comment.

Someone asked, "Do you remember anything about her? I remember visiting her in the nursing home."

Switching to another person, one individual said, "I think Annette must have been a better parent."

"Yep, I have nothing but fond memories of her," was the response.

Another storyteller began by saying, "One of the letters from Dad…"

I was amazed by what I heard. All were gaining clarity and understanding as they shared memories around the circle. I struggled to type and stop listening for a minute or two. I listened to similar conversations when I was a young boy, and I've tried to pass them along to my son and my daughter and their families. Some of those stories will help their children better understand their heritage. My heart was happy because these folks were sharing memories from days past. One day, like Eric and Tracie, those youngsters in the circle will be helping other young listeners better understand their elders by sharing stories from their lives. Some of the stories told then will be the ones they heard this morning.

After concluding my writing for the day, I went to the BCI and spent time with my friends. I returned to my cabin and, as I went to bed, remembered my good fortune by being in the woods of Brown County.

I spent the next morning at the state park, hiking along one of the trails for an hour, surrounded by fall's splendor. Along this trail is a waterfall, water slowly running over the rim and falling into the lake below. Even the water was slowing down in anticipation of winter. Along the trail, I heard an unfamiliar sound. I stopped and listened, trying to figure out what the sound was and where it was coming from. In a few moments, I realized the sound was the gentle wind whistlin' a beautiful rhapsody through the tops of the mighty evergreen trees huddled close together all around me. I stood as silent as I've ever been and listened to the soothing movement of the wind through the trees. What a peaceful reminder of the grace within which I stood. Even when the sounds come in the thunder of the storm, the song of the wind whispers of the world's majesty, just as the music did that day.

I spent the afternoon and evening with friends and came back to spend time with Professor Tansey, write about my day, and take one long, last look at the moon overhead. I went to sleep thinking about my ride home the next day, a ride promising both sadness and anticipation.

After getting a good night's sleep, I read my daily devotional, dressed, and made my last visit to the coffee shop. I read the morning papers and wrote in my journal, recording my reflections on this visit and deciding whether "the third time is the charm." In my journal I noted that I went to the woods that third time anticipating my answers to the above questions. In fact, I came, having done what I don't like doing, creating preconceived notions about answering the question that began this chapter. I came fully expecting I would not return as a writer and storyteller. Will I be back? Do I need to return? Do I want to return? My final journal thought was that I would not return to the woods. I felt I had heard the stories I wanted and needed to hear, met the people God put in my path while there, and wrote what needed to be written to help me rediscover my authentic path. Therefore, my third visit was the charm because I knew I had learned what God wanted me to learn while there.

I said good-bye to Professor Tansey and thanked him for his hospitality. I checked out, found Charlie at the parking lot, said good-bye, and began my long drive north. Each trip I had taken with me fond memories of my visit. That third and final trip was no exception.

Is it Time to Make New Friends and Hear New Stories?

Although I thought I was finished with my runs to the woods, the authenticity of the people I met and the stories they shared seeped into my being. I realized the same anticipation and joy from previous trips were still there as I drove into and out of Brown County. I thanked God for allowing me the return trip and the gifts I continued to receive, gifts of conversations with dear friends, lots of laughter, and reminders of the strong connections I felt to my spot in the woods. Interestingly, both the confusion and the understanding continued with each trip. I understood more and more why I was drawn to my woods. I needed the peace, the friends, and the serenity I found there to move me back to my authentic path. However, gaining insights often leads to more questions. I make this statement with enthusiasm and hope. God continues to allow my faith to grow as He lovingly prepares me for my next calling.

Like the hero on his or her journey, I returned home with freshness and anticipation surrounding me, ready to share my experience with those I found as I arrived. Many friends and acquaintances still did not completely understand why I went to the woods in the first place. I didn't expect them to understand. However, as I shared the experiences from each trip, they gained in their understanding. I talked about the setting and its impact on my inward journey, a sense of inner peace as I continued to come closer and closer to having answers to those questions I took to the woods. The time span from my first to my third visit was over a year, giving me the opportunity to reflect and gain additional clarity that resulted from my trips to Brown County. As I gained this kind of clarity, I was able to more clearly explain to others why the trips were already in place for me before I found them. The clearest message I received from my retreats to Brown County was the desire to write and speak full time. I didn't know when that dream would be realized, but I knew my heart was telling me to move down that path. I knew I could write anywhere, and I knew I had a story to tell that people needed to hear. Part of that story would come from my writing, but other parts would come from my speaking and professional coaching.

Reflecting on this third trip, I noticed I didn't write as much as during the earlier two visits to the woods. I didn't stay as long this time, which accounts for some of the brevity. However, I wondered if another reason had to do with my friends and their stories. Those I met did become old friends. Was it time to make new friends and hear new stories? I wrote earlier I now know I can hear stories wherever I go.

CHAPTER 15
Lessons from Art and Charlie

In late fall, 2005, I lost my two dearest friends in Brown County, one to death and the other to geography. Charlie died on December 29, 2005. His long and hard-fought battle with colon cancer was finally over. A friend had called in November to tell me Charlie had entered the Veterans' Hospital in Indianapolis and the prognosis was not good. She and I agreed on a date we would go together to visit Charlie in the hospital. I drove to Nashville the evening before our visit. The morning we were to leave to drive to Indianapolis, I received an urgent phone call from my university, informing me of an emergency and mandatory meeting that afternoon. Knowing I did not have time to both visit Charlie and get to the meeting on time, I cancelled my plan to visit my friend. After learning of Charlie's death, I immediately thought of Dad. I had missed my chance to say good-bye to my dad because of the excuses I made about my hectic schedule as a high school principal. Realizing the impossibility of knowing when someone will die, I look back on both Dad's and Charlie's deaths regretting beyond belief that insignificant work priorities prevented the good-byes I so wish I could have said.

In keeping with his well-known sense of humor, Charlie asked that no service be held for him, instead wanting his family and friends to gather and remember him with smiles and laughter. At (where else) The Hotel Nashville, friends toasted the life Charlie Alber led, sharing tales of his escapades and adventures. Robbie Bowden and Slats Klug sang "In These Hills," that special memory of his beautiful Brown County by which Charlie wanted to be remembered.

I have written about Charlie's love of motorcycle racing. At a very early age, he got his start in racing at the Stoney Lonesome Motorcycle Club and raced there for many years. Later in life Charlie was still very active in the Club, encouraging young riders to follow their own dreams of becoming major dirt track racers. Charlie's final wish was that his daughter spread his ashes at a race in Charlie's honor. As I thought about his request, I've pictures hundreds and hundreds of young racers grinding ever deeper into the earth Charlie's ashes, continuing to keep alive one of the most important aspects of his life.

My final thought of Charlie's death went back to a statement he made during my first trip to the woods. He said, "I don't think He wants to deal with me. I'd probably get up there and wanna reorganize everything." Well, God was ready to deal with Charlie, but I also imagined this gentle spirit was up there reorganizing everything, with an ever-widening grin on his face.

In late fall 2005, not too long before Charlie's death, Art moved to Seattle to live with his daughter. I was in Nashville the week before Art left, so I did have a chance to say good-bye to a new friend who quickly became an old one. As I listened to Art telling me of his imminent move and looked into his eyes, I was once again reminded that our lives are a series of paradoxes. The sadness Art expressed about leaving his dear Brown County home of many years and his many friends was blended with the excitement and wonder he felt for the life awaiting him around the next curve in the road. Art had a real-life experience with the change process, the sadness of an ending, the uncertainty of that neutral zone before he got to Seattle not knowing what awaited him there, and then the anticipated excitement of a new beginning. After he moved, I tried several times to contact Art in Seattle, but to no avail. I could not find a phone listing for him in the area.

The loss of these two dear men allowed me to reflect on the gifts I received from them and shared with you. Why did I share with you so many of the stories I heard from Art and Charlie? The answer is simple: I was drawn to their stories, for they helped me regain a sense of understanding in my life and find some connections among the questions that began my quest. I shall always hold in my heart their personalities, their always-happy demeanor, and their stories. Although Charlie was only four years older than I and Art 20 years older, I had created in them a father image that I didn't see growing up next door in Columbus. Just as I allowed God to begin fathering me during this journey, I realized I had also wanted Art and Charlie to play that same role.

The wonderful, poignant stories Art and Charlie shared with me were probably very familiar to the many folks who lived in Brown County. In fact, as I listened to their stories, quite often someone around us chimed in to finish the story one of them started. But I couldn't finish their stories. Although familiar to those around them, the stories from those two friends were new, wonderful, refreshing, and inviting to me. The stories were told from their hearts and went directly to *my* heart.

Art and Charlie began as new friends who quickly became old friends as they helped me find my heart in Brown County. We all have places to travel where we find our heart. I began finding mine while surrounded by the woods, the solitude, and the sense of community I found there with these two men.

As I thought about Art and Charlie and of words I could use to describe them, I focused on their desire to have a blend between self and others. This attribute identified my struggle to help myself by helping others. It also embraced the questions I brought with me and those important items I packed in my suitcase as I began my journey.

Losing these two men from my life caused me to reflect on the lessons I learned from them, all connected to who they were as men along journeys of their own. During our time together I realized the journeys they were taking emulated ones I was trying to find for myself. Additionally, I knew that the attributes I found in Art and Charlie were the very ones I was struggling to bring into my own personal journey.

I Quickly Discovered the Genuineness and Transparency in Art and Charlie. Art and Charlie "peeled all the layers off the onion," revealing their souls. What you saw is what you got with those two guys. They had no masks to wear, so I saw the same person every time we met. Folks in Brown County learned to be open and honest with Art and Charlie. I saw this transparency every time they talked with friends and I was part of those conversations.

Caring, Concern, and a Welcoming Heart Come Back Full Cycle. Art and Charlie welcomed this outsider and made me feel at home, their caring about me amazing. Charlie always asked others how they were doing, and he always wanted to know how a particular friend or relative was doing, especially if he or she was ill. Art and Charlie never met a stranger.

I've said this before, but almost everyone I met while with Charlie asked how he was doing. Remember Dee's question as she gave him his Hug a Lady Day embrace? "How are you, Charlie? I worry about you." Dee's concern was a direct reflection of how she felt about Charlie. The concern he had for others was evident in the numerous times I heard Charlie ask Dee that same question.

A young man whom I saw most every day at The Daily Grind joined Charlie and me there one morning and shared a news story he read in the paper and saw on television. A local law enforcement agent was seriously injured in a motorcycle accident. Everyone in the coffee shop was concerned. The young man said the accident victim was unconscious. Charlie immediately left and upon returning said he called a friend who said the injured man had regained consciousness. As Charlie was leaving, the young man said, "If you need someone to go with you to the hospital, I'll be glad to go along."

As sensitive and selfless as Charlie, Art made daily phone calls to friends he knew who were ill. He took them flowers and, when he couldn't see them, always asked mutual friends if the illness had improved. All of Art's friends expressed genuine sadness when he decided to leave his Nashville home and move to Seattle to live with his daughter. At the same time they admired Art for realizing that, at age 84, he should no longer be living alone, but they were going to miss him fiercely.

Giving and Receiving Is Cyclical and When We Look for the Good in Others, We Also Find It in Ourselves. Whatever a friend asked Charlie to do, he immediately responded, "I can do that." All of Charlie's long-time friends in Brown County talked of how he would do anything to help someone. Dee, from The Nashville House, told about the many times Charlie came to her house to help her with a problem at the house – heating, plumbing, electrical – it didn't matter. Charlie was there to help. Before he developed colon cancer, Charlie was, as folks described him, robust, muscular, and handy at fixin' most anything. One time, Charlie repaired an elderly lady's porch. She was out of town at the time and never knew the name of the Good Samaritan.

One evening at dinner I said to Charlie, "To achieve all you've achieved in life, you must have worked very hard." Charlie thought for a moment and said, "Not really. I was just in the right place at the right time. I loved it all." Although Charlie was a multi-millionaire, he always wanted to give of himself to others. They, in turn, gave to him, especially as his illness got worse and he couldn't do as much as he wanted to care for himself.

Art was also a very giving person, often helping folks financially when they were in need. He helped his son set up his medical practice in Arizona. His generosity returned to him during that horrendous period after his son's suicide, for he found the gifts that he needed from Robert's friends and colleagues.

As I Saw the Honesty in Art and Charlie I Reflected on That Attribute in Myself. During all the years he lived in Brown County, Charlie never once locked his car. He kept valuable items in "my office," as he called his car, but he knew they would be there when he returned. On fall weekends Charlie did his "parking lot" job, collecting cash from visitors. Many times he told me, "They pay me way too much for what I do." He said he could easily pocket some of that cash and "no one would know the difference." But Charlie would never do that. The honesty stretched way beyond Charlie. If I lost my wallet in Nashville, I knew someone would find it, find me, and return it. Most importantly, folks there were honest and forthright with their feelings. I *always* knew their comments to me came from their hearts. Understanding this honesty was such an inviting feeling because I responded with honest feelings.

Unlike those in Brown County, I have not always been trustworthy in my dealings with others. I lied and I kept my secrets. I escaped to the office during those times I did not want to be at home, even though I didn't have work to do. I kept my gambling and drinking a secret as long as I could. I once again began smoking after twenty-seven years. I was a closet smoker and didn't want any of my friends, or Bonnie, to know. Having kept my secrets and told my lies made it very difficult for me to trust others, because I knew they shouldn't trust me. I learned both trust and honesty from Art and Charlie. I quit hiding behind my secrets and lies, because I stopped engaging in those behaviors.

Observing the Unassuming Behavior in Art and Charlie Helped Me Get My Ego Blended with My Essence. The ego I nurtured in the suburbs meant nothing in the woods. Although dramatic differences in economic status existed in Brown County, the playing field was leveled when friends gathered. I couldn't tell the millionaires from those who didn't know when their next meal would appear. Again, Charlie was an excellent example of this characteristic. If a person met Charlie on the street, in his dirty jeans, red, loose suspenders, stained T-shirt, sloppy shoes, and unshaven face, he might think he would be one looking for his next meal, but he wasn't. Art too met with much success in his life, but he rarely talked about his many accomplishments. I, on the other hand, was quick to share my successes with anyone who would listen, I mean *anyone*! I didn't have time to hear of the positive contributions of others because I was too busy sharing my own. I didn't listen and let others share because I was too full of myself. As I spent time with Art and Charlie I learned how insignificant my accomplishments were.

I Learned the Importance of Both Wandering and Wondering. Through the stories they told, I found the souls of these two surrogate fathers, but I also found the wandering they did up and down the hills and hollers, seeking an even greater sense of authenticity. They searched with their hearts and never got lost even though Brown County was full of back road crossroads. Brown County was full of back road crossroads. Because Art and Charlie knew how to maneuver those crossroads they found their way sooner and easier than I. As I watched and listened, I followed their lead as I searched to reclaim my authentic path.

I Learned to Love These Two Men as They Did Me. People in Brown County both expressed and received love openly, their openness causing me to do the same. As I said, each of Charlie's friends loved him from the bottom of his or her heart and would do anything for him. He returned that love without hesitating for a moment. This sincerity was not reserved only for Charlie. He paid forward that love to others.

Life's Challenges Neither Defeated Art and Charlie Nor Robbed Them of Happiness. Both Art and Charlie had a world of struggles in their lives, the same struggles as humans anywhere else. The ways they chose to handle those struggles amazed me. Seldom did I see these two men without a smile on their faces. Thinking about my conversation with Charlie that night when he said, "I loved it all," I remembered Rabbi Harold Kushner's book, *When Bad Things Happen to Good People.* I reflected on all the "bad things" that have come Charlie's way during his lifetime: he's been involved in some horrific, life-threatening motorcycle accidents; he lost his 42 year old son a year ago following a heart attack; he was divorced from the woman "I still love"; he survived failed business ventures; he was diagnosed with colon cancer in February, 2004; he was diagnosed with a non-malignant tumor on his back; he was deaf in one ear and only had 30% hearing in the other; during his late years he stuttered because "my mind works faster than my mouth"; he used a walking stick for balance; he was very feeble and lost a lot of weight. How did he keep his happy disposition? He kept it because he rose above it all, made his peace with God, and led the life he coveted – one day at a time. Most often when friends asked him about his day, he said, "I've had a wonderful day." Charlie always looked for the positives in his own life and the lives of others. People here knew all too well about

Charlie's struggles, but his happy disposition allowed them to learn an important lesson: we determine our own happiness.

Art lost his son to suicide but he, too, exuded happiness. He was closer to a sense of peace about his son's death when I met him, allowing him to become the joyful person he was before that tragedy.

God cannot protect us from the suffering we experience in our lives since we cannot escape the consequences of our humanness or our choices. But if we are connected with God, as Art and Charlie were, we receive His unlimited love and compassion for us as we suffer. He is there when we need Him, just like Art and Charlie were.

I want to summarize this lesson with a statement I began using several years ago: Tell me who you walk with and I'll tell you who you'll become. I walked with Art and Charlie for almost two years, sometimes in person and sometimes in my writing. At the end of that part of my journey I hoped beyond hope I was becoming more like them.

CHAPTER 16
My Desert Oasis

If we want a free and peaceful world, if we want to make the deserts bloom and man grow to greater dignity as a human being – we can do it.

Eleanor Roosevelt

My Minister and His Message

To catch sight of my authentic self, I went to the hills of Brown County, The Cenacle Retreat Center, and I also traveled to the desert. In March, 2005, I boarded Southwest flight 2779 and flew from Chicago to Albuquerque. After a three-hour drive the next morning, I was at Ghost Ranch, New Mexico, where I spent six days in solitude, surrounded by the beauty of the desert. I hoped to find the desert blooming in me so that I could grow to a greater dignity as a human being as I continued to listen for my inner voice.

The 21,000 acre ranch has a long and fascinating history which includes cattle rustlers, ghosts, poker games, atomic scientists, dinosaurs, dudes, and Georgia O'Keeffe, who spent years capturing on canvas the beauty of this place. I found out about Ghost Ranch one day while having lunch with my minister Clinton Roberts. He and his wife Deb were the Co-Associate Pastors at my church. Clint knows well my current crossroads experience, my various retreats these past two years, and the writing I was doing. During lunch Clint asked, "Ed, have you ever been to Ghost Ranch?" I told him I didn't know about Ghost Ranch, so he went on to explain a little about the conference and retreat center that opened in 1955 when the Presbyterian Church took ownership of the land. He also said he had been there three times for personal retreats. During our lunch, Clint said at least four times, "Ed, you have got to go to Ghost Ranch." We finished our lunch and went our separate ways. Not knowing about this beautiful place, I wasn't sure why Clint suggested I go there. A couple of weeks after that luncheon engagement, I saw Clint at church. "Did you ever follow up on the Ghost Ranch idea?" he asked.

"No, not yet, "I replied.

"You should look into it. I think you would find some time there helpful to you as you continue to work on your writing." The next Tuesday I called Ghost Ranch and talked with Gary Salazar, who was in charge of retreats for the center. I booked my accommodation, and, like my response to my other retreats, I felt such a rush of anticipation. The very next Sunday I saw Clint in the hallway before church. I could not wait to tell him I would soon be off on my next adventure. The vestibule was full of Sunday morning worshipers, but Clint yelled down a long hallway to where Deb was working in her office. "Hey, Deb. Ed's going to Ghost Ranch!" Then to me he said, "Be sure to take lots of pictures and tell me all about it when you get back."

Meeting Art's Friend

My plane touched down right on time. I was so excited about my week-long adventure. However, before going to the desert, I spent Palm Sunday with Jane Harmes the minister who so masterfully conducted the very difficult memorial service for Art's son, Bob, after his suicide at her church in Placitas, New Mexico.

Jane was busy preparing last minute details for this important day in the Christian calendar. Still, she took time to give me a huge hug. The service was beautiful, and the choir sang a traditional Easter Cantata. I met several of her parishioners during my time there. Las Placistas Presbyterian Church is a very welcoming community. I felt as if I were right back in Brown County, talking and laughing with my new friends, all of whom extended me a warm hello. The membership was small, so as a newcomer I stood out among the crowd, just as I did when I first arrived in Brown County.

After church, Jane and I had a chance to spend some time together over lunch. The warm and caring voice I heard last summer on Art's audiotape of his son's memorial service became real as Jane and I talked. Very quickly we began sharing our individual stops along our journeys. We talked a lot about our struggles with depression. We discovered we share common interests in several authors, having attended lectures, seminars, and workshops over the years conducted by these individuals. We talked some about *Lessons from the Porch*, and she wanted to know more about my current writing and the reason I was doing that writing at this time in my life. I shared my four crossroads experiences and explained why this current fifth time at a crossroads had brought me to New Mexico.

As it turns out, Jane was considering a new calling in her life at exactly the same time I was. She was planning to stay at her church the same amount of time I planned to stay at Aurora University before we both retired and moved on to our new adventures. Jane struggled with many of the identical fears as I, which included breaking through our current comfort zones; feeling uncertain about financial security; taking risks; accommodating a completely new, less structured life-style; wondering if we could really follow our new callings; continuing to find happiness and personal meaning in our lives; finding ways to be of service to others; figuring out if we were really ready to venture forth; and, finally, wrestling with the fact that we could meet with failure in our new callings.

I felt connected with this lady from the moment I heard the tape of Bob Jahnke's memorial service. That connection was strengthened beyond belief as Jane and I talked about our present and future lives. God, I know You allowed me to spend time with Jane Harmes.

The Grandeur of Ghost Ranch

I said good-bye to Jane after lunch and headed toward my destination. The drive to Ghost Ranch was spectacular, north on Interstate 25, then a shortcut around Santa Fe, and finally some narrow, winding roads ending at an elevation of over 6,500 feet. I tried to do the impossible, both drive and look out at the vistas all around. The giant, flat-head buttes rising abruptly above the surrounding land, the snow on the mountaintops, and the desert vegetation were overpowering in their beauty. I especially noticed the cactus plants, already showing their long, cone-shaped spring flowers. Some were a deep violet while others were yellow. I remembered that during the winter months, they were tiny, sleeping seeds, protected by the strong, upright arms of the cactus plants. They were being nourished in preparation for their return at this time of year.

On the last lag of the trip, I drove thirteen miles from Bodes General Store in Abiquiu to the entrance at Ghost Ranch. I followed the long, curving, dirt road to the administration center, registered and found out which cottage was mine. Until I arrived at Tamarisk, my cottage, I thought it a bit strange that I wasn't given a key. Once I got there, I realized there were no locks on the doors. At first I felt uneasy. There I was on a 21,000-acre ranch with no way to lock myself in my quarters and no way to keep others out. My concern went away once I realized the total trust that must pervade this place. Only the hospitals where I received treatment for depression offered this same sense of trust. Suddenly just the simple fact of not having keys to my living space brought a connection with my past.

Tamarisk, without phones or televisions, had striking similarities to my three cabins in Brown County. My room, with a single bed, opened to a small living area with a sofa and three chairs. Down the hall were a bathroom and another sleeping room identical to mine. Fortunately, no one was staying in that other room. I had the living space to myself and did not have to share the bathroom with anyone. The furnishings were minimal, again reminding me of the Spartan accommodations I loved in Brown County.

The primary difference between the two settings was my view once I stepped out the door. In Brown County I saw the beautiful woods surrounding my cabins. At Ghost Ranch I had a spectacular view of the mountains. Describing the mountains was difficult because they are so awe-inspiring. I thought and thought of appropriate words, but they didn't come to me. Describing the beauty in southern Indiana was, initially, equally difficult; however, I spent more time there, was familiar with the area, and the words finally came.

More than the scenery surprised me about Ghost Ranch. First of all, I did not know when I made my reservation that in 2005 the Presbyterian Church, USA, celebrated its 50th Anniversary of ownership of this 21,000-acre paradise. In 1955 Arthur and Phoebe Pack donated all of Ghost Ranch to the church, except for a small portion purchased in the late 1930s by artist, Georgia O'Keeffe. When she arrived in New Mexico in 1933, she said, "When I got to New Mexico, that was mine. As soon as I saw it, that was my country."

I soon got wonderfully lost in the very loose structure I imposed on each day, once again reminding me of my retreats in Brown County and The Cenacle Spirituality and Retreat Center. I began each day at the Meditation Garden. I was the only one in the garden during my thirty-minute silent meditation. This spot is a small yet beautiful parcel just behind the original Pack home. The adobe house provided a sight barrier and protected the garden on two sides, and an old, decaying, wooden fence protected a third side. The fourth was open to the mountains well beyond my reach but not my sight. While in the garden I repeated the prayers I said each morning on my back patio at home. As I finished my prayers, I felt a sense of peace even greater than I felt with my surroundings. I thanked God for making it possible for me to visit Ghost Ranch, just as I thanked Him for his guidance in helping me choose Brown County, The Cenacle, the ocean, and the mountains of North Carolina.

Because of the elevation the mornings were always cool. After finishing my meditation each day, I returned to Tamarisk to read and write inside in the warmth, allowing the temperature outside to warm up a bit. Most mornings it either rained or snowed a short while, but by early afternoon, the sun was high overhead, and the sky was a beautiful, deep shade of blue.

Finding the Tower with a View

As each day got warmer and sunnier, I wanted to get outside and enjoy it to the fullest. Ghost Ranch has nine marked hiking trails. I walked each of them during the week, but the most impressive one was the path to Chimney Rock. The path to the 1,500 foot summit is full of curves and switchbacks, similar to the back roads in Brown County. Like those roads, the trail at times is quite narrow. My fear of heights caused me to stay well to the inside of the trail, and I tried not to look over the outside of the curve. When I did look, I felt an ache in the pit of my stomach, but I trudged on. Fortunately, I remembered a sign at the beginning of the trail warning me to bring a good supply of water. I went to the Trading Post and bought the biggest bottle I could find, and I'm so glad I did. By the time I reached the top, after a two hour climb, the bottle was over half empty.

The walk to the top was invigorating. The dirt trail was steep, so I stopped along the way to drink some water and luxuriate in the beauty surrounding me. As with other, much different paths in my life, I thought of turning back at several points, thinking, "I can't do this. I will never reach the top." However, as I climbed, I saw other hikers at the top, barely visible because they looked so tiny and far away. Seeing them and remembering God's words to me from the front seat of our tandem bike, I kept pedalin'. When I reached the top, I congratulated myself. For once in my life I didn't turn back before I realized my dream.

Before telling you of the surprise I found at the top, I want to share the source of my motivation to complete my goal. During one rest stop I was captivated with what I saw on the side of the mountain farthest away from me. As I sat on a big boulder, I studied the unmelted snow remaining on the side of that mountain. As my focus sharpened, I saw the partial image of an angel left in the snow. She was incomplete, but in her unfinished beauty, I knew she was encouraging me to fly to the top of Chimney Rock. If other travelers looked at this same snow mass, they probably saw different images, if they saw anything at all except snow. But for me my angel was there telling me my dream was within reach. I began my ascent once again.

At two different stops along the way to the top of Chimney Rock I saw stacks of small, flat rocks placed there by hikers who preceded me. By the time I saw them, the stacks were quite tall but well balanced. I carefully placed my small rock at the top of each tower, realizing that as I did so others would hike the trail after me and place their rocks on top of mine.

For me this simple act of stacking the rocks reflected the sense of community I felt there. Each rock touched the one both above and below it, just as we touch those with whom we are in community. In placing my rock, I had to cooperate with previous hikers so that the tower didn't tumble and destroy the sense of togetherness I felt both with God and with the fellow travelers I would never know.

Arriving at the top, I knew why I was there. As I turned in every direction, I had the most humbling sensation in my life. I knew I was looking at one of the miracles of God's loving work. A bald eagle soared effortlessly overhead, its wings spread to their fullest length, and it glided, using the updraft of the wind coming through the mountain valleys below. The eagle represents the boundless spirit of freedom. Living as he does on the tops of lofty mountains amid the solitary grandeur of nature, he has unlimited ability to seek the freedom he represents. As I thought about these representations, I recalled the words to the song I included earlier "I Wish I Knew How…" In that song the artist, Nina Simone, sang these words: "I wish I could be like a bird in the sky. How sweet it would be if I found I could fly." Her words fit so well with the eagle's flight I saw, and I realized the eagle and I have much in common. We both seek freedom, and I was living in the solitary grandeur of nature, hoping to continue discovering the boundless spirit I was looking for since that first day in Brown County.

At the top of Chimney Rock I saw many mountain ranges within the 21,000 acre ranch. To my utter amazement, I found the viewing point I was looking for.

Because of the altitude, I saw those same four paths I discovered atop the tower at the crossroads but couldn't find when I climbed the tower that day at Brown County State Park. The images along those paths I saw atop Chimney Rock had changed dramatically since I first saw them at the beginning of my journey.

The view to the north was not so hazy this time. The witches and demons gave way to more angels, whose wings were no longer hidden behind them. With greater clarity I saw the road sign marked Spiritual. The sense of fear I've felt about the meaning of God in my life was diminished, and I was able to admit that my sense of peace and comfort increased during the two years since I looked out of that first tower.

The adventurers I initially saw were still there as I looked eastward toward my Personal path. The knights in shining armor had driven away the highwaymen and warriors. The beautiful peacemaker, with the long, flowing blonde hair, was dancing with the images I saw. Lots of little boys and girls, each pair holding hands, replaced the arguments, looks of fear, and silence. I knew Little Eddie was there among them. It was raining, so they were all dressed in matching yellow rain slickers, hats, and boots. They were laughing and singing as their boots found the biggest water puddles. As they landed square in the middle of each, their laughter echoed through the mountain ranges. My Personal path was much more serene. The potential danger from the highwaymen and warriors was gone. Little Eddie had found his place among the other boys and girls who were having such fun.

Looking toward the south, I once again saw a familiar landscape. Soon I found the Professional road sign with its arrow pointing straight ahead. I realized I recognized this path more clearly than the other three because I spent more of my life along this path while ignoring the others. My co-workers were still there. However, this time I saw fewer arguments, a sense of cooperation abounding. More of those along the path seemed more self-confident as their feet moved them along. I saw myself among the images, a huge trash can beside me with the word "Masks" stenciled on the side. The trash can was filled to the brim with images of myself I have known over the years. I saw people along the path asking me questions. I listened a lot and talked very little. I encouraged them to find their own answers inside them, thus leading them to the decisions they wanted and needed to make. I asked questions of others, but I realized I was not seeking their advice or their answers to my questions. I simply wanted them to listen. I noticed I felt good about living from within rather than from without. I walked straighter and with more self-assurance than at any other time in my life. Finally, my own image had grown dimmer along my Professional path. Struggling even to find myself interacting with my colleagues, I felt I wouldn't be on that path much longer.

As I turned toward my western view, I finally saw the path with the "Authentic" sign on the pole next to it. An even greater sense of calmness surrounded me because the marker for this path was more distinct than when I first saw it from atop the tower many months ago. I understood my sense of peace as I realized the telling of my story through my writing gave me a tranquil feeling I had not recognized before. Throughout my writing, I often referred to reclaiming my authentic self. A few times, in earlier parts of the book, I did use the word path, instead of self. At those times, I didn't know for certain that the words were the same. I was feeling more confident about my earlier thoughts. This path meandered up a steep mountain I saw in the distance. As I studied the path, I found another pattern left behind by the winter snow. I didn't see another angel but a series of what I thought were half circles leading to the top. I assumed the circles were completed around the other side of the mountain I could not see. The snow's melting pattern also created differently patterned lines connecting the circles one with the other all the way to the top. I was reminded of the labyrinths I had walked in my town of Naperville and at The Cenacle Spirituality and Retreat Center.

I stayed on top of Chimney Rock for a long time, sitting on one of the enormous boulders. I could not help but look all around me and say a prayer to God for encouraging me to take a hike I never thought I could complete. I descended Chimney Rock more quickly than I climbed it. The entire hike took four hours, but it seemed like four minutes as I got to the base, stopped, looked up to the top one last time, and reflected on my experience.

Stumbling Upon My Authentic Path

While at Ghost Ranch, I walked my third labyrinth. The now familiar concentric circles were set at the base of the beautiful rock formation called Kitchen Mesa. Mesas are the smaller siblings of the buttes I saw on my drive to Ghost Ranch. Before beginning my winding path through the labyrinth, I sat on a rock, anticipating my journey.

As I sat on the rock, I realized that on my previous two walks I purposely put my thoughts and feelings in a magic file cabinet next to the entrance, locked the drawer and moved into the labyrinth free of clutter in my mind and heart. This time I wanted to carry my thoughts and feelings with me. I wanted to keep with me the questions I had when I first went to Brown County and the struggle I had finding my way out of the crossroads. This time I wanted God and me to walk the labyrinth together. I asked Him to provide continued guidance, to help me keep Him in front showing the way, and to help me release the struggles I kept too deeply inside as I entered the other two labyrinths. I also recalled the lines in Dante's *The Divine Comedy* where he uses labyrinthine terms to say, "Midway along our road of life, I woke to find myself in a secret dark wood; for I had lost the narrow path… Yet there I found my path for good."

As I entered the labyrinth, I thought about its structure. It is the same wherever one finds a labyrinth, anywhere in the world. But each time I've walked the labyrinth, I have had unique feelings because I was at differing points along my way toward once again finding my authentic path. When I walked the labyrinth in Naperville, I had just returned from my first trip to Brown County. During that walk I wanted to increase the clarity of that retreat. As I entered the second labyrinth at The Cenacle, I remembered my other retreats that summer – my second trip to Brown County, my connection with the hero's journey, my trips to the ocean, and my providential meeting with the dean as I began the fall semester at my university. I connected the cyclical path of the hero's journey with the same circle I would travel in the labyrinth. I also remembered the words of author Caroline Adams I quoted earlier: "You are on the path… exactly where you are meant to be right now."

During this third walk I felt ready to find the synchronicity of my disparate solitary experiences, and I asked God to help me find the connections among those different retreats. I felt my legs getting heavy, and I knew God had tied weights securely around my waist, encouraging me to take my journey slowly enough to understand the meaning it had for that time in my life. I looked up to see the beautiful mountains completely surrounding the labyrinth, and I looked down to find my way along the path. I recalled my hikes in the woods of Brown County where I was reminded to look both ways. I also thought about my brief conversation with the Chicago Cub fan as he got up from his chair in the mezzanine courtyard and helped me enjoy the hummingbirds hovering above.

I continued thinking about the constancy of the labyrinth's structure. I understood something for the first time: Each labyrinth has its own unique look in its distinctive setting. The uniqueness of the physical setting matches perfectly with the changing thoughts and feelings I had as I entered each labyrinth.

As I continued my slow pace, I felt the weights around my waist falling one by one to the ground. My step was lighter, not faster, but much less encumbered.

Arriving at the center of the labyrinth, I saw a huge boulder awaiting me. Just as the setting itself, the center of each of the three labyrinths was different. In Naperville's smaller labyrinth no centerpiece exists, just a small space to stand and reflect. At The Cenacle an old tree stump provided a resting place.

As I sat absolutely still, I heard a quiet inner voice telling me that the labyrinth's constant structure represents my unwavering love in God and the confidence that He is working out His perfect plan through me. My inner voice also told me that, although the physical characteristics of the labyrinth remain constant over time, the unique environments I discovered parallel the changes I find in my beliefs about God's unrelenting love for me. As I allow my beliefs about God to grow in my soul, I see God with different eyes, eyes that extend God's meaning in my life. Those extensions will never cease.

I took time to search my soul for the meaning of my authentic path. When I began writing *Lessons from the Crossroads*, I thought I needed to find the authentic path out there just waiting for me. As my writing evolved throughout the book, so did the understanding of my authentic path. I didn't need to find the path, rather I needed to rediscover the path I've had all my life.

I was not looking for a physical path but one I carry in my soul. I reflected on the day in Brown County when Charlie and I were standing in the middle of the field in Helmsburg. There I realized I was findin' home as I revisited childhood memories that would never have seen the light of day had he and I not spent time together that Saturday many months ago. I also wrote that home for me is also the physical place where I grew up. The labyrinth is a physical place, but also it is the meaning and memories I have deep in the recesses of my very being.

I knew the authentic path I was trying to rediscover would also have distinctive characteristics. Rather than stumbling upon a new authentic path, I needed to discover again the path I've always been on that held the greatest meaning at any given time, the path toward answering the questions I took to my first retreat in Brown County, and the path to my soul. As I've written, much of my adult life was full of what was best for me. I was very selfish, and you've read many examples of this character trait. My selfishness took many forms along all three of those paths I saw at the crossroads. I lost my authentic path. As I have worked to replace selfishness with selflessness along my spiritual, personal and professional paths, I am again walking my authentic path. The path I tried to reclaim was unique because it represented needs that were highly personal to me. No one can walk the path as I. The nature of the other three paths that combine to help me redefine an authentic path changes over time. As I sat on the rock and reflected on my retreats, I discovered that, among other things, my authentic path represents a place for meditation, an experience for prayer, a call to bust free of my comfort zone, a trigger for growth, and an opportunity to consider the questions surrounding me at any particular moment.

Understanding the personal nature of each path brought me to the thought that the labyrinth itself represents the searching I was doing to get back on my authentic path. I know the labyrinth represents for me the blend between my inner and outer self. As I walked the path, I constantly moved from the inside out and from the outside in, along one synchronous, circular trail. During my journey inward I realized that journey will continue to be affected by the part of me exposed to the world. My friends in Nashville became a strong outer force that tremendously impacted my inner journey. Just as I sought solitude, while at the same time needing to be in community with others, I cannot fully understand the search for my inner voice unless that voice is cognizant of my outer life.

However, when I began this journey, I had lost that inner voice that I found while writing *Lessons from the Porch* and once again became overly influenced by what others wanted of me rather than what I wanted of myself. My small, inner voice increased its decibel level as I walked the labyrinth at Ghost Ranch.

As I walked, I recalled the changing images I saw along my personal, professional, and spiritual paths. Because I reflected on those paths as I moved along the labyrinth's circle, I felt a braiding together of my personal, professional, and spiritual paths with my reclaimed Authentic path, similar to braiding different strands of hair into one single, tight braid where the individual strands are no longer detectable.

I also thought of my earlier writing about the connections between wandering and wondering. I was wandering along the path, but I wondered as I walked about the meaning the labyrinth holds for my life. I had two affirmations about my earlier thinking that not all who wander are lost as long as the journey of the feet is accompanied by the journey of the heart. The wandering and wondering are not separate activities – as I had thought over the years – but rather they emerge contemporaneously along a circular path.

As I sat on the big rock in the center of the Ghost Ranch labyrinth, I gained a clarity like I've never known in my life. I finally understood the meaning of the authentic path that has always been there for me since before I was born. I didn't recognize it until I understood that I had traveled the other three as separate paths, never seeing connections. I had different masks for each of those disconnected parts of my life. Until I recognized that my masks were not allowing the authentic Ed Poole to see the light of day, I never saw the interconnections among them. I led three separate lives, depending upon which path I was on at that time and which masks I wore as I walked that path. God, in His infinite wisdom, allowed me to walk those three paths separately, knowing all along I would discover the folly of the decision He allowed me to make. He also knew, eventually, I would find the inseparability of those three paths. As I sat on the rock at Ghost Ranch, I saw those three paths all coming together for the first time. I no longer felt the need to travel them separately. I couldn't find my ever-present Authentic path until I understood what had been happening along the other three. At an earlier point of my understanding, I had been following an unconnected life path that hid my authentic path.

I learned my core set of values from my parents as they nurtured me. God chose the parents He wanted for me, because they held the values He wanted me to have. As I grew and matured, two phenomena emerged: I retained some of those values I had at birth while at the same time altering others to match my life's flow. Until writing this book, I didn't recognize I have retained more of my parents' religious beliefs than I ever thought possible. Even after finishing *Lessons from the Porch*, I still had much inner work to do in understanding and accepting this new revelation. Because I walked the other three paths separately, I didn't internalize their overlapping core values until I sat on that rock.

Once I understood my authentic path, while sitting on that Ghost Ranch boulder, I revisited my core values. I also realized that my beliefs, intertwined with my core values, evolve over time. As long as the evolving nature of my beliefs doesn't contradict my core values, I continue down the authentic path I did not recognize. If I feel the dissonance, I know I have lost my authentic path. I definitely felt this discomfort when I took that first retreat to Brown County. I just didn't know from where the discomfort came. At those times, I need to question and find out what's causing my angst and the need to rediscover my authentic path. I need to go back and re-examine my core values to see if my belief structure is still aligned. If the alignment is not there, I need to stop, take a time out, and understand the disconnects. The time out I chose this time was my retreats God knew I needed to take. As I sat on that rock, I also saw the labyrinth path as circular, allowing the person walking the path to return to the place he or she began and see the ending differently from the beginning. I thought of the hero's journey, another circular adventure, where the hero arrives home and also sees it differently from when he or she left to begin the journey.

Just because I finally realized I have always had an authentic path doesn't mean life is easy down that path. There will always be work to do. My danger is becoming so comfortable along that authentic path I am unwilling to recognize when the path is no longer aligned and what I should do to create that alignment I sought as I wrote this book. Moving along the path that continues to hold my heart will be uncomfortable and full of hard work, perhaps even stressful at times. But if I resist the stress and discomfort, I meet even more resistance and stress.

All of my life's lessons brought me closer to the path I needed to find as I wrote *Lessons from the Crossroads*. The lessons I learned came from the other three paths. By the inward journeys I took along those paths, I was able to recognize the path I was seeking.

While sitting at the center of the labyrinth, I recalled the meanings for "authentic" and "path" I found in the *New World Dictionary*. Among other words, the dictionary used "genuine," "that can be accepted," and "trustworthy," in defining authentic. Genuine means "sincerely and honestly felt or experienced." The word path means "track or way worn by footsteps; trail." For me these words signify that I have been along this path before. Since the authentic path is mine and mine alone, who else but me could have traveled down it?

After sitting on the boulder over an hour, I got up and retraced my steps, arriving at the point where I began and seeing it for the first time. My heart sang as I left the labyrinth. And there was no possible way the song I heard and the spring

I felt in my feet could have been there had I not had the precise experiences along my journey that led me to Ghost Ranch. God allowed my series of retreats, and the writing accompanying those retreats, to unfold in their logical and natural order. I had no idea I would end up at Ghost Ranch. I could not have known that. I didn't know where my next retreat would be until I was ready to find it. My journey did indeed evolve as I moved closer to God and allowed Him to point my way toward my authentic path.

The Alfalfa Field

A gigantic alfalfa field was right across the road from the main administration building, which is right next to Tamarisk. The last night I was there, while I drove back to the ranch from dinner, my headlights caught at least thirty deer eating the alfalfa in the field. I turned the car at a slight angle so the lights would allow me to see them better. A few got skittish and ran away, but many stayed right where they were. I remembered the big field of hay in Brown County and my last night there when I lay in that huge field of hay.

I got out of the car and walked toward the alfalfa field. Realizing the deer were more nervous than I, I ventured forth. I lay down in the field just as I had in Brown County and stared up at the stars overhead. Because of the 6,500 foot altitude, the stars were even more brilliant than in Brown County. The sky was black. I lay in the field for about thirty minutes, thanking God for directing me to this beautiful place. The moon was full, creating shadows all around me. I still had a difficult time realizing I was in a place that reflected such a brush stroke of God's beauty. Standing up and walking to my car, I found my clothes were wet from the light dew in the field. Just as in Brown County, I could not have cared less that I wore wet clothing. I returned to Tamarisk to spend my last night at Ghost Ranch. The next morning I took one last look around. I packed my bag, closed up my laptop, checked out, and drove down the winding dirt road underneath the large Ghost Ranch welcome sign.

Leaving Ghost Ranch

I left Ghost Ranch with two lessons indelibly burned into my soul: After much searching, I once again saw my four paths from atop Chimney Rock. I noticed the differences in the images I found this time compared to the first time I saw them through the four windows at the top of those 71 tower steps at the crossroads. Secondly, I once again found my authentic path while walking along the labyrinth. And I understood that my authentic self and my authentic path are one in the same. When I am my authentic self, I am on my authentic path. When I lose sight of the authenticity of who I am, I stray off my authentic path and need to find my way back. If I had not been exactly where I needed to be, at the precise time God wanted me there, I could never have found these lessons. They had been waiting there for me forever. I just needed to get there to find them. I wanted so badly to turn my Ghost Ranch experience over to God and simply wait to see what He had in store for me. Before driving under the huge posts at the entrance to Ghost Ranch, I pulled my car over to the side of the road, turned off the engine, and sat in the stillness. I asked God to guide me and help me make meaning of it. More so than during any other retreats, I did let go and let God direct my thoughts and emotions as I left. I was aware of God's presence and the significance of my sojourn to Ghost Ranch, New Mexico, another life-changing moment in my life.

CHAPTER 17
Understanding My Authentic Path Didn't Remove the Fears

When I began writing, I didn't know what my fears were. I knew they were there, as they often have been when I felt the need to expand my comfort zone. Finding the authentic path that God put in place before I was born helped clarify the fears that were part of my journey. The struggle for understanding and clarity never escaped me, and I never want to be free of either the questions or the answers. Sue Monk Kidd used her own words to describe the journey toward her authentic path, words that hold such meaning for me. Her strong desire to be the person others wanted her to be captures much of my adult life. Eventually she realized that being directed by the wishes and expectations of others was losing its meaning. I am slowly but surely coming to that same realization in my life. She said, "The over arching roles that created the theme song for my life -- Perfectionist, Performer, Pleaser, Good Little Girl, submissive church goer, passive and traditional wife – began to lose their music. It's anguish to come to that place in life where you know all the words but none of the music." Kidd's thoughts and mine are so very similar. I was a good little boy. I went to church when I didn't want to. I was passive growing up. And I have filled the roles as a husband and father that resembled what I saw at home. I began struggling with changes I needed to make in those roles to improve the image Eric and Tracie find in their views of what a father should be and do, views I did not see, or recognize, growing up.

I've always ended conversations with Eric and Tracie by telling them I love them. We give hugs and kisses when we meet and when we part. We talk often on the phone. We all initiate those calls – Eric and Tracie with each other, and each of them with me. They are willing to share their problems with me, and I always try to listen and encourage. At the time of this writing, Eric's work as a real estate broker in southern Oregon had taken a bad financial turn. He struggled with what other work he could find to support his family. I kept telling him the plan for his life and that of his family had been in place before any of them were born, and God's plan would play itself out in the way He intended. I added Eric and his family to my morning prayer mantra, not specifically asking God to provide this or that, but to help Eric and Stacy be aware of the messages He was sending them.

Although I was often an absent father when Eric and Tracie were growing up I now have a strong desire to be present, either physically or spiritually. I have also been present, as often as possible, for my four granddaughters, who all are wonderful young human beings; while I am not trying to make up for my absence with Eric and Tracie, I realized I missed a lot of fun times with my own kids, and I don't want to miss those with my granddaughters.

Eric and Tracie also discovered their dad's fallibility and his humanness, for which I am very grateful. Both of them had their dad up on a pedestal. While I appreciated their love and respect for me, at the same time I knew they had put me in an inappropriate place in their minds. In part through their anger toward me when I left home, I was taken off that high position. As the three of us have talked about why I left home, I removed most of my masks, and they saw their father with a very confused soul and spirit. They continue to love me deeply, but I wonder if they replaced some of that unconditional love and respect with a lack of trust they formed toward their father as I struggled to rediscover my authentic path.

Understanding My Authentic Path Didn't Remove the Fears

My struggles with finding the way out of the crossroads sent me off on my retreats into solitude and community. My struggles also brought forth questions. Questions that emerged from the eight I took with me to the woods helped me discover the path carrying me from the present moment toward the dreams down my authentic path. Writer Zora Neale Hurston said, "There are years that ask questions, and years that answer." I knew the year to ask my questions was the year I fell from the helicopter. I knew eventually there would come a year when I found answers. The three years of writing this book were an ongoing reflection on those questions I took to Brown County.

I struggled to place those questions in God's hands, and I continued to struggle with how to pray to God to help me be in the present, knowing the present is the only place I can truly be. Often I forget that I've unconditionally turned my life over to God. And when I do remember to turn it over to God, why do I always want His immediate response to appear in bright, flashing, neon lights? I know God doesn't work with me that way. Secondly, His answers will come, not as bright lights but as subtle messages that I must be open to.

As I learn to wait and listen, my legs often get this very heavy feeling like the weights I felt when God and I began our labyrinth journey at Ghost Ranch. Perhaps those are the times God is telling me to slow down, live in the moment, and not fret about what I've asked of Him. Maybe God is sending me the answer in these words: "Ed, you're doing fine right now. If you need me, I'm always around, but you can make it on your own for awhile. Live a bit more with the questions."

As I was writing this section of the book, a friend sent me some wonderful thoughts. These thoughts came from an unknown author and in part said, "Listen-up: I am God! Today I will be handling all your problems. Please remember I do not need your help. If the devil happens to deliver a situation to you that you cannot handle, do not attempt to resolve it. Kindly put it in the SFGTD (something for God to do) box. It will be addressed in MY TIME – not yours. Once the matter is placed in the box, do not hold on to it or remove it. If it is a situation that you think you are capable of handling, please consult Me in prayer to be sure that it is the proper course of action. Because I do not sleep nor do I slumber, there is no need for you to lose any sleep. Rest my child."

I am taking tiny steps these days while realizing the value of waiting and hoping. As I wait and hope, the beauty of fall is ushering in the cold of winter, bringing with it a different beauty and, for me, a time to slow down, be in the moment, and reflect. It was 5 degrees above zero this morning in Chicago, with a wind chill factor of minus 10 degrees. I thought about those hot, humid summer days in Brown County. The cold, biting wind yesterday and today gave me a lethargic feeling like the slow drip of molasses on a hot stack of pancakes. I wanted to stay inside and hunker down where it was warm.

As I hunkered down, I felt the darkness settling in around me. Recently, while searching for the light within, I discovered I have SAD – Seasonal Affective Disorder. For many people this condition surfaces when the sunlight of spring, summer, and fall gives way to the gray, dreary days of winter. From December through February, I can string together a lot of sad, unhappy days. I need the sunlight to brighten my soul and my outlook on life. When Chicago gets a huge snowstorm in early December and the weather turns cold, the snow stays around, turning gray and eventually black along the roads. Three years ago I bought a special SAD light and placed it on my desk at work. The rays come in through my eyes, going directly to the chemicals in my brain, encouraging them to believe it is a bright, sunshiny day outside. My special light helps keep my soul alive during the cold Chicago days. SAD slowly begins to surface in November. It hits me hardest in the dead of the Chicago winters. Nearly everyone is affected in some way by the change in seasons, and those of us already suffering with depression are affected the most.

Many don't understand why the blue days string together this time of year, and especially during the holiday season. This lack of understanding increases our isolation because many who are blue or depressed just do not feel like participating in many of the traditional holiday activities. Like me, many who struggle with depression become anti-social at this time, the antithesis of our normal outgoing personalities. About an hour before I wrote these words, that weighty feeling came back to my legs and stayed for a long time. I know God was telling me to slow down, take time for me, relax, and reflect.

During one recent holiday season, our son, daughter-in-law, and granddaughter visited from Oregon. One day we took Allie to a magnificent hands-on science museum in downtown Naperville. This world of science provides wonderful opportunities for young children to experience a variety of science concepts while actually being involved in the experiments. When we arrived, the place was jam-packed, at least 200 young people scurrying around in the various rooms. I was there only a few minutes when I said I just couldn't stay any longer. I drove home and returned to get the crew when they were ready to leave.

Another holiday season, however, I thought I escaped the holiday blues. I said earlier my new medications for BiPolar2 helped me feel much better. I hoped they would see me through that holiday period. Although I did not have the same level of sadness as earlier years, it was back just the same. I was blue. I didn't want to be around a lot of people. I wanted to retreat within myself. Those who do not understand depression said, "Aw, come on, Ed! It's the holidays. You should be happy. You're letting this myth of sadness around the holidays become a self-fulfilling prophecy. Get out and do something. Keep busy. Let the sunlight radiate out from your depths." The thoughts, well intended, came from friends who did not see past the surface observations to find the soul, much like those who don't realize the tip of an iceberg sticking above the water's surface reveals only ten percent of its size. I found myself walking aimlessly around the house during that holiday time, as if I could not decide what I wanted to do next.

During the time of darkness, I try to remember that frozen, sleepy seed taking cover in the ground. That seed (me) needs extra care during the cold winter months. This season also gives us many blessings. A friend sent me a holiday card with this saying: "May you find among the gifts wrapped beneath your tree the most wonderful gift of all – the child you used to be." During the winter months, I try extra hard to find L'il Eddie.

I Am Fearlessly Afraid of the Future

When I began *Lessons from the Crossroads*, I heard two messages about change from that tiny voice within. One message was to stay with the comfort I found at that time in my life, and the other message was to take a risk and make some changes. I discovered I may never pursue my dreams and find fulfillment from within the current cozy life I felt at that time. Leaving comfort zones is supposed to be hard. At times I feel so unprepared to leave my current life and go out into the unknown. The poem "How Dare You" floated in and out of my heart. At times I knew the answers to the questions that poem asks, and at other times I seemed clueless. I often forgot that each time I break through my comfort zone, my level of comfort always expands as I travel along my journey.

If I am so afraid to follow my dream, why did God put it before me in the first place? Why doesn't He just take my fears away? God, I believe, wants me to find the courage to follow my dreams, letting my faith grow in anticipation of a new calling. I have to remember that courage is not the absence of fear. To heed the call to follow my dreams, I have to act in spite of my fears. When we follow our dreams, we admit to God we really cherish the wonderful gift He has put before us. That tug-of-war I felt as I considered whether or not to return a second time to Brown County, metaphorically, was all about breaking through my comfort zone and living with the questions.

I had to face head-on a life-altering question about my dream to write and speak: Is it worth standing and protecting? If I don't fight for my dream, or if I ask anyone else to approve my dream, I have lost control of my gift.

What were the fears about pursuing my dream to write and speak? What was holding me back, keeping me in my comfort zone?

1.) Will I have enough money?

"All this sounds great, but what about the money?" The NFL football player Cuba Downing, Jr., in the movie *Jerry McGuire*, kept shouting to his agent, Tom Cruise, "Show me the money!" At times, I've felt the same anxiety about my need for financial security, but if I take away the emotions I feel about money, then money becomes a tool to use toward realizing my dream. The money becomes a means to an end, not the end itself.

Most of my emotions about money go back to what I saw growing up. Mom and Dad never had much money. I remember as if only yesterday, each Friday Mom and Dad both brought their paychecks home. Mom went to the bank and cashed them. Then she returned home and dutifully placed ¼ of the cash needed to pay each monthly bill into a separate, small, brown envelope kept in a metal box in their closet. At the end of the month, she had the exact amount of money she needed to pay each bill. What they were able to save was set aside for their later years, years they were never able to enjoy.

Mom had great skills in managing finances. She stretched the money they had to take care of her family, paid off our house long before the mortgage due date, sent her son to an expensive private college, and left a financial legacy for my sister and me. I remember a trip we took to Oklahoma to visit my dad's brother, Uncle Johnny, the only time I saw him. I was about ten, and my sister was fourteen. Mom got one hotel room for the four of us, and when my sister asked why we were all staying in one room, I piped up and said, "Oh, Mom probably wants to save some money." I clearly remember the disappointed look on Mom's face as I blurted out these words. Only much later in life did I realize the gifts of my mother's financial management. I wish I could have understood her financial prowess much earlier. She saved for the days the rains came, and she saved for the days the rains didn't come.

I'm wondering how many rainy days have to come along before I run out of money. If that day arrives, will I create new and exciting ways to provide an income sufficient to live on? Can I let go of my need for financial security and just get out there and explore?

2.) How will I spend my more unstructured time after years of a lot of structure?

Immediately I realized I had absolutely no trouble making good use of my time during my retreats. I loved allowing each day to unfold without any structure. I tried to stay out of the way and let my days happen! I didn't look at my watch often, but when I did, I was amazed how quickly the time slipped away, unnoticed. I wrote earlier about the fun I had and the reality that I can be with just me and have a great time.

I had a new dream after my retreats: purchasing that cabin I've mentioned before and following Jon Katz into the wilderness of the unknown. I've imagined a huge stone fireplace in the center of the main room. I have a big stack of logs on the front porch. I'm sitting in front of a roaring fire, looking out the window as the snow falls gently and steadily on the pine trees surrounding the cabin. The heavy snow is causing some of the pine branches to bend almost to the ground. For one of the few times in my life, I hope it snows all night. I'm just going to sit here, be warm, get more wood from the porch when it's needed, and maybe stay up all night being grateful for God's blessings in my life. At daybreak, I see the snow has come close to the bottoms of the cabin's windows. I smile, put some more wood on the fire, make some steaming hot chocolate, grab my book, and settle in for a long, wonderful day.

Learning to appreciate days with less structure also means not racing to provide structure. My sense of appreciation grows as I learn to wait, letting the day provide the structure, rather than allowing a pre-determined structure control the day. T.S. Eliot said, "I said to my soul, be still, and wait... So in darkness shall be the light, and the stillness the dancing." In my unstructured days, I wanted to find the light and learn to dance. I wanted to wait for the music to begin.

Waiting and listening in the silence without structure in my days are difficult for me. I haven't seen waiting as a very important event, a time to reflect on what I have asked God and to live with the questions which I turned over to Him. I had not stood still for ten years, waiting and listening in the silence. If there was no other reason to find my places of solitude, there was that one. I needed to reconnect with myself, to drop off the map for a while. Waiting also allowed me to find new meaning for my unstructured time. If my days are filled with events, I miss that time to reflect and to enjoy looking out the window at the snow. I realized that my impatience surfaces when I come close to those dark holes in the sidewalk where the demons I fear remain hidden.

Becoming patient and seeing wait time as the opportunity to reflect make me more comfortable with unstructured time. Until I went on the retreats, my life was full of structure. I had schedules calling for me to be at a variety of places at specific times. Following my dream includes structured times, but self-imposed, not placed on me by what others want me to do with my time. I welcome the possibility of that change in my days.

3.) Am I being selfish in pursuing my dream?

I know I can follow my dream and do so in an unselfish way. I realized the unselfishness of taking care of myself during my stay at Linden Oaks. I realized I couldn't give over to anyone else the major responsibility for my own care.

When I care for myself, however, at the expense of ignoring the needs of others, I revisit my narcissistic personality and fall in love with the reflection I see of me. I was also in love with my ego, for unhealthy reasons. My ego has to be involved in my dreams, but it is joined by my essence, my soul, as I follow the authentic path my dream giver provides. To use Parker Palmer's words, "Of course, knowing when we are speaking from the soul rather than the intellect or ego is difficult, since the intellect and ego insist that *they* are the center of our lives, and *they* speak the voice of truth. It takes time to learn to distinguish between the various voices within us and even more time to get regular access to the voice of soul."

Much of my self-aggrandizing behavior was to gain the approval of others, and I assessed my own self-esteem on the basis of what others thought of me. Loving myself means I accept myself as a worthy person because I choose to see myself that way. Loving myself also means I am deserve the gifts I receive into my life. As a young by, I learned it's better to give than receive. I felt guilty when I received compliments, feeling I didn't deserve them. As I wrote, I realized I do deserve the blessings God grants me every day.

    Taking care of myself does not mean I abandon others in the name of being good to myself. Abandoning others, while selfishly looking after Ed, has been my main course of action for many years. Let me give you an example. Until recent years another manifestation of my Bi-Polar2, which I did not recognize at the time, was spending money. When my emotions were in their more manic state, I wanted to spend money. I bought clothes, books, and CDs like you wouldn't believe – all for me. Because I was handling the finances, I did not let Bonnie know about my extravagances. But when the monthly credit card bill arrived, which I never allowed Bonnie to open, I was astounded at the bottom line total, unaware I had spent that much money last month! Somehow I worked my way out of the financial jam, holding the spending secret, thus allowing me to stay in control of the finances, but control was simply an illusion. In truth, I didn't care how my spending affected other family members. If I wanted it, I bought it. When I bought clothes, I bought only the best, most expensive name brands I could find. I hid the clothes in various places until I felt safe enough to bring my purchases into the house. When I wore a new piece of clothing and Bonnie asked, "Is that new?" I would always say I had it awhile but just hadn't worn it in a long time. As in high school I was still trying to impress others with what I wore. My clothes filled two large closets, relegating Bonnie's to a tiny one in another bedroom. My selfishness often sent Bonnie to discount clothing stores for Eric, Tracie, and herself.

    I didn't feel this selfishness as I began my inward journey three years ago. If I didn't find a way to know myself better, how could others know the real me? I wanted people to know me for who I was becoming. During the writing, I began to view this journey as a selfless, rather than a selfish, process.

4.) Can I find happiness and meaning in my life?

As I approached the end of *Lessons from the Crossroads*, I felt happier than I had felt in a long time. I attributed this feeling to two factors: (1) my new medications for BiPolar2 and (2) my retreats in 2004, 2005, and 2006. What was God telling me as I considered this question about happiness and meaning in my life? Elsewhere in the book I've written about happiness – how to find it and how to define it once found. I've realized I can find happiness and meaning only from within. I can no longer find them in the lives of others, nor do I want to! Happiness and meaning in my life most certainly will not come by listening to the expectations others have for me.

New happiness and meaning began to grow in February and March, 2004, with my diagnosis of BiPolar2, and they continued as I found those times to be alone with myself, searching for a way to find the relationship between happiness and meaning in my life. With the right combination of both, I began to quench my desert thirst through writing, reading, speaking, resting, refreshing, and reflecting. The decision to be happy is mine. Happiness has both appeared and disappeared in my life. When I couldn't get back on my authentic path that I saw very faintly from the crossroads, I was unhappy without knowing why. Some of the unhappy times also appeared when my depression was at its worst. Interestingly, some of my happiest times came as I gained control of my depression and found new meaning for my life.

5.) What if I don't make it?

As a new journey begins, I need enough confidence in my faith and myself to be honest with myself, to be prepared to say, "I may not be successful in this venture." Admitting this possibility does not mean I shouldn't try. I haven't always thought this way. Right after I finished my doctorate, I was offered a teaching position at the University of Georgia. I was scared to death. I wanted to go, but I didn't want to go. I knew nothing about my porch, my fear of moving off it, and most especially the process of traveling hundreds of miles to Athens, Georgia. I did not want to break out of a comfort zone I had known for years in southern Indiana. Something about that faraway place triggered a tenuous feeling in the pit of my stomach. Yet a part of me wanted to give a shot at this new experience.

One afternoon I talked about this offer with my minister, a wonderful and caring soul. After a long conversation, Bill Laws asked, "Ed, are you prepared to go to Georgia and be a complete failure?" WOW! Very quickly I told him I wasn't in any way prepared for failure. What a strange question. I only thought in terms of succeeding at whatever I tried, not realizing, as I do now, that some of my best lessons come from what doesn't go well in my life. For example, my mishandling of the family finances, my experience as a superintendent of schools, and my propensity for being selfish were wilderness experiences in my life from which lessons came. At the same time my life was full of successes. I had been successful in high school, college, teaching, and my advanced degree work. Bill listened with a smile as I told him all the reasons I would not fail. Bill said, "Maybe you should get ready to fail." Somehow, at that point in my life, I was hoping for more positive advice, not realizing Bill's advice was so very wise. I loved the teaching at Georgia, but I did not thrive in the "publish or perish" environment I found there. I knew I would not be successful in an environment that exposed my insecurity and disinterest. I left my position there to move back to my familiar Indiana and take a public school administrative position.

Also, I was not prepared to understand the words of author Sue Monk Kidd when she said, "I thought if I gave up my safe, prescribed role… and risked being a writer, the sky would fall. I went around muttering 'What if I make a fool of myself? What if I fail? What will my family think if I leave a perfectly good career? And for what? To be a writer, for pete's sake. How absurd.'" I didn't know a single thing about being a college professor, but I also didn't think I might fail.

Much has changed in my life since then, primarily because of the intervening 33 years since that conversation. Thinking about my question "Can I make it?" I know I can make it, but I'm prepared for rough times along the way. I am better prepared for the rough times now because I've had many such experiences since realizing that my dreams for success may not be the path God wants me to travel. This question, Can I make it? assumes I must be willing to explore, to bust the comfort zone, to move in some direction, to accept the possibility of failure, and to learn from those failures.

Professionally I failed as a superintendent. Without knowing how to do that job well, I struggled during the entire time I held that position. I didn't know at the time why I was struggling so much. Much of my role as a superintendent required me to confront leaders in the teachers' union. I did not like these confrontations. I did not like working with the Board of Education, the majority of whom changed between the time I was appointed and began the job. The majority of board members who chose me no longer served on the board. In reality, however, being a superintendent prepared me for my next job as an associate superintendent where I worked in areas that brought me greater happiness and meaning. I was responsible for all the instructional programs in the district, and I worked with many committees as we collaborated to improve student learning. I tell my students, as they ask me the very same question about making it, "You will never know unless you try, and if you find the job is not what you want, you now have this important information and can move in other directions." Eventually this piece of advice to my students became internalized, and I can now follow my own advice.

In following the advice I offered my students and thereby enhancing the possibilities of following my dreams, I must make the best decisions I can at the time. Looking back, I haven't always made the best decisions I could because the basis for those decisions came from an imbalanced perspective. I didn't know how to balance what I wanted with what God wanted for me. I didn't see the connections between my heart and my head, so I listened only to my head. My heart never had a chance to blend with my head. I rebelled so greatly with my sense of spirituality, so I ignored the critical need to include my soul in my decisions.

6.) Can I move in and out of comfort zones?

I thought about my comfort zones even before the first visit to my woods in Brown County, and I have written about my difficulties in leaving comfort zones to scale new mountains. As I write this, I am amazed about my current thoughts relative to my comfort zones and my willingness to address one in particular. Where am I in my quest to understand if God is asking me to pursue a new calling to write and speak about my life journeys? Now I'm wondering if my fear is not about having the courage I need to leave the familiarity of my job but rather about fearing I might stay in my safe environment at the university too long. I wonder what impact doing so might have on my soul. This thought just required a 180-degree turn in viewing my comfort zone. Through writing *Lessons from the Crossroads*, I discovered many of my fears have been misplaced. I never thought about reversing the fears of leaving or staying in my comfort zone.

On a regular basis I get additional affirmation from God that a new calling is waiting. I always tell my graduate students, "It's one thing to get into a new job when you feel you're ready. Of equal importance comes when you know when to get out of that job to pursue other dreams." My experience has been some folks don't always know when they should go on a quest for new adventures, through retiring or just moving on. They stay where they are too long. When this settling in occurs, co-workers sometimes remember those last few months or years, focusing on negative events that may have occurred during that time working with people who "retired" but continued in their jobs. When we're ready to leave but don't, we often behave as if we did leave but didn't. Instead of remembering all the good we did while there, colleagues focus on what we didn't do while we stayed too long.

I am struggling to discover why comfort zones keep me where I am. My comfort zone is always with me. It expands or shrinks in direct proportion to the amount of fear I feel for my new adventure. We feel safe in our comfort zones. We know who we are and what we can accomplish. While there, we feel happy. We do not want to leave everything we know for everything we don't know. We have problems, but we've learned either to live with them or to solve them. We don't know what problems await us outside the zone, so why in the world do we want to go out?

One day, going into the Starbucks in downtown Naperville, I overheard a conversation about comfort zones. I went there to write and read, again relishing in my definition of solitude, combining the noise of customers buying their favorite morning drinks with my own sense of silence. After writing for an hour, I went outside to get some fresh air.

Two gentlemen were talking right outside the door. While eavesdropping, I found out one is a local business owner, the other a local real estate broker. They were looking across the street at a recently vacated, 5900-square-foot building. The real estate broker was pointing out the benefits of the new location, trying to pique the interest of the businessman, whose business is now in a different location outside the downtown area. After a ten-minute conversation with facts and questions being relayed back and forth, the businessman ended the conversation by saying, "It really all comes down to my comfort level. I know what I can do where I am. I can't picture how a new location would work out."

7.) Am I ready?

Answering this question when I wrote the first page of *Lessons from the Crossroads* would have resulted in a resounding no. I had no idea writing this book could cause me to consider answering yes. Readiness, like happiness and meaning in my life, is a relative term. Part of becoming ready is in direct proportion to the journey along my authentic path out of the crossroads. Being ready is a state of mind, a willingness to see the readiness, because I believe I am equipped to move out on faith and faith alone.

Becoming ready is all about preparing, looking inward, having dreams, standing in front of the full-length mirror to take ownership for myself, and anticipating a new journey on the other side of my comfort zone. Blaming other people, past events, poor personal choices, and the consequences of those choices will insure I let go of my dreams, not encouraging Little Eddie to get out there and explore. Happiness brings meaning to my life. In *Spoon River Anthology* George Gray said, "To put meaning in one's life may end in madness. But life without meaning is the torture of restlessness and vague desire."

I resigned my university teaching position on March 31, 2006, leaving a profession I enjoyed for over thirty years. As I wrote this section, I had been gone from that profession only four months. As I thought about my resignation, I knew I now needed to answer that first question I took to Brown County: Should I leave the field of education to write and speak full time? I felt really good about my decision. I was ready to write and speak on a full time basis. This decision, however, put me on a new journey where I had much to learn, and I was delighted about this new opportunity to find out more about myself.

I had to begin learning the skills of an entrepreneur, a set of skills I had not needed in my educational profession. I had to reinvent myself, not only learning entrepreneurial skills but also developing the tools to market my books and myself to others. I also had to understand how to find those people and organizations to which this marketing should be directed. I attended several seminars and workshops centered around the topics of marketing and of self-esteem and self-confidence. Much of my adult life my self-esteem and self-confidence came from the masks I wore. Letting go of those masks during my ongoing journey of self-discovery left me feeling, at times, like I wasn't good enough or strong enough to put myself out there in a whole new arena. I realized, however, that if I could not gain more confidence in myself and feel better about who I was becoming, potential clients would see these inadequate character traits and not hire me. I hired a professional success coach who was helping me make those transitions. I was feeling good about the progress I was making because the progress was not limited to my abilities to sell books or gain speaking engagements but also included my journey of feeling better about who I was becoming as a person.

I just identified seven fears that existed at one time in the middle of the crossroads. Explaining them with the above thoughts doesn't mean the fears are gone. They may be diminished somewhat but still there. Whatever decisions reveal themselves as I search for the authentic path always awaiting me, the fears will remain until I find that path. Even then I expect them to stay with me but, I hope, in some smaller form. I am also certain other fears will rear their ugly heads in the next several months as I continue to find my way down the authentic path. Usually I cannot identify my fears as explicitly as I just have. More often they remain unidentified blobs in my mind and heart. Being able to write them down was a step forward for me.

CHAPTER 18
Lessons from the Crossroads

As I reflected on my retreats, I discovered parts of Ed Poole I didn't know existed. However, the discovery process is never-ending. After I finished *Lessons from the Porch*, I forgot I had not learned all of the twenty-two lessons I described in that book. I even forgot that I ended the book by saying, "I'm still right smack dab in the midst of the struggles." The struggles continued, and those lessons I did learn are still a work in progress.

This book is replete with new struggles and also continues to be a work in progress. Because I shared my own lived experiences, I had to read, reread, and reread my writing. If this process seems meticulous and repetitious, it was. But this work was necessary. I had to absorb my writing to the point that the words were true to my story and to me. Finally, I saw the wholeness within the separate yet connected chapters because I believed it was there. At that point, certain lessons began emerging, surfacing as I saw the interactions present among them. These lessons are interdependent. Like the questions I brought with me in my heart as I went to the woods, each lesson depends on all the others for its definition and meaning. For this reason, I restate ideas to show the connections. I cannot do otherwise; I cannot view the themes as separate, independent entities.

Lesson #1: *I Want to Write and Speak: Answering the Call*

I *do* want to write and speak. That statement moved out of me as quickly as my fingers could race across the keyboard. Finally I was willing to risk leaving my university position to follow that calling. I believe God presents more than one calling, one dream, in our lives. While we are in one calling, God is preparing us for the next, allowing our faith and confidence to grow to a point He feels we are ready to receive His newest dream for us. My calling follows the permission granted by God, my heart, and my soul: "Get out there, Eddie, and explore." If I don't allow that grace into my life, how can that most sacred part of me become involved in finding my next calling?

God has used a variety of ways to get my attention. Twice He got my attention when I was hospitalized with depression. Other times, He got my attention when I realized the pain of not heeding His call was more than I could continue to endure. When I discern a calling, I know God wants me to use my giftedness, given by His grace, for others. When I am able to live in harmony with my gifts, I move into my calling, like moving with the flow of the river. Real synchronicity occurs for me when my career path and the path of my calling are the same. My career will lose its meaning when my call to action moves in another direction. I feel that disconnect now. My career of 40 years was moving away from what I believe God is presenting me as a new calling. This new calling demands I once again move along my authentic path. I finally knew He was preparing me for my new calling.

I have a strong sense that earlier callings gave me the strength to choose my various career paths. Those paths were not ill chosen. They provided great joy and a sense of accomplishment within my chosen profession. However, because my soul was not always there, those paths never allowed me to feel the peace I yearned for in the connections among the personal, professional, spiritual, and authentic Ed.

Lesson #2: *I Can Write and Speak Anywhere.*

Having said I want to write, *can* I write, and if so, *where* do I write? I wondered earlier if the ease with which I wrote in all the various places was a function of the encouraging, peaceful, and beautiful surroundings or the reality that I was ready to write. After considering this question, I truly believe I can write anywhere, and I am ready to write and speak. I cannot minimize the impact of the new friends I met as well as the beauty and wonder of these stops along my journey. I've said many times I'm at this particular crossroads along my journey because God wants me here for now. I don't know if He will continue to want me here in the future. I'm leaving the guidance to Him. He is one guide who will not leave because His work with me will never end.

The people I met and the stories I heard allowed me to gain new insights about who I am and how God wants me to live out my life. Because I met my new friends and heard their wonderful stories at just the right time, I don't believe I gained these insights from merely being in the right place at the right time or being plain ol' lucky.

If God wants me to pursue my dream, He will make certain the people I meet, the gifts I receive, my guides, and the experiences I have are placed on the path along my journey, no matter where I find myself. However, my heart has to be open to the messages and the questions God is sending.

Though not everyone can escape to the woods, spend time at an ocean retreat, or fly to New Mexico to relish in the beauty of the desert, I found the place is not important. What I choose to do wherever I am allows me to better understand my authentic self. I believe all of us can designate a specific time each day to take care of ourselves and ponder our questions, find time alone to journal and to reflect. The outcome of our alone time is most important, and we can achieve this outcome in different settings. Wherever we find the retreats in our soul, we will feel a sense of being lost for a while. During this time, God is calling us to continue growing and recovering what is lost and orphaned within us.

He also wants us to stand still in the precious present to allow the growth to move deep within our souls.

In much of my life, I looked for the *next* moment, the *next* job, and the *next* community. I went on this way for years, waiting for the next event in life, moving full speed toward it, and trying to control an outcome I wanted. I spent much time looking back toward my past, trying to learn from where I'd been. However, when I dwelt on my past, I often stayed there too long. As I thought about my past and my future, not trying to dwell in the former or *be* in the latter, I asked myself, "Will my reflecting help me find my way out of the crossroads?" I knew the answer to this question was yes. I also know the answers to the question I posed for this lesson: I can write and speak. I can bust through my current comfort zone to do so, and I can write and speak wherever the environment I'm seeking presents itself.

Lesson #3: *I Have Found the Joys of Telling Stories through Our Voices and Our Songs*

I once heard a story about what we carry with us to pass along to future generations. The storyteller was visiting the Chicago Museum of History and stopped in front of an exhibit titled "Sacred Bundle." The bundle he saw contained the small number of artifacts a particular tribe held as sacred. One of the tribal elders was charged with protecting its contents and bringing those artifacts to all tribal campfires.

As the tribe gathered, this respected member of the tribe reminded others of the significance and hallowed meaning of each item in the sacred bundle. Telling these stories insured future generations would understand the tribe's culture.

Each of us has our own, unique, sacred bundle containing the stories that explain to future generations and to ourselves those parts of our lives we want to better understand and pass on to others. Unlike those early tribal elders, we may not be able to carry our bundle of stories in a small animal hide. Instead, we often have to carry those stories in our hearts. No matter how we define the container we use to transmit the culture, we must do so. Our stories are *the* best means we have to help the young understand the journeys, the struggles, and the inner peace of the old. They allow us to begin the process of turning ourselves inside out and sharing thoughts and feelings that are way down deep and have never before surfaced. The young and old clustered on the main floor that day at the Abe Martin Lodge were sharing their stories from the sacred bundles carried in their hearts and minds.

Every single person on my retreats who told me his or her stories, as we "sat around our campfires," told them from the sacred bundles in their souls. The stories were not only full of specific events but also, and more importantly, included the meaning each teller had in his or her heart. Believe me, those stories will keep alive for future generations the lives of all those I met. I will always remember the sacred bundle stories my friends in Brown County shared with me.

During a recent trip to Key West, Florida, I met a crusty old guy, Peter. As we became friends, hanging out at the Schooner Wharf Bar, Peter told me an amazing story from his sacred bundle. Peter's story was not one of joy but of closure, leading to a life-altering decision.

Perhaps you have read the book by Sebastian Junger or seen the movie, *The Perfect Storm*. It's the story of the ill-fated day that the boat, the *Andrea Gail*, sunk off the southern New England Coast on October 28, 1991, as a result of the greatest storm in modern history.

Accompanying the *Andrea Gail* on this extended hunt for swordfish was the *Hannah Borden*. Peter was a crewman on that sister ship. The captain of the *Hannah Borden*, Linda Greenlaw, the first woman to ever skipper a sword boat, tried to warn Billy Tyne, skipper of the *Andrea Gail*, about the coming storm, but apparently Tyne and his crew decided to ride it out.

Ten days after Tyne's boat went missing, a propane tank with the letters AG painted on its top and a long line beacon were discovered washed ashore on Sable Island, 120 miles southeast of Nova Scotia. Peter is the one who retrieved these only remaining artifacts from the *Andrea Gail*. He finished his story, looked at me through his tear-filled eyes and said, "Ed, that's the last time I ever set foot on a fishing boat."

Peter told me this story from the sacred bundle he carries in his heart and soul. Although not in any way a joyous story, it is one, I'm certain, he will carry in his bundle until the day he dies. And his experience changed his life forever.

Some folks in Brown County share their sacred bundles in the songs they sing. I wrote earlier that many customs, beliefs, and stories of Brown County pass from generation to generation through songs about the history of that place. Songs have always been an important way to tell stories because all songs contain within them a story. Almost every era in our country's history has songs unique to that period of time. Some of those songs center around conflict: the Revolutionary and Civil Wars, World Wars I and II, and the Vietnam War. Most of the songs remind future generations of the triumphs and defeats experienced during those conflicts. Other stories are told through the songs of most every decade, the '20s through the '90s. We understand many of the joys and sorrows of those decades by listening to the stories in the songs. Not every song is sung from a sacred bundle, but most are.

Lesson #4: Our Memories Provide Common Threads for Findin' Home

Findin' home includes my memories of the physical places I've lived, *a function of geography,* and my meaning of faith I discover in my portable home, *a function of my soul.* The changing winds swirling about me reminded me to come home to myself, to try to become who I truly am and struggle to reclaim my soul. These winds also showed me common threads among those memories.

The words to the music I heard in Brown County brought back many common threads and memories from my childhood and early adult years. I know memories are the triggers that bring our past into our present, helping us understand who we are and what we are as members of the human race. Without memories, our lives lack definition and purpose.

Recalled memories of my past help me grow and evolve as a person. I am who I am because my past joins the present in my soul. I have learned many lessons by awakening my memories.

The memories present themselves as common threads and themes that connect *all* the stories I heard while on my retreats. Every single story had some relationship with one or more of the questions I had. I found some part of myself embedded within each story. And, through the storytellers' authentic selves, the expressions on their faces, and the questions we asked each other, I know my stories found places in their hearts and souls. The gift of these memories helped me reclaim my authentic path out of the crossroads.

I've talked a lot about connections I discovered during my retreats. I saw a kinship all around me. Therefore, I saw that life itself is a confluence of all those parts that define who we are. Still, because each of us discovers different connections, our lives differ.

Lesson 5: *God Planned My Journey so I Could Find the Path*
I've Always Been Traveling

Finding the path to my authentic self is a journey I struggled with most of my adult life. I found the authentic self, as it was defined at that point in my life, three times – when I found Joshua and he helped me leave the superintendency; when I left the hospital and wrote *Lessons from the Porch*; and when I discovered the responsibility I had to release my demons in the sidewalk's hole and write this book. Then I got caught up in the busyness of my daily life, and my authentic self eluded me. I did not take time to remember myself within the tasks surrounding me each day. Perhaps forgetting was my way of escaping newly found lessons that I didn't understand and perhaps feared.

Searching once again for my authentic path had everything to do with those queries that launched my retreats as I struggled to find the inner peace that allowed me to let go and let God give me enough light to find my lost authentic path. However, doing so was the only way I could rediscover the lost part of my soul. Unknowingly, I circled all around my questions most of my adult life. I did so because even though they were there, I didn't know it. Until ten years ago I took no time to discover the questions and then live through them to some answers. I came to the heart, the center, of those questions this last time I fell into the crossroads. When I landed in the crossroads and began searching for my way out, I knew what I needed. I needed guidance.

Lesson #6: *Not All Who Wander Are Lost*

As I noted earlier, for years I had my wondering and my wandering in reverse order. I took off to places unknown before I knew who I was or why I was walking down that unknown street, and I always fell into the deep hole.

During those earlier years, I only knew about wandering with my feet, and *then* only with my mind. Because of my time on my retreats and the message on the T-shirt from the Life Is Good store, I have grown to understand the significant connections between wandering and wondering. Until that time, I saw these two concepts as sequential and unconnected. The flapping butterfly wings and the quivering shrub were messages to me about all of life's many wonderful and meaningful intersections.

Once I understood the connections of wondering and wandering, I saw the necessity of considering them together, as one, not separately and sequentially. I am limited if I believe I wander only with my feet and mind. The limitation is a mighty one because this singular kind of wandering, which demands movement, excludes the critical components of my heart and my soul. I need all four as I stand still and wait.

The truth is, if I wander with my heart and soul first, I can find my way back home even before I wonder about a new calling. My heart and soul *always* precede my mind and feet. I wandered to Brown County, the Cenacle, the labyrinth, the ocean, and the desert, all the time wondering what God wanted me to do next with my life.

After I spent four months in the hospital in 1996-1997, wondering about who I am, God helped me see that I must call a halt to all my activities and get to know myself. My career identified me. I knew who I was as an educator, but I did not know me beyond that, as a human being. During the year and a half I didn't work I read many books, trying to find my identity from the words of others. Reading the thoughts of other authors helped to a point, but their words became a crutch, a dependency, which still kept me from the work I needed to do. In 1998 I began writing *Lessons from the Porch*, continuing, initially, to rely on the thoughts of others. Gradually I came to trust my own words. Then in late 1998 I got busy with my work at the university and consistently found many convenient reasons to avoid understanding Ed Poole.

When I returned to the question of why, with all my professional successes, I wasn't happy or fulfilled, I had no answer. A voice inside me continued its familiar, singular thought: "I need…need…need" or "I want…want…want." My needs and wants were resting only in my eyes and my head, not in my heart and my soul. My ego and my essence were not connected, and my essence, my soul led me back to my authentic path. Telling my story in *Lessons from the Porch* became a new beginning of my journey, an authentic path out of the crossroads; however, I still couldn't identify my inner needs because I didn't spend enough time trying to gain this understanding. I thought rereading my book would remind me of my struggles. How could I assume new struggles were not just around the next curve in the road? How could I help others if I couldn't help myself?

As I thought about the title of this lesson *Not All Who Wander Are Lost*, I cannot tell you how much I cherish the message on the T-shirt I bought that day in the Life Is Good shop. Had I not gone into that store and found the T-shirt that now means so much to me, I would never have seen the power of wandering with my heart and soul. Again, I thank God so much for encouraging me to turn left, walk up the steps, and find such an important message.

Lesson #7: *Blending "Being," "Knowing," and "Doing" Is Critical to Reclaiming My Authentic Path*

When this lesson emerged, I knew it would be a difficult one for me to write about. The blend I sought was being (my soul), knowing (my mind), and doing (my body). Primarily the difficulty arose because I had not been very successful at the blend this lesson suggests. I wrote earlier that I have often been a human doing, not a human being. Since I did not know my authentic self, the blend was based on the masks I wore which eventually fooled even me. Not only did I not know Ed Poole, but I also did not want others to get behind the masks to see the shell of a person that lived behind them. My masks served my roles as a husband, father, school administrator, church participant, community leader, and neighbor.

The insight I've gained on the need to blend my wandering with my wondering helped with this lesson because I saw the three concepts identified with this lesson as also being interconnected

I wanted to know; I wanted to be in the moment; and I wanted to do what God wants me to do. Were those three parts of me at odds with each other, or did all three occur simultaneously? I knew my mind, body, and soul were getting connected, and I took God up on His offer to get reacquainted. Because I now believe in my heart this connection is true, I must be able to see these three parts always depending upon each other for both understanding and action. When one of the three is overemphasized, the other two, by default, diminish in the blend.

Author Oriah Mountain Dreamer gave me insight into the need for a blend of being, knowing, and doing. She said awareness of our ego is that part of us that connects with the patterns of changing "thoughts, feelings, sensations, and life situations" necessary to understand our humanness. Essence awareness is "the consciousness of the eternal inherent being we are." This awareness does not worry about the minutia of daily living. At another point, she stated, "Life without essence awareness lacks meaning and connection. Life without ego awareness lacks fire and direction." Being human, we are a complete entity, a blending of both essence and ego.

My ego is a combination of my knowing and doing, the mind/body connection. My essence, my soul, is reflected in my being. My ego wants me to see that I am a human being having a spiritual experience whereas my soul wants me to understand that I am a spiritual being having a human experience. My ego put me on my personal and professional paths at the crossroads. I did not understand, before I wrote *Lessons from the Crossroads*, that these two paths were connected to my ego. For much of my adult life, along those two paths, my ego tried to keep me separated from my soul. It did this by continuing to allow me to control these two paths but did so out of love so I would understand, some day, that my ego had grown too large to be healthy. Strengthening my ego, without including my spiritual journey, also caused me to continue living in the victim archetype. The enemy was out there somewhere, and because my true being was hidden behind my masks, I didn't know how to forgive others or myself. My ego and my essence are crucial because the former keeps me anchored in my human experience, and my essence provides that same anchor for my spiritual experience.

My being, my spiritual path, was an unknown entity until I took the inward journey of self-discovery to find my soul. This inward journey was the primary reason I began my retreats, bringing with me those eight questions I took to Brown County my very first trip there. My being keeps me anchored in my spiritual journey. Through my writing I discovered why I had not seen the connections among three of those paths I found as I looked out the tower at the crossroads. At the same time, I began to understand why that authentic road sign was so very hazy and unfamiliar.

Author Sue Monk Kidd used her own words to describe essence and ego when she said, "A strong ego, aware of its boundaries, is crucial to wholeness and healthy functioning… We can't do without it. The problem arises when the ego becomes egocentric, an unavoidable human condition… These egocentric patterns make up our false selves… They become the masks we wear. In order for the ego to relinquish its central position, my hardened structures must be cracked open. This process opens the way for the gradual shift of centers, a deep restructuring away from the ruling needs of the ego toward the Self."

Earlier I wrote that my ego has most always been out in front of me, driving me longer and harder to do more, and I always found myself swallowed up with the tasks of daily living. As I did more and more and achieved greater recognition for my accomplishments, my ego kept growing and growing, leaving little space and time to consider what is eternal and infinite within me. Long before I did, God noticed the ingredients I had blended were way out of proportion. By moving from job to job, I attempted to release my inner struggles but continued to keep the blend out of proportion because I didn't consider those struggles before I left for my new adventure.

The blending of being, knowing, and doing allowed me to see those three paths braided and interlocked, leading me to regain my authentic path. My authentic path has always been within me, the blending of how I can be in the present, what I know, and what I do. That self, that path, is what I found while sitting on that rock in the middle of the labyrinth at Ghost Ranch.

Lesson #8: *By Replacing One Picture with Another I Changed Fear to Hope.*

Earlier I introduced George Gray one of the fictional characters in *Spoon River Anthology*, who has this uncanny ability to look back from his grave to read what was etched on his tombstone. I also wrote that one of my greatest fears is that I'll be lying on my deathbed, lamenting the fact that my life was just like George's. I will have lived without lifting my sail and catching the winds of destiny wherever they take the boat. I will have been afraid to put meaning in my life because I feared this meaning could end in madness. I feared I would never have learned that putting meaning in my life, regardless of the outcome, helps me to once again find my authentic path. As a daily reminder that I did not want my life to end up like George Gray's, I framed his lament and hung it on my office wall. I carried that reminder from office to office for twenty years.

During one of my visits to Brown County I was looking for a painting of the beautiful 1838 covered bridge built by Aaron Wolf at the entrance to the state park. Although I visited every art gallery in the area, I didn't find one. However, I did find a local artist who said she would paint one for me. On my last visit to Brown County I purchased her oil painting of my beloved bridge. I returned to my office at the university, eager to find a prominent place to hang the picture.

To my chagrin, I found the available wall space was already taken with other pictures. Then my eyes fell on the George Gray wall hanging, the one I've read almost daily for twenty years. Instantly I knew I was seeing his words for the first time with my new eyes, a view I gained through writing this book. At that moment I realized I no longer needed George's sad life as a reminder of my own. As I lifted Gray's epitaph from the wall, I had one of the most relieved feelings I have ever enjoyed.

The Aaron Wolf painting represents the hope I've found in my life since that very first visit to the park, now over three years ago. The George Gray epitaph represented a life I no longer plan to lead. As I lifted George from the wall, I knew, for the first time in twenty years, that I will not end up on my death bed repeating George's words.

Lesson 9: *During the Writing Process an Intruder Became a Welcomed Guest*

Earlier I introduced you to Portia Nelson's book *There's a Hole in My Sidewalk*. Her writing hit me like a ton of bricks when I was hospitalized a second time with depression. I felt I was that hole, and I kept finding it over and over again.

Reflecting on the growth and guidance God gave me through the labyrinth of this writing, I remembered the words of Sue Monk Kidd: "It's a contemplative work. It means descending into self, into God, into the deeper labyrinths of prayer. It means listening to disinherited voices within, facing the wounded holes in the soul, the denied and undiscovered." I discovered the holes were not in the sidewalk at all but inside *me*, deep within my soul, just like my understanding of home. I carried the holes with me every day, whatever I was doing. They were portable. Over the years, the holes in me had been getting wider and deeper, following me wherever I went.

Just like a hole in the sidewalk keeps getting wider and deeper if not repaired, the holes inside me needed repairing to prevent decay. The repairs I give to my own holes not only prevent deeper erosion but also allow them, over time, to begin filling up, not with hard and permanent concrete but with the soft and malleable understanding I gain through the materials used to repair them. The ingredients in the material not only allow me to release the pain there but also give me the craftsman's skills necessary to fill my holes with hopes, dreams, self-confidence, and the strength needed to bust comfort zones.

The repairing process began the moment I realized my own responsibility in getting out of the holes I created. This writing provided the materials I needed to begin filling my holes. I rediscovered my authentic path, and I knew I no longer needed to find another street to walk down. I just needed once again to recognize the authentic path that has always been accessible, but one I have lost at times in my life. I have more hope and self-confidence now than at any other point in my life, including the time after finishing *Lessons from the Porch*. I remained in the victim mentality after finishing that book, and even though I thought that writing brought me the peace I sought, I later realized once again I lost my authentic path. My ego still dominated my human experience, and I continued to control my job and my family. I have vowed, this time, that I will not forget the power of the soul in repairing my holes in the sidewalk. I am still in the learning process relative to the twenty-two lessons in my earlier book. Thinking I had learned them all as I finished writing and believing those were the only twenty-two lessons I ever needed to live the life I thought God wanted me to lead caused the holes to harden and decay.

Throughout my life, several different holes have appeared in my soul. Many of the holes kept getting wider and deeper because I ignored them. I did not know how to fill them. Each hole needed repairing with different material. My holes, described below, appeared when I was young and increased as I reached adulthood:

The emotional vacuum I felt growing up:

The absence of feelings, love, and affection displayed at home, along with the lack of identification with my dad, created the first hole in my soul. I craved the human contact I didn't find at home and filled that hole with girlfriend after girlfriend and with my other friends. I ran with an older crowd, looking for older males to cover the hole left by the lack of identification with Dad. Like a baby to his mother, I clung to any and all relationships I could find. I always fell hard for each girlfriend I ever had. At the time she was providing what my mother wasn't.

Loneliness:

I was often alone *and* lonely as a young boy. Feeling alone is one thing, but feeling lonely is quite another. Both parents worked hard, and they were gone a lot. I remember every Saturday morning sitting alone in front of the TV, watching Gene Autry, Roy Rogers, and Hopalong Cassidy westerns, imagining I was the hero rushing in to save the damsel in distress. Even as a young boy I identified with the heroes I found on television. I ran home from school every afternoon to find my favorite spot in front of the TV so I could watch American Bandstand. I saw myself in front of the cameras dancing with Donna.

I repaired my loneliness hole with a variety of experiences. I sought the companionship of others. I wasn't always discerning in the companions I hung out with, causing me to push the envelope of my faith-based beliefs. I was in that unique position in high school of being able to travel back and forth between my do-gooder friends and others who were the more problem kids. I learned to drink, smoke, and have sex as I hung with this latter group. When my guilt became unbearable, I returned to my friends who never caused any trouble for anyone, in or out of school. The interesting dilemma for me was I enjoyed my life more with the problem kids than with the do-gooders, who were the popular, smart, and well-respected students. Mom and Dad did not know about many of those excursions, which only encouraged me to try more and darker adventures across that conservative, religious, line-in-the-sand between right and wrong.

Religious upbringing:

I felt uncomfortable with the religious beliefs handed me as a young boy. I did not know where the discomfort came from, but it existed. I filled this hole with resentment and anger until later in life when I realized I could repair the hole with a different set of beliefs, a new understanding of God in my life. I adjusted those early beliefs to fit the current meanings religion and spirituality have in my life.

My depression:

I had the same feeling both times I was hospitalized with depression: Initially I didn't feel it was my responsibility to dig my way out of the hole. The gift of both hospitalizations was realizing the only way to dig my way out of the depths of depression was to grab a shovel. Both hospitalizations became gifts; the first gave me the courage to write *Lessons from the Porch,* and the second gave me the introspection to write *Lessons from the Crossroads.* Most likely I've been at some level of depression for much of my life. Until ten years ago I had handled it myself. Then I understood one of my greatest strengths was to give in to the depressed feelings and start digging.

Guilt and shame:

I was raised on guilt! I knew I wasn't the nice little boy all the adults at my church and elsewhere thought I was. When I felt guilty for something I had done, I felt the shame that went with the guilt. I rebelled against those stifling religious beliefs I got growing up in my church. I was scared of hell, but I kept on pushing the envelope. In spite of my dad's warning, "Son, if you ever get a girl in trouble, just don't bother coming home," I had sex with my high school sweetheart, Donna. At one point in that relationship we went through one agonizing month, thinking she was pregnant. For that entire month my mind was ablaze with guilt and shame, primarily because I couldn't imagine what Mom and Dad would say. Donna was not pregnant, but we continued having sex.

I added to my feelings of guilt and shame by stealing. For a period of time my dad was superintendent of our Sunday school at church. Part of his responsibility included collecting the money that was given the church during this time in the Sunday morning service. He allowed me to go to each class and get its collection plate. On the way back to the church office I slipped some of the money into my pockets. Since my parents were never home on those Saturdays I watched the marathon westerns on television, I rode my bike to the Knotty Pine restaurant down the street, using some of the money I stole from the collection plates to load up with burgers and fries. Then I returned home to eat and watch TV. Eventually Mom found the large stash of change in my room. Once again Dad said, "Don't you know you made your mother cry?"

When I was in high school, I worked in the men's clothing department at a prominent store in Columbus and stole merchandise, not money. I was trying to impress my wealthier high school friends by wearing the same kind of clothing they did. Periodically I slipped a shirt, a sweater, or a pair of slacks under my top coat and carried it out of the store. I always felt like one of the crowd as I wore my stolen clothes to school and to parties.

I was dishonest in the classroom too. I finished in the top ten academically with my high school class of over 400 students. However, no one knew that I cheated on many tests during those four years in order to make those good grades. I always studied, but I couldn't memorize the material, and I can't memorize information to this day. The teachers and administrators at my high school thought I was such a fine student and a nice young man.

With all of the above happening, I knew my parents would be crushed if they found out. The guilt and shame I felt were unbelievable. I pushed myself into a very low level of self-esteem and self-confidence. I knew I let my parents down, even knowing they were unaware of my many adventures to my dark side. To this day I have trouble letting go of guilt and shame. Even though I know a loving God forgives me, I still have great difficulty forgiving myself.

Unconditional Love:

As a young adult I didn't love very well, and I didn't know how to receive love. I always thought I could never be capable of an unconditional love that lasted a lifetime. Writing *Lessons from the Crossroads* gave me a refreshing perspective on loving and being loved unconditionally. This realization came from that inner journey to find my heart, my voice, and my way out of the crossroads.

Earlier I wrote that the love I saw and felt at home carried conditions and judgments. I was going to hell every time my parents discovered one of my adventures that ran smack head-on into their religious beliefs. Because I didn't understand, until later in life, the kind of love my parents <u>were</u> able to give me, I developed deep within me a certainty that I had not grown up being loved unconditionally and didn't know how to either offer it or receive it. Unconditional love means being willing to forgive, and for much of my life I didn't feel I deserved to be forgiven. Now I do feel, and know I am, forgiven and I need to forgive others for hurting me, failing to give me what I needed, and trying to control me.

The six sidewalk holes I just described are much, much shallower as I finished writing this book than when I first began. The growth through my writing also required that I revisit the poem *How Dare You*. I changed as a person and a writer. Because my writing is cyclical, I returned to where I began and recognized it for the first time. My poem you read earlier identified my fears and defiance. Although happy where I was in my life, I felt the strong urge to move on. But I was afraid to change me. I wanted to know what awaited me as I found my path out of the crossroads. Realizing I don't know in my heart what I haven't experienced, I rewrote the poem to reflect the changes in me these past couple of years. Here is the rewritten version of the poem:

A Welcomed Friend

A new calling seeps into my soul.
I now recognize the calling from my welcomed, invited, and known friend.

Lessons from the Crossroads

I know who you are. I know what you want. And I'm glad you found me.
You interrupted my life, causing me to question what I want to do – how
I can be open to your nudges and how I can put you in the front seat.
You sent your angel whose wings are now spread so wide I can hardly see the tips.
She is going to teach me to fly.
The world I thought brought me comfort, predictability, and contentment
is no longer my world. You saw behind my masks and taught me to
see behind them as well. I jumped head first into the mysteries of
my journey because I felt you right beside me, encouraging me to
"Get out there, Eddie, and explore!"
I am overwhelmed with your patience, blessed with your presence
in my life, and I'm ready to "hit the road" with you in the front seat.
When the unrelenting waves pound the shore, I know you will remind
me of my own special wave you gave me when I was born.
I now know I'm responsible for the lessons I'm learning. I know
this because you've helped fill in the missing pieces.
Please, dear God, help me to remember all this as you
join me along our path out of the crossroads.

Ed Poole

I had great difficulty finding the words to describe the wonderful journey I had writing this book. It began with a simple, unplanned, yet beckoning call to the woods of Brown County. I returned again and again, and I wrote and read in many other places during my sojourn toward greater self-understanding. When the backwoods and dirt roads were straight, I picked up speed. When they were steep and full of curves, bends, and switchbacks, I slowed down. At those times, God invited me to enjoy the journey and prepare for the next downhill run. When the climb seemed insurmountable, I remembered God's words as He looked back and smiled, "Just Pedal."

The friends I met, the stories I heard, and the sense of community I found wherever the roads led have blessed me beyond reason. I tried my best to keep God in the front seat, aware at times He was taking me to scary places. While at those stops, I was always rewarded with gifts, knowledge, emotions, and courage to continue my journey.

I now know for certain this book could not have been written at any other time in my life. God knew I was not ready before I began writing, and because he knew the pain and struggles that drove me to Brown County, He wouldn't let me wait until some future point. It wasn't that He was impatient with me. In His infinite wisdom He allowed me to see that I could no longer grow as a person if I didn't experience the wonderful process He laid before me. He invited me on a hero's journey I didn't know I would make. He also knew that, when I returned home, I would see it with new eyes, those eyes that I found while sitting on that rock in the middle of the labyrinth at Ghost Ranch. I am so grateful I became aware of His invitation to get the words out of me and onto paper.

I also know for certain I would not have wanted God to choose any parents other than the ones He gave me. Without those two specific individuals in my life, I would have never grown into the person I am today and similarly would not understand the absolute necessity to continue that growth. Believe me, I could never have written those last few sentences had I not experienced the journey God put before me three years ago.

Before I walked out of the crossroads and onto my authentic path, I decided to walk back over to the tall, stone tower I found after the dust settled from my having been pushed out of the helicopter. The door was open this time, so I climbed the 71 steps to the top. I rushed to the first, then the second, and finally the third windows. The road markers that hung so tall and stately with the words Personal, Professional, and Spiritual on them were now dangling from a tiny, thin wire and moving back and forth in the lazy afternoon breeze. I thought the signs were about to fall off their posts. I could no longer read the words on the markers. In fact, the three paths no longer existed. Large fields of bright green grass were now growing where the paths were.

The fields were flooded with every imaginable wild flower waving lazily in the breeze like the three signs and displayed every color in the rainbow. I thought of the beautiful wildflowers I found in Brown County and at the Cenacle and Ghost Ranch. I ran to the fourth window. When I looked out, I saw a brilliantly painted road marker with the word Authentic on it. The path was circular and resembled my labyrinth. I could tell this path now included those events and people I found along the other three paths because I could see some of them and I recognized some of the activities from each of the other paths. I knew my dream had come true: My personal, professional, and spiritual paths had become entwined and a part of my authentic path. With a broad grin on my face, I walked back down the 71 steps and headed toward my only remaining path. As I looked back the tower began to disappear, and I knew it had served its purpose.

I cannot find the words to adequately describe how much I have changed through the writing, and someday I will find the words to explain how much better I feel about myself as I once again travel down my authentic path. I anticipate with great joy the next curve in the road.

EPILOGUE
A Talk with God

    I want this part of my journey to end with an imaginary conversation with God. Although the conversation is, in reality, one I imagined I had with God, I thought about it so much our talk became real. I don't need to believe that I had the conversation in order to see its value in my life. I need only have an open heart and soul.

    Ed, before you finish writing, I want to talk with you. I want to remind you of what you've said in your book, hoping this conversation will help you look back with fondness on new lessons you've learned and forward with hope for a brighter and more meaningful future.

    So, what are we going to talk about?

    Let's start with this. Ed, it's time for you to know that I'm the one who pushed you out of the helicopter and into the crossroads on that day over three years ago.

    YOU! Why did You do that? I was lost and alone when I landed in that crossroads, and I ached all over from that fifteen-foot drop! I can't believe You did that!

    I did so with love, Ed, because it was time for you to get back inside yourself and rediscover the authentic path you had lost sight of, the one I put

you on before you were born. Just as I got your attention ten years ago when you went into the hospital and again three years ago when you again went into the hospital, I needed to grab your attention, and I did. You are so stubborn sometimes, and I don't like taking such drastic measures. But I've found doing so is the only way you know how important these times are in your life.

But, God, why is this time in my life so important? Why not next year, or the one after that? Why now?

You have some major decisions to make, and most often you've been afraid to make those life-changing decisions. I know, you've made many decisions that have *changed* your life. But have they been life *changing*? I put the tower there for you so you could climb those 71 steps to the top and look out on your four paths. I also locked the door after you left because you needed to understand those four paths and their meaning to you. I knew you were going to make some significant journeys between then and now. You needed to keep your initial image of those four paths in your heart so you could find their meaning for you. All people have paths down which they journey, Ed. Their lives represented in the paths they walk are different; therefore, the paths are not the same as yours. Some don't recognize them, and those who do sometimes continue to see them as separated from each other. You immediately recognized the importance of seeing them all as part of your authentic journey and have tried to find the connections among them by writing *Lessons From the Crossroads*.

But, God, what about all those questions I first took with me to Brown County?

Don't you remember what you wrote about that? Life is all about being able to live with your questions and not hasten too quickly to some ill-defined answers. After you finished *Lessons from the Porch*, you thought you had *the* answers to all your questions. Not only did you not have all the answers, but also the answers you did have ten years ago now have different questions; plus you have a whole litany of new questions. I think you forgot that your entire life is a process, a journey, and you never get to definitive answers. You need to keep asking questions over and over again. Answers you've found through your struggles have been good answers at the time, but they don't always remain good answers. In this book, you're really making a full circle back to some of those same questions you had in *Lessons from the Porch*. You're just using different words to ask them. The questions you are asking now cut deeper into your soul. You are seeking inner peace and personal control like never before. You want to stop leaning on others to find your own peace and to tell you what kind of person you are. Ed, you are very capable of searching for these answers. You are searching for ways to open your heart to the messages and questions I am sending you. I've never seen you be so interested in listening quietly and patiently for My thoughts and hopes for you. Finally, I see you looking for the paths I want you to travel. I have a big smile on My face right now, Ed. I cannot make your decisions for you, but if you can sit in the silence, listen, and pray, you will find those decisions that have both your heart and Mine in them.

> But how is this time around different from the last time, in terms of my questions?

You and I have rediscovered each other and moved out of our imprisonment in that lost cabin, an imprisonment you imposed on both of us. I allowed it because I hoped you would finally find Me there. And you did. But I thought for a while you would never get the message. I sent Joshua to help you, and he did just that because you finally let him do his job. He was always there to help, but you never asked him until fifteen years ago. Until you began this writing, you had given Me "lip service." I don't feel you really believed I was there to help you and love you unconditionally, and it's good for others to know that about you. You finally are having the patience to listen and the wisdom to learn, just as you've said about storytelling. It works, Ed.

> God, sometimes I've been afraid of You, and I haven't known how to pray to You for your guidance.

Throughout your adult life, Ed, you have carried around your guilt and shame like a badge of honor. You've had all those feelings stuffed in that heavy

bag right on your chest. The weight has been oppressive, but I know you thought all that weight was just how life was supposed to be. I have heard you say so many times to others that I forgive all human beings for their past, present, and future transgressions. I know you believe this in your heart, but at times the belief becomes overpowered by the demons in your hole in the sidewalk. And because I've known you even before your mother began nourishing and loving you in her womb, I do understand fears and frustrations. For so many years you saw Me as an avenging God, someone you feared. Every time you did something you thought went against those early religious tenants, the guilt and shame swept over you again and again. I've been hoping you can cut a hole in that sack, put it on your back, and let that guilt and shame fall right out the bottom, into the crossroads. You're doing better, but, like all humans, you have a ways to go. Many people do not even know they have their fear packed tightly in that bag hung around their necks and carried on their chests.

How can I let go of those early religious beliefs, God?

Well, I'm not sure you need to let go of them. You wrote about the importance of adjusting your beliefs to find meaning in your present life. Why do you think you're unlike so many others? You're not, believe Me! You are spending a lot of time trying to understand the adjustments you are making in your belief structure, and I applaud you. It's hard work! Ed, you are so much like so many, many other human beings I've created or will ever create. You really do want to do what's right, but you slip, slide, and fall once in a while. You need to know you're making great progress. Instead of lamenting what you haven't done, rejoice in the growth you've made. Ed, don't be so quick to discount those early religious beliefs you learned at your church in Columbus. They are still more a part of you than you will ever know. They are a part of the home you found that day in Brown County. Cherish them and applaud yourself for remolding them to fit your present life. You have been angry at your parents for putting you in an environment that ingrained those beliefs into your being. Maybe you should be grateful to them instead. You have continued to put your parents and you in an untenable position. I remember as a teenager, each week you would sit in front of your TV and watch The Ozzie and Harriett Show. Over time you created this idealized image of parenthood based on what you saw on those TV shows. You wanted your parents to be like Ozzie and Harriett, never realizing that you were not seeing the real parents that appeared on TV. Your parents were who they were, and you cannot make them into people they could never be. You were a victim of victims, just as your parents were victims of their own parents. The only way they knew how to show their love to your sister and you was by providing for and protecting the two of you. And you've acknowledged those roles they played so well. Ed, there is no perfect parent-child relationship, but you *have got* to let go of this nice little victim story you've built for yourself for too many years. Do you remember looking through that box of old pictures? You wrote about the love you saw in your parents' faces, love for each other and for you. You have also focused too much on never hearing the words "I love you" from your parents. I think now you truly believe their actions showed you their love. Words mean nothing without actions, and their actions spoke louder than any words they could have said to you. So many times you have said to others, "What you do shouts so loudly people can't hear what you say." In this instance that thought has a positive, rather than a negative, ring to it. Your folks were doers, and you are finally beginning to understand that everything they did was for your sister and you. They worked, saved their money, provided for the entire family, and sent you off to college which was one of their greatest gifts to you. Ed, your parents weren't shown any other way to love their children than how they were shown love. That is not their fault. Let me remind you of Christmases almost twenty years ago now when Eric and Tracie were in high school and college. You had probably every clothing catalog from every major company, and you bought and bought and bought gifts for them from those catalogs and had them shipped to you at the office. Now do you understand why you did that? Buying "things" for your kids was how, at that time, you thought you showed them you loved them. Up to a point the gifts were nice, but now you know your kids needed more from you than the gifts: They needed you to be present for them, to hug them, to ask them how you could help them as they struggled through difficult times in high school and college, to let them know you loved them in ways other than buying clothes. Don't you see, you couldn't always provide them what they *really* needed during those critical years in their lives, because *You* didn't know how to share with them what they wanted so badly? Fortunately, you realized what was happening, and you do not go overboard now during the holiday season. You have tried mightily to be present for them, to offer your help, to listen when they talk to you, and to ask them questions that will get them back on whatever paths they are on. It's time to see the importance of your anger and embarrassment as helping guide you back toward your authentic path at the crossroads. Your mom and dad so wanted you to be surrounded by those early beliefs, and you've been the better person for having them. This is good news, Ed, because you know full well that as you struggle, you come closer and closer to finding that authentic path.

God, why have I always thought I didn't know how to be a good parent for Eric and Tracie?

You were a much better parent for your kids than you think. Bonnie has told you this, and so have Eric and Tracie. But, you did dump onto Bonnie many of those parenting responsibilities, and you wrote about abdicating these responsibilities to Bonnie. Basically, you got out of the way. Do you remember visiting Eric and his family last fall in Oregon?

Yes, I do.

What were the special thoughts and feelings you took away from that visit?

The "aha" I felt was truly being present for Eric, Stacy, Allie, and Aimee. That visit was the first one I made by myself. During every other single visit when Bonnie and I went together, I pulled the same act with my kids and grandkids that I did when Eric and Tracie were young. As soon as we arrived, I gave to Bonnie the opportunity of being with all four of them.

I went into Ashland, visited bookstores, walked through music shops, read at the library, and went to my favorite bars for a drink. She had all the fun, and once again I missed out on opportunities to spend time with my family. I know that now. This last visit, however, there was no one to whom I could turn over those parent and grandparent activities. I spent every moment possible with Allie, Aimee, and their parents. We went to the park several times to play. The little girls and I watched their "Baby Einstein" DVDs, and Allie and I watched *at least twenty times The Beauty and the Beast*. And, it was all such fun. During that visit Eric and I had over an hour just to sit and talk. He shared he felt we had been pulling away from each other these past few years. He talked about having me up on that pedestal, but now I was not there any more. I told him it was about time. At the conclusion of our wonderful conversation we agreed to move forward from that point and stay in closer touch, and we have! You know, God, I found out I do know how to be a parent and a grandparent.

Ed, what a major revelation for you! It doesn't matter how long it took you to get there; you're there now, so remember what you just said.

Thanks. Now that I am adjusting a parenting belief system I've had inside me for years, I have another question, God. Am I really *adjusting* my early belief system, or am I giving up on those beliefs? I wonder about this a lot.

Again, just remember what you said in *Lessons from the Porch* about how you and I both adjust our beliefs. You said that I change and evolve over time just as you. And you had some questions about this statement from those who read *Lessons*.

I do remember the questions.

If you don't mind, I want to amend one of the thoughts in that earlier book.

Please, go right ahead.

I both change and don't change my beliefs.

I'm afraid, once again, I don't understand, God.

Let Me try to explain it to you. The basic tenets of your faith were brought down from the mountain by Moses. Those are sacred and holy and do not change. I know you don't like the word "absolutes," but these ten statements *are* eternal truths. However, within their absolute parameters, I have adjusted My beliefs even *before* the beginning of all time, just as you are doing in your life. Don't throw out those beliefs; just adjust them. You have tended to have tunnel vision about your early beliefs. Take off the blinders and hold yourself open for the fact that God does change.

Okay, I can accept the changing part of You, but I don't understand yet just how You do change. How do You do that?

Perhaps, Ed, the *unchanging* part of your understanding of God is the fact that I *can* change. Your understanding of life is constantly growing and evolving. So is mine. And the process never ends for either of us, or anyone else, for that matter.

But what about my thoughts concerning "religion" and "spirituality"? Do these both change as well?

They sure do! You will continue to have both religious and spiritual experiences in your life. See them for what they are – opportunities to match your own sense of these two concepts against what you are experiencing at any present moment in time. Take what helps and leave the rest. I will love you for that. Many people today think they already know everything there is to know about God. So, they get lulled into this false sense of security that there is nothing new to learn. They are wrong! I know you feel you do not need to go to a physical building – temple, church, mosque, or synagogue – to worship Me. I do not need to be worshipped. Take time daily to talk with Me, wherever that might be. You've said before that you like to commune with nature. You will find some of the best religious and spiritual parts of yourself outside the physical structures. As a little boy you got an unintended message about Me when you attended the physical building called East Columbus Church of

Christ. You talk about having the hell scared into you as a boy. For that part of your religious experience I'm sorry. Even if I had wanted to spare you from those early feelings, I could not have done so. Your life then, and now, is playing itself out in its natural and logical order. Think about how those early beliefs have provided you a wonderful barometer for making your current decisions. You know, better than at any other time in your life, which beliefs you want to keep in your heart and soul and which ones you want to release. How could you have your current comparisons if those early beliefs had not been as much a part of you as you thought? Do you remember the rationale Bonnie and you adopted to give Eric and Tracie a religious experience when they were growing up? You both said, at some point in their lives, one or both of them may decide not to attend church or have religion as a part of their lives. However, in order to make an informed decision, Bonnie and you said the kids needed an experience upon which they could later base their decisions. Without that religious experience they would have had nothing to compare their later beliefs to. And you have been just the same way. Do you understand this? Sometimes I feel religious people want to keep you from hell while spiritual ones are those who have been through hell. And all of your wilderness journeys have given you diamonds you've polished as you walked through the hot, barren deserts – your own, self-imposed hell.

> And, as you know, I feel some of my best lessons about life have been learned while in the wilderness. I haven't perished in the desert. I've gotten to the other side of those difficult times in my life and have been the better for them. I've learned from them.

Yes, you have. How many times have you written, and said to others, that all people already have within them all the answers to every question they will ever have in life? Ed, all the wisdom you will ever need is within you right now and has been since before you were born. Use it! Believe in it! What if this entire writing has been about discovering the spiritual side of you and using that discovery as the connection to your authentic path? I'm sad that the religions of

the world tend to put people into cubbyholes and unnecessarily divide them, rather than unite them. There is even competition among the various religions, which divides people even more. Spirituality is a term that unites people. You can tear down the walls of your religious compartments and bring people together. Each time you talk with others about your wilderness experiences, they can identify some of their own. Both your religious and spiritual sides are important, so please don't deny either in favor of the other. You like the word blend instead of balance. This part of our talk is a perfect time to remember the value of blending religion and spirituality in your life. And your spirituality has grown these past several months. You rediscovered your spiritual path from atop the tower and as you climbed to the top of Chimney Rock at Ghost Ranch. You see the importance of integrating your spiritual path with your personal and professional journeys in order to once again find your authentic path. But, and this is important, Ed: Once you get to one mountaintop, there are always new mountains to climb. Once you get to the top of one mountain, understand the wisdom there (just as you did on Chimney Rock), and then use that wisdom to see the beginning of your next peak experience. Remember what Eric told you? You do the uphills to enjoy the downhills. It is with great joy that I tell you the mountains never end, and they keep changing. Ed, why do you think I asked your minister, Clint, to encourage you to go to Ghost Ranch? I knew while you were there you would find your authentic path while walking the labyrinth. I also knew you would rediscover your four paths at the end of your hike up to Chimney Rock. You wrote about the differences you saw the second time you got a clear view of them after that long, sometimes tiresome hike. But, you kept going, and I was right behind you pushing you forward. The reason you couldn't see above the trees on top of the tower in Brown County is because you were not ready to revisit your paths at that point in your journey. Why do you think I purposely put you at Ghost Ranch when I did? Do you remember the first time you went to Brown County and saw the granddaddy longlegs spider? Let Me refresh your memory. You were sitting on the porch at your cabin,

Epilogue: A Talk with God

drinking a Coke. The drink was about half gone when a granddaddy longlegs came cautiously up to the bottom of the can. He slowly surveyed the bottom of this "mountain" and then slowly began his ascent to the top. About halfway up this cold, slippery obstacle, the spider slid back to the table below. Valiantly he tried his ascent two more times, getting closer to the top each time yet sliding back down to the bottom of the can. After the third attempt he scurried off to find his next challenge. Do you remember what you thought as you observed the spider's attempts to get to the top?

Well, I have to admit I don't. Do you?

Yep, I do, Ed. You realized that the spider showed great spunk and courage as he tried three times to meet his challenge before taking off for other mountains to conquer. Most of the time in your own life, you haven't come close to matching that spider's tenacity as you faced some of your challenges. You ran off much earlier, unfortunately never knowing if you could have conquered your mountain. Like granddaddy longlegs, each time you got a little higher but not high enough to find your way out of the crossroads.

I think I'm beginning to see this part of our conversation. But there are still some important pieces to fill in.

Which ones?

Even though You told me to put my guilt and shame in the sack with the hole in it and put it on my back, I still struggle with three areas – my absence as a father and husband when Eric and Tracie were young, my propensity to put myself above others, and, finally, my tendency to need to control the lives of others – specifically my family and friends. And these three all seem connected.

Ed, what we're talking about here is very difficult to internalize. Don't expect to see it all at once because time will pass before you really believe everything I'm telling you. But, let Me talk about each of these three struggles you've had for a long time. Like the lives of most people, your early life was all about being as successful as you could be in your chosen profession. Even

though you didn't know it at the time, those same two roles of protector and provider you came to see in your parents were deep within you. Don't carry around the guilt that you wish you could have spent more time with your family. Maybe you could have found ways to spend more time with them, but you just didn't. You are more like others than you think. Sure, there were times when your ego got so big your essence got pushed to the side. There were times when you fed off what others said about you. And do you know the result of this positive feedback? You just worked harder and harder, to get more and more praise for your work. You are learning how to accept praise, but to do so in terms of who you are finding from your inward journeys. Until about fifteen years ago there were so many times when you didn't trust your own voice over the voices of others. But you didn't know how to listen to your own voice. You didn't even know you had one. You allowed your low self-esteem and lack of self-confidence to grow. Your parents didn't always understand how very important it was to help you feel good about yourself. You listened to the compliments of others when you were young and didn't have this praise affirmed at home. So, why wouldn't you grow up placing your own life in the hands of what others said about you? Ed, you've said in this book that your parents did the best they could. Can you really see this? Can you believe it to the point that your sight allows you to get back to your authentic path?

    Okay! Okay! Let me think about what You just said. This is a hard one for me.

    I know. Let Me shift to your second struggle, putting yourself above others. You've talked about being a "me-firster" for much of your life, putting yourself and your needs above those of family and friends. I agree with you, but I also feel you've been too hard on yourself. Remember how you felt when you were a patient at Linden Oaks and you kept getting the message to take care of yourself? You thought about this idea and realized you have been given the awesome responsibility of caretaker for yourself. This is no small thing, Ed. Just as you wrote that the story of any one of us is, in part, the story of all of us, the life of any one of us contains, in part, the lives of all of us. As soon as you can believe what I just said, you will see that you can help others while at the same time helping yourself. The two cannot be separated *if* you see all of humankind connected. As you follow those paths with your heart, your soul will tell you what is best for you and for others. When you feel conflicted about the blend of serving self and others, your soul will know what is best for others even if you don't think you are doing what is best for you. It takes a while to get to this point, Ed. But, in giving up yourself for others, you will find a new, more sacred self. I promise! Here is the positive part of all this: You want to spend time trying to understand yourself, and I applaud you because I know it's hard work!

Well, God, that's two out of three of my current struggles. What about my need to control others?

You've talked about being in control, and I agree with you. What you don't understand is I was right beside you even at those times when you made decisions you thought served your own self-interest. I could not keep you from making those decisions; however, I hoped you would learn from them. Sometimes you did, and sometimes you didn't. You kept falling into the same hole in the sidewalk. The providential moments you wrote about, those times when a decision was obviously an accumulation of a long series of earlier decisions, were those times in your life when you finally saw something because you came to believe it. Now you and I are on that tandem bike, but you're just learning how to ride it. Sometimes I feel we're having a tag team match as we scamper back and forth between the front and back seats. But, that's okay. You now see the tandem bike as a way for us to help each other grow and evolve.

OK, God. Just one more question, for now. Have I really chosen my authentic path out of the crossroads?

My friend, only you can answer that question. And you can't begin to answer that question until you begin your journey down the path that will allow you to devote much of your time to writing and speaking.

I do believe your metaphor of the labyrinth will hold meaning for you in the future – up to a point.

What do you mean, "Up to a point?"

Seeking your authentic path, your authentic self, is a critical journey. Some never take it. I like the idea that you want to be the same person in all aspects of your life, and I believe you're on the road to seeing this idea because you believe in the labyrinth. Remember what you wrote? Labyrinths have a double meaning for you: The consistency of how they are created reminds you of the unwavering, constant beliefs you have and continue to accept. The changing part of labyrinths is represented by the different settings in which you find them. So with labyrinths it seems to me you have captured two essential elements: the constant structure within which you want to live and the flexibility you found in the various labyrinthian environmental settings representing the opportunities you're seeking to grow and change your life *within* the consistency in your life you so badly want and for which you will continue to search. Are you with me?

I hope so, God.

So do I because I never *ever* want to use the drastic measures I have to get your attention: your two hospitalizations and the shove out of the helicopter.

Believe me, God, when I tell You I hope You don't either.

Great! I want to leave you with two final thoughts: First, Do you remember the song by Dan Fogleburg titled *Run for the Roses*? I know he's one of your favorite singers. In that song, Fogleburg says: "It's a chance of a lifetime in a lifetime of chance, and it's time that you joined in the dance." Ed, the game has already begun. Get in it! Second, please know that as you follow your bliss along the path that currently holds your heart, My peace is ever there. Amen.

About the Author

Much of Ed's professional life was in public education. Within that field he was a high school teacher, middle school principal, high school assistant principal and principal, associate superintendent for instruction, and superintendent of schools. Ed also taught fifteen years full-time at The University of Georgia and Aurora University, as well as part-time at Indiana University, Butler University in Indianapolis, Northern Illinois University, National-Louis University, and North Central College. He was Education and Training Director for Cummins Engine Company, a Fortune 100 company, located in Columbus, Indiana.

Ed resigned his last university teaching position in April, 2006, to found Lessons for Your Journey, Inc., and to devote himself full-time to those paths which hold his heart. Those paths include Ed's experiences as a writer, public speaker, success coach, storyteller, and a consultant, facilitator, and trainer to both profit and not-for-profit organizations. For over twenty years Ed has written and presented extensively throughout the United States on organizational change, the dynamics and alignment of organizations, leadership development, organization development, and executive coaching. Ed has developed programs for school districts, universities, and Fortune 500 companies.

There are several ways you may contact Ed:

Address:
3108 S. Route 59 - Suite 124-213
Naperville, IL 60564

Phone: 630.674.4480 - FAX: 630.364.3929
E-mail: epooleiu71@aol.com - Website: www.TheLessonGuy.com